D0881195

POWERING Search

POWERING
Search

The Role of Thesauri in New Information Environments

Ali Shiri

ASIST Monograph Series

Published on behalf of the
American Society for Information Science and Technology by

Information Today, Inc.
Medford, New Jersey

First printing, 2012

Powering Search: The Role of Thesauri in New Information Environments

Copyright © 2012 by American Society for Information Science and Technology

All rights reserved. No part of this book may be reproduced in any form or by any electronic or mechanical means, including information storage and retrieval systems, without permission in writing from the publisher, except by a reviewer, who may quote brief passages in a review. Published by Information Today, Inc., 143 Old Marlton Pike, Medford, New Jersey 08055.

Publisher's Note: The author and publisher have taken care in preparation of this book but make no expressed or implied warranty of any kind and assume no responsibility for errors or omissions. No liability is assumed for incidental or consequential damages in connection with or arising out of the use of the information or programs contained herein.

Many of the designations used by manufacturers and sellers to distinguish their products are claimed as trademarks. Where those designations appear in this book and Information Today, Inc. was aware of a trademark claim, the designations have been printed with initial capital letters.

Library of Congress Cataloging-in-Publication Data

Shiri, Ali, 1968-
 Powering search : the role of thesauri in new information environments / by Ali Shiri.
    pages cm. -- (ASIS&T monograph series)
   Includes bibliographical references and index.
   ISBN 978-1-57387-454-0
   1. Information storage and retrieval systems. 2. Information retrieval. 3. Subject headings. 4. World Wide Web--Subject access. I. Title.
   Z667.S57 2012
   025.04--dc23

                                                                2012029189

President and CEO: Thomas H. Hogan, Sr.
Editor-in-Chief and Publisher: John B. Bryans
VP Graphics and Production: M. Heide Dengler
Managing Editor: Amy M. Reeve
ASIST Monograph Series Editor: Samantha Hastings
Editorial Assistant: Brandi Scardilli
Cover Designer: Shelley Szajner
Copyeditor: Dorothy Pike
Proofreader: Penelope Mathiesen
Indexer: Enid Zafran

www.infotoday.com

To my wife, Fary (Farzaneh),
for her love and unstinting support,
and to my precious daughter, Kimia

Contents

Acknowledgments

I would like to acknowledge the support, encouragement, and advice of several people who have directly or indirectly contributed to this book. First and foremost, I would like to express my deepest gratitude to my colleague and friend, Dr. Alvin Schrader, who willingly and meticulously read and edited the entire manuscript and made it a more readable and consistent work. I am truly indebted and grateful to my graduate assistant, Maria C. Tan, who patiently spent hundreds of hours contacting a large number of organizations and people to seek permission for the screenshots that I have included in this book.

I would also like to thank my colleagues in the School of Library and Information Studies at the University of Alberta, in particular, Dr. Toni Samek and Dr. Margaret Mackey for their sincere support and encouragement. My gratitude goes to my students for their valuable research and teaching support over the years. My very special thanks to Dr. Samantha (Sam) Hastings, ASIS&T Monograph Series editor, and to the members of her editorial board for their many useful comments and suggestions. I am truly grateful to John B. Bryans, editor-in-chief and publisher, and Amy Reeve, managing editor, of the Book Publishing Division of Information Today, Inc., for their great support throughout the process. I would like to acknowledge all of the publishers, institutions, and people who have granted me permission to include screenshots of their products and services.

I would like to acknowledge the sabbatical leave granted by the University of Alberta Faculty of Education, without which I would not have had enough time to complete this book.

Finally, I wish to express my heartfelt thanks to my wife, Farzaneh, and my daughter, Kimia, for their genuine support, patience, and encouragement throughout the writing of this book.

Introduction

In the 1990s, a number of researchers noted that it appeared likely that in the near future, thesauri would be used more frequently during retrieval than at input. Since my own first paper on thesauri, titled "Thesauri on the Web: Current Developments and Trends," which was published in *Online Information Review* in 2000, several web-based projects and services, such as digital libraries, bibliographic and full text databases, open archives, content management systems, portals, and digital archives, have made use of thesauri in a wide variety of contexts.

This refocusing of the use of thesauri within information retrieval systems now means that it is imperative that information professionals take cognizance of the potential of thesauri as essential components of the largest information retrieval environment ever created, namely, the World Wide Web.

Powering Search is designed to provide a comprehensive treatment of information retrieval thesauri as search and browsing tools for user interfaces with a broad range of information retrieval systems, from bibliographic and full-text databases to digital libraries, portals, open archives, subject gateways, and linked data repositories. The book focuses particularly on user interface features and functionalities that can be designed, developed, and used on the basis of the knowledge structures inherent in thesauri.

A specific objective of *Powering Search* is to bring together research, development, and scholarship from areas such as information retrieval, knowledge organization, human computer interaction, information architecture, and information search behavior to emphasize the importance of effective and efficient user interfaces to thesauri for the purpose of supporting users in their information search process. This book examines the ways in which information retrieval thesauri, with sophisticated semantic networks, have been and are currently being used in a wide variety of web-based search and browsing user interfaces. These interfaces include research-based as well as operational user interfaces that have been developed to facilitate users' subject access.

Furthermore, the book provides a detailed discussion of empirical evaluations as well as usability studies that have made use of print or online thesauri by a broad range of users, from online search specialists, indexers, and catalogers to end users. These studies have provided valuable insights for creating thesaurus-enhanced search user interfaces.

The overarching argument of this book is that even though several well-established thesauri are used in a broad range of web and non-web information access and retrieval systems, many of these systems do not exploit thesauri to their full potential to support end users in their search and interaction processes. Of particular importance are the ways in which thesauri and their semantic assets are presented to users in search user interfaces.

The focus of many of the books written on thesauri, controlled vocabularies, and knowledge organization systems has been exclusively on library and information professionals, indexers, and catalogers, as well as on the construction of thesauri and controlled vocabularies. Even the books and articles that discuss user interface issues do so from thesaurus construction and thesaurus management perspectives, not from those of end users.

This book takes a new approach to thesauri by examining, analyzing, and synthesizing perspectives, projects, practices, and services from a variety of communities that share an interest in thesauri and their functions and that are not closely collaborating. Drawing on the research on search behavior, usability studies, search user interface, information architecture, and interactive information retrieval, a set of guidelines and best practices is proposed for the design and development of thesaurus-enhanced search user interfaces.

Chapter 1 provides an introduction to information retrieval thesauri and highlights some of the recent trends in the use of thesauri as search aids, including faceted search, exploratory search, and interactive term suggestion.

Chapter 2 contextualizes thesauri in models of information search behavior and interactive information retrieval.

Chapter 3 analyzes the use of thesauri as sources of search terms in user-centered query formulation and expansion studies.

Chapter 4 provides examples of new information environments on the web that have made use of thesauri as search and browsing tools, including digital libraries, portals, subject gateways, and open archives.

Chapter 5 discusses the treatment of thesaural interfaces in the recently revised thesaurus construction standards in the U.S. and the U.K.

Chapter 6 examines and compares numerous research-based prototypes and commercial user interfaces enhanced with thesauri.

Chapter 7 describes user interface features and functionalities developed for multilingual thesauri and meta-thesauri in Canada, the U.S., and Europe.

Chapter 8 discusses various evaluative approaches and strategies adopted to assess users' impression and understanding of thesaurus interface features and functionalities.

Chapter 9 proposes a set of guidelines and best practices for the design of thesaurus-enhanced search user interfaces.

Chapter 10 concludes with a discussion of current trends and developments in powering search in new information environments that are associated with digital libraries, search user interfaces, query formulation, social tagging, and the semantic web.

This book aims to provide a comprehensive view of thesauri for user searching and browsing in ways that are relevant to an international readership. With that in mind, the primary audience for this book is students, instructors, researchers, and practitioners who are active in the multiple areas of information organization and representation on the web, information architecture, metadata-enabled information access, and searcher education. Scholars, researchers, and practitioners who are involved in user interface and interactive information retrieval design can also benefit from the practical and design guidelines. Finally, the theoretical and practical aspects of *Powering Search* can be useful for organizations and institutions such as digital libraries and digital archives, museums, and web portals that are active in information and records management projects.

CHAPTER 1

Thesauri: Introduction and Recent Developments

This chapter introduces information retrieval thesauri and highlights some recent trends in the use of thesauri as search aids, in particular search and end-user thesauri. Addressed here are the differences among thesauri, taxonomies, and ontologies, along with the role that thesauri have played in the development of taxonomies and ontologies. This chapter also covers recent research trends that focus on the provision of semantic support for user interfaces provided by major search engines, areas such as faceted search, exploratory user interfaces, and dynamic term suggestion functionalities. The notion of social tagging is introduced, and a number studies that have compared controlled vocabularies and social tags are reviewed.

1.1 Thesaurus: A Brief History

The term *thesaurus* as a reference tool dates to the publication in 1982 of *Roget's Thesaurus*, and this, or some modern equivalent, is what most people have in mind when they think of a thesaurus (Broughton, 2006). Developed by Peter Mark Roget, *Roget's Thesaurus* is still the most widely used English language thesaurus, organizing words and their meanings in a systematic manner to assist people in identifying semantically related terms.

1.1.1 Information Retrieval Thesauri

The history of information retrieval thesauri can be traced back to the 1950s. Detailed accounts of the history of information retrieval thesauri can be found in Vickery (1960), Gilchrist (1971), and Aitchison and Dextre Clarke (2004). There is agreement that in the context of information retrieval, the word *thesaurus* was first used in 1957 by

Peter Luhn of IBM. The first thesaurus used for controlling the vocabulary of an information retrieval system was developed by the DuPont organization in 1959, and the first widely available thesauri were the *Thesaurus of Armed Services Technical Information Agency (ASTIA) Descriptors*, published by the Department of Defense in 1960, and the *Chemical Engineering Thesaurus*, published by the American Institute of Chemical Engineers (Aitchison and Dextre Clarke, 2004).

In the 1970s and early 1980s, commercial online database providers such as Dialog made use of thesauri alongside their bibliographic databases to enhance the quality of search. Chamis (1991) reported that in the 1980s about 30 percent of Dialog databases had either a printed or an online thesaurus. Many online databases now use thesauri for vocabulary control.

The introduction in 1974 of the first international standard for the construction of monolingual thesauri gave rise to the popularity of thesauri in various scientific and technological subjects. Several thesaurus construction standards have been developed during the past three decades: international standards (ISO 2788: 1986; ISO 5964: 1985); British standards (BS 5723: 1987; BS 6723: 1985); and UNISIST standards (UNISIST Guidelines, 1980, 1981). The U.S. standard on monolingual thesaurus construction, American National Standards Institute–National Information Standards Organization (ANSI/NISO) Z39.19, was published in 1993.

The advent of the web and the rapid growth of web-based information retrieval systems and services such as digital libraries, open archives, content management systems, and portals prompted international, U.K., and U.S. standards organizations to make revisions and changes to accommodate the demands of the electronic environment. The international standard ISO 25964-1 (2011), *Thesauri and Interoperability With Other Vocabularies*, revises, merges, and extends both ISO 2788 and ISO 5964 standards for the development of monolingual and multilingual thesauri. Guidelines for BS 5723 were replaced by BS 8723, *Structured Vocabularies for Information Retrieval*. BS 8723 was superseded by ISO 25964-1 in 2011. Details of the standard can be found at the British Standards Institution's website (www.bsigroup.com).

The new U.S. standard ANSI/NISO Z39.19, *Guidelines for the Construction, Format, and Management of Monolingual Controlled Vocabularies*, was published in 2005 and revised in 2010. Its new designation is ANSI/NISO Z39.19-2005 (R2010).

Major emphases in these changes and revisions were interoperability, electronic and web-based applications, thesaurus displays, and coverage of a wide range of vocabularies used in information retrieval systems and web-based services. In the field of information architecture, there is a firm belief in the advantages of staying close to the accepted standard. According to Morville and Rosenfeld (2007), these advantages are based on the following assumptions:

- "There's good thinking and intelligence baked into these guidelines.

- Most thesaurus management software is designed to be compliant with ANSI/NISO, so sticking with the standard can be useful from a technology-integration perspective.

- Compliance with the standard provides a better chance of cross-database compatibility so that when two companies merge, for example, it will be easier to merge their vocabulary sets." (p. 214)

1.1.2 What Is an Information Retrieval Thesaurus?

A thesaurus is a tool designed to support effective information retrieval by guiding indexers and searchers to consistently choose the same terms for expressing a given concept or combination of concepts (Dextre Clarke, 2001). Aitchison et al. (2000) define a thesaurus as "a vocabulary of controlled indexing language, formally organized so that *a priori* relationships between concepts are made explicit" (p. 1) that can be used in information retrieval systems ranging from the card catalog to the internet. The ANSI/NISO Z39.19 (2005) standard provides the following definition of a thesaurus: "A controlled vocabulary arranged in a known order and structured so that the various relationships among terms are displayed clearly and identified by standardized relationship indicators." Some of the long-established and well-known thesauri are the Medical Subject Headings, also known as the MeSH Thesaurus, in the area of medicine and allied sciences, the Art and Architecture Thesaurus (AAT), and the Thesaurus of ERIC (Education Resources Information Center) Descriptors.

Standard thesauri incorporate three types of term relationships, namely, equivalence, hierarchical, and associative. Equivalence relationships are usually defined as relations between synonyms and quasi synonyms, for instance, between *computer languages* and *programming languages*. This type of relationship provides an alternative access point for the user during searching. Equivalence relationships are shown by the notation UF (Used For).

Hierarchical relationships are assigned to terms that have various levels of specificity. For instance, the term *libraries* is a narrower term for *digital libraries*, while the term *user interfaces* is a broader term for *visual user interfaces*. These broader and narrower relationship types allow a user to semantically navigate in an information collection from terms that are general to more specific terms and vice versa. The boarder and narrower term relationships are shown by the notations BT (Broader Term) and NT (Narrower Term).

Associative relationships are designed to create relationships between terms that do not have equivalence or hierarchical relationships but would be conceptually or mentally related, for example, between *information overload* and *information filtering*. This type of relationship is represented by the notation RT (Related Term).

The following entry from the *ASIS&T Thesaurus of Information Science, Technology, and Librarianship* illustrates the various types of term relationships:

> **Internet**
> UF Cyberspace
>   Information highway
>   Information superhighway
> BT Telecommunication networks
> RT e-mail list servers
>   ftp
>   gophers
>   Internet search systems
>   National Research and Education Network
>   Network computers
>   Newsgroups
>   telnet
>   Web TV

Another characteristic of standard thesauri is their inclusion of scope notes. A scope note is a definition of the term or an explanation of its meaning and use in a specific database. The notation SN represents scope notes in thesauri.

1.1.3 Thesaurus Displays

There are several different methods of displaying thesauri on paper and on the computer screen:

- Alphabetical displays showing scope notes and equivalence, hierarchical, and associative relationships for each term

- Hierarchical displays generated from the alphabetical display

- Systematic and hierarchical displays showing the overall structure of the thesaurus and all levels of hierarchy

- Graphic displays of varying sorts (Aitchison et al., 2000) using arrows, family trees, or two- and three-dimensional visualization techniques (an extended discussion of user interfaces for thesauri appears in Chapter 5)

Guidelines for the design and construction of thesauri are beyond the scope of this book. Readers interested in this area should consult the practical manuals developed by Aitchison et al. (2000) and Broughton (2006).

1.1.4 Thesauri as Knowledge Organization Systems

The literature of indexing, thesaurus construction, and subject access and information representation categorizes thesauri as controlled vocabularies. Thesauri have also been classified as *knowledge organization systems* (KOSs) (Hodge, 2000; Broughton et al., 2005), a term coined by the Networked Knowledge Organization Systems Working Group (NKOS) at its initial meeting at the Association for Computing Machinery Digital Libraries 1998 conference in Pittsburgh, Pennsylvania. Hodge (2000) explains the use of thesauri and other types of KOSs on the web in these terms:

> Knowledge organization systems are used to organize materials for the purpose of retrieval and to manage a collection. A KOS serves as a bridge between the user's information need and the material in the collection. With it, the user should be able to identify an object of interest without prior knowledge of its existence. Whether through browsing or direct searching, whether through themes on a web

> page or a site search engine, the KOS guides the user
> through a discovery process. (p. 3)

NKOS is devoted to the discussion of the functional and data models for enabling KOSs—such as classification systems, thesauri, gazetteers, and ontologies—to function as networked interactive information services that support the description and retrieval of diverse information resources through the internet. The American and European NKOS groups have held annual workshops in conjunction with the Joint Conference on Digital Libraries and the European Conference on Digital Libraries, providing a venue for research, development, and evaluation of KOSs on the web. Thesauri and their applications have been the focus of many presentations and publications in these workshops.

1.1.5 Uses and Functions of Thesauri

A thesaurus may be employed as an indexing tool, a searching aid, or a browsing and navigation function. As an indexing tool, a thesaurus can be used to assign indexing terms to a given document collection. Many bibliographic and commercial database providers use a thesaurus for indexing purposes.

As a searching tool or a query formulation support feature, thesauri can be used as an interactive term suggestion tool or as an automatic query expansion support functionality.

In the interactive term suggestion approach, users are presented with a list of terms to choose from. This can be the result of matching an initial query term with the thesaurus terms to provide synonyms or semantically related terms for the user's guidance. In the case of automatic query expansion, a thesaurus can be used to automatically add terms from it to the query terms a user has initially submitted in order to improve or enhance the retrieved results. Thesauri can provide a browsing user interface in which thesaurus terms and their relationships are presented on the user interface to assist users by making term selection a more engaging and interactive process. An extended discussion of thesauri as supporting tools for query formulation and expansion is provided in Chapter 3.

All of these uses and functions have been adopted by several generations of information retrieval systems, from traditional indexing and abstracting commercial databases to current web-based digital libraries, portals, repositories, and open archives. Aitchison et al.

(2000) note that thesauri may be used for both indexing and searching, for indexing but not searching, and for searching but not indexing. These uses are associated with the ways in which a thesaurus can be developed and incorporated into an information representation and retrieval system.

Additional uses of a thesaurus as noted by Broughton (2006) are as a source of subject metadata and query formulation and expansion, and as a browse and navigation tool. In his discussion of the functions of thesauri, Soergel (2003) comments that they can facilitate the combination of multiple databases or unified access to multiple databases in the following ways:

A. Mapping the users' query terms to the descriptors used in each of the databases

B. Mapping the query descriptors from one database to another (switching)

C. Providing a common search language from which to map to multiple databases

Another useful and interesting function that he refers to is document processing after retrieval, for instance, the meaningful arrangement of search results and the highlighted descriptors responsible for retrieval.

1.1.6 Types of Thesauri

The types and uses of thesauri depend largely on the ways in which they are constructed and incorporated into an information retrieval system. The well-known types of thesauri can be categorized as follows:

1. Standard, manually constructed thesauri: These are standard subject-specific thesauri with equivalence, hierarchical, and associative relationships, used in the indexing and retrieval of print and digital collections. Some databases and information retrieval systems use these thesauri for indexing purposes only, while others present these tools more explicitly to end users to support their search term selection.

2. Search thesauri: Search thesauri, also referred to as end-user thesauri and searching thesauri, are defined as a category of tools enhanced with a large number of entry terms that are synonyms, quasi synonyms, or term variants that assist end users in finding alternative terms to add to their search queries (Perez, 1982;

Piternick, 1984; Bates, 1986; Cochrane, 1992). Aitchison et al. (2000) note that the role of thesauri here is usually to assist users in searching free-text databases by suggesting search terms, especially synonyms and narrower terms. A number of searching thesauri have been designed and developed (Anderson and Rowley, 1991; Lopez-Huertas, 1997; Knapp et al., 1998; Lykke Nielsen, 2001) and have been evaluated in query expansion research (Kristensen and Jarvelin, 1990; Kristensen, 1993; Kekäläinen and Jarvelin, 1998). A searching thesaurus can also provide greater browsing flexibility. It can allow users to browse part or all of a thesaurus, navigating the equivalence, hierarchical, and associative relationships. Terms (or the combination of preferred and variant terms) can be used as predefined or "canned" queries to be run against the full-text index. In other words, a searching thesaurus can become a true portal, providing a new way to navigate and gain access to a potentially enormous volume of content. A major advantage of the searching thesaurus is that its development and maintenance costs are essentially independent of the volume of content. On the other hand, such thesauri put much greater demands on the quality of equivalence and mapping (Morville and Rosenfeld, 2007).

3. Automatically constructed thesauri: These thesauri are constructed with computer algorithms and are not as semantically well-structured as standard manually created thesauri. A wide range of statistical and linguistic techniques have been developed to build such thesauri. Unlike hand-crafted thesauri, corpus-based thesauri are constructed automatically from the corpora or information collection, without human intervention. There are two different methods of extracting thesaural relationships from text corpora, namely, co-occurrence statistics and grammatical relations (Mandala et al., 2000).

4. Linguistically and lexicographically focused thesauri: The well-known examples of these thesauri are WordNet and *Roget's Thesaurus*. WordNet is a manually constructed thesaurus, available electronically, and has been used in many information retrieval experiments for query expansion purposes. It is a general purpose thesaurus and therefore lacks the domain-specific relationships found in standard thesauri. *Roget's Thesaurus* is also available in electronic format and has been used in information retrieval experiments.

1.1.7 Knowledge Organization Trends

Several researchers have studied research and development trends associated with knowledge organization in general and thesauri in particular. In her review of knowledge organization research between 1998 and 2003, McIlwaine (2003) highlights thesauri initiatives as one of the recent trends along with such topics as terminology, internet, search engines, resource discovery, interoperability, visual presentation, and universal classification systems. Williamson (2007) notes that, currently, controlled vocabularies of various kinds (e.g., thesauri and taxonomies), as well as other kinds of information structures, are deemed to have an important role to play. She says it is clear that thesauri have now assumed a role as a search tool. She provides a discussion of the application of thesauri on the web between 1997 and 2006 with a particular focus on their role in searching, browsing, and navigation.

Recent developments in the use of thesauri highlight how pre-web applications and standard tools such as thesauri are being used to make metadata more usable. As the organization of knowledge and information continues to evolve in the digital environment, it seems evident that the relevance of core principles of knowledge organization will remain high, despite shifting trends. These principles will most certainly help enhance both the browsability and searchability of emerging web-based environments, such as digital libraries, content management systems, institutional repositories, and virtual learning environments (Saumure and Shiri, 2008).

Subject analysis in general and the use of thesauri in particular enjoyed a flurry of interest in the 1970s and have recently become a focus of attention again. The scholarly community carrying out work in this area has become more diffuse and grown to include new groups such as information architects (Schwartz, 2008). The need to improve users' browsing, navigation, and experience in digital information spaces has brought both controlled vocabularies and thesauri to the center of attention.

1.1.8 Emergence of Thesauri Search Tools

With the development of the web, the use of thesauri is coming to the forefront of knowledge organization studies. New trends in developing thesauri have also been emerging since the advent of the web (Saumure and Shiri, 2008).

Over the past 15 years, numerous researchers have discussed the status, suitability, importance, and diversification of the function of thesauri in the new information environment. Aitchison et al. (2000) have noted that the role of thesauri is changing but that they are likely to remain an important retrieval tool. This shift in the functions of thesauri is viewed as an expansion, including a role for thesauri not only in performance enhancement in full-text systems but also as tools for use on websites; in intranets; and for indexing, search statement expansion, and visual organization. While initial proposals for the use of thesauri focused on their ability to ensure consistent analysis of documents during input to information retrieval systems, these tools have increasingly become vital as aids to effective retrieval. Indeed, in the near future, it appears likely that thesauri will be used more during retrieval than at input. Thesauri can complement full-text access by aiding users in various ways: by focusing their searches, by supplementing the linguistic analysis of the text search engine, and even by serving as one of the analytic tools used by the linguistic engine (Milstead, 1998).

To reassess the functions and capabilities of thesauri in the digital age, any revisions to thesaurus construction standards should take into account at least four essential areas: 1) the nature and function of thesauri in full-text databases, 2) term definition and all types of term relationships, 3) dynamic and interactive display of thesauri in the digital environment, and 4) thesauri as support for the internet (Williamson, 2000). In a discussion of the importance of providing browsing capabilities for thesauri and subject headings, Olson (2007) notes that in many abstracting and indexing services, users are forced to switch between the thesaurus and the database in order to form an understanding of the references and relationships between terms and to make effective use of thesauri in support of searching. To make knowledge structures such as thesauri more browsable, she suggests that emphasis needs to be placed on the references and relationship types and on their visibility to searchers.

Shiri and Revie (2000) note that although there are few operational information retrieval systems that have effectively incorporated thesauri as search and retrieval aids, we are witnessing an increased enthusiasm among thesaurus developers to make their tools available on the web for potential applications. The reasons for this enthusiasm and the increasing availability of online thesauri are closely linked to five key issues associated with the emergence of the web:

1. The colossal growth of information resources, demanding better subject identification

2. The migration of traditional information resources to the web, calling for more consistent subject approaches

3. An urgent need for resource description and discovery through reuse of existing information management tools such as controlled vocabularies

4. Problems associated with the quality of unstructured information retrieved from the web

5. The need to provide users with knowledge structures such as thesauri for rapid and easy access to better-organized information

Shiri and Revie introduce some of the early developments associated with the use of thesauri on the web, such as thesauri incorporated into web-based databases, stand-alone thesauri, thesauri in multithesaurus search systems, and thesauri in subject gateways.

Miller (2003) argues that, as the use of the web becomes widespread, the problem of semantic organization of information will become more and more urgent. To address this problem, he suggests that a thesaurus should be constructed on the basis of the maximum possible number of terms and their synonyms, objective relations between terms, multiple languages, and receptivity to new terms. Lykke Nielsen (1998) suggests that future thesauri should also function as search tools to support users in analyzing and conceptualizing their information needs, in locating and choosing appropriate access points, and in refining requests as well as queries. However, today's pressures for intuitive end-user access and seamless flows of information from one system into another compel new thinking about ways of designing, implementing, and presenting vocabulary search tools (Aitchison and Dextre Clarke, 2004).

Thesauri have been used to develop organizational taxonomies for library and information science (Wang et al., 2008). Gilchrist (2003) comments that taxonomies use both classification and thesaurus techniques, and it is interesting to note how similar some of the techniques are in automatic indexing and automatic categorization, this being largely a matter of granularity. Taxonomies may also use a combination of classification and thesaural techniques applied to a wider range of object types; museums documentation and image retrieval may be mentioned here as areas in which the object types pose particular problems and in which other techniques are being developed. Faceted classification techniques can be used to provide a framework on which taxonomies can be built. The focus on noun forms and unit concepts popular in thesauri can be adopted to provide a more consistent approach to taxonomy construction. In a discussion of the past 50 years of knowledge organization, Dextre Clarke (2008) writes as follows:

> As the taxonomy buzz-word spread around, many information professionals seized a different opportunity. They rescued their existing home-grown thesauri, subject heading schemes and classification schemes, dusted them off a little, and re-branded them "taxonomy." The controlled vocabulary had now become more popular than ever before! (p. 433)

These developments suggest that the terms *thesaurus* and *taxonomy* have been loosely and interchangeably used and that some people who have used the term *taxonomy* were unaware of the long-standing research and development behind thesauri and their construction standards.

Gruber (2009) notes that "an ontology defines (specifies) the concepts, relationships, and other distinctions that are relevant for modeling a domain and the specification takes the form of the definitions of representational vocabulary (classes, relations, and so forth), which provide meanings for the vocabulary and formal constraints on its coherent use" (p. 1,964).

A quick analysis shows that there are a number of similarities between *ontologies* and *thesauri*, namely, in their treatment of concepts, classes, and relationships. Therefore, it is not surprising that these two terms have been used interchangeably, and confusingly, in the literature. A very good example of this confusion can be found in the terms used to refer to WordNet, a large lexical tool for the English language. It has been called a *thesaurus* in numerous information retrieval studies during the past decade, but it has also been called an *ontology* by the World Wide Web Consortium and a *taxonomy* by some researchers.

However, one of the key characteristics of ontologies is that they provide a more formal and detailed set of conceptual constructs and relationships than do thesauri, and the formalization lends itself very well to the web environment. As Gruber (2009) suggests, ontologies are used "to exchange data among systems, provide services for answering queries, publish reusable knowledge bases, and offer services to facilitate interoperability across multiple, heterogeneous systems and databases" (p. 1,965.)

An analysis of these functions shows that they are common to both thesauri and ontologies. Therefore, development of any high-level, sophisticated, and machine-processable ontology can benefit from the conceptual and semantic structures inherent in various existing thesauri. Gilchrist (2003) suggests that the main characteristic that thesauri, taxonomies, and ontologies have in common is that they all address natural language. Soergel (1999) refers to a recent interest in ontologies as classification tools in such areas as artificial intelligence, linguistics, and software engineering and notes that "indeed, once these communities increased their awareness that there is not only a problem of classification but also of terminology, 'ontologies' included lead-in vocabularies as well, and became full-fledged thesauri"(p. 1,120.)

His argument points to the fact that scholarly communities outside library and information science identified the need for classification and used the term *ontology* without actually benefiting from the long-standing research, development, and standardization forming the basis of numerous well-structured controlled vocabularies such as thesauri and classification schemes. He calls for collaboration among these various communities to create better information access systems.

From an information architecture point of view, Morville and Rosenfeld (2007) comment that thesauri are expected to be more widely used in the coming years as they become a key tool for dealing with the growing size and importance of websites and intranets. One advantage of thesauri is their tremendous power and flexibility to shape and refine the user interface over time. Not all of the capabilities can be exploited at once, but one can user-test different features, learning and adjusting incrementally as one proceeds.

A review of the literature on thesauri and their applications and functions in the new digital information environment identifies a wide range of ways in which thesauri can be made more suitable for the new search environment. Some of the more common approaches are as follows:

- Revising thesaurus construction standards to facilitate the development and use of thesauri. The British and U.S. thesaurus construction standards have recently been revised to reflect current changes and development in the areas of thesauri and other types of controlled and structured vocabularies.

- Using a wide range of user-based and document-based techniques for thesaurus construction, including bibliometric approaches, term co-occurrence analysis, word association tests, transaction logs, and data-mining and web-mining technologies.

- Enriching thesauri by incorporating a larger number of terms and relationships so as to provide a vast entry vocabulary to support users' initial interaction with the information retrieval system. Search thesauri are one example of these tools that may support free text searching.

- Enhancing the semantic structure of thesauri, such as expanding the relationship types within a thesaurus or covering a broader range of relationships among terms.

- Constructing more-sophisticated user interface features and functionalities. Many information retrieval systems and databases have a thesaurus but do not provide seamless, straightforward access to the thesaurus to support end users in their search process. This kind of access can be designed in such a way as to make thesaurus structures more explicitly visible for browsing, searching, and navigation purposes. Interface design techniques and strategies that combine browsing and searching can be adapted to provide more dynamic and interactive interfaces.

- Using thesauri for interactive (visible) or automatic (invisible) query formulation or expansion to support users' information interaction.

- Using thesauri as sources of subject metadata. Many thesauri are now being adapted to provide consistent subject description in well-known metadata standards such as Dublin Core.

- Using existing thesauri to organize and visualize web-based information systems and services. Examples are websites, intranets, content management systems, portals, and subject gateways.

- Using existing thesauri to develop simplified or more sophisticated knowledge structures for organizing and representing disciplinary or multidisciplinary web-based applications.

- Employing multilingual thesauri for web-based cross-lingual information retrieval.

- Bringing into play user evaluation of thesauri and their usefulness within the context of web-based information systems and services in order to provide insight into the ways in which thesauri may support users' search behavior.

1.2 Thesauri and Information Architecture

The Information Architecture Institute (2005) defines *information architecture* as the art and science of organizing and labeling websites, intranets, online communities, and software to support usability and findability. Rosenfeld and Morville (1998), in the first edition of *Information Architecture for the World Wide Web*, were among the first authors to introduce the information architecture community to thesauri and controlled vocabularies. They note that the relationships in standard thesauri can be useful for determining the labeling of the different levels of a website.

While the terms of a thesaurus can be adapted, however, the website designer needs to remember that the narrower and the more specific its vocabulary, the better the thesaurus terms will perform for the website. For example, if the site users are computer scientists, a computer science thesaurus will "think" the same way that its users do. In choosing a labeling or KOS, the authors particularly emphasize the importance of taking into account the types of users and their information search habits.

A successful website will have a well-organized knowledge structure that accommodates users' search and interaction behavior. Constructing and using a controlled vocabulary impose an important degree of consistency that supports search and browsing. A thesaurus on the back end can enable a more seamless and satisfying user experience on the front end (Morville and Rosenfeld, 2007). Even though the first thesauri were developed for libraries, museums, and government agencies long before the advent of the web, Morville and Rosenfeld believe that information architects can draw on these decades of experience.

Designing labeling and organization structures for websites and intranets can benefit from the characteristics and features of thesauri. Synonym management is the most important function of a thesaurus used as part of a website. The mapping of many synonyms or word variants onto one preferred term or concept is an important feature allowing users to deal with the ambiguities of language during their searching and finding experience (Morville and Rosenfeld, 2007).

Thesauri have come back into our everyday life via the web. More than a tool to get more and better words, thesauri are used to create a web of interconnected terms to help people find information (Wodtke and Govella, 2009).

The Argus Center for Information Architecture polled its membership about subject matters with which information architects are concerned. Based on the responses of 241 participants between February 9 and 21, 2001, survey results showed that some 54 percent of respondents felt that controlled vocabularies and thesauri were among the subject areas with which information architects are concerned (Zhang et al., 2002).

Thesauri, taxonomies, and topic maps have been compared and discussed as tools that assist information architects to develop better user interfaces for their websites and intranets. Thesauri provide a much richer vocabulary for describing terms than taxonomies do and so are much more powerful retrieval tools. As can be seen, using a thesaurus instead of a taxonomy would solve several practical problems in classifying objects and also in searching for them (Garshol, 2004). Other researchers have demonstrated that all the characteristics of standard thesauri, such as broader, narrower, and related terms, as well as scope notes and synonymous terms, can be effectively used to create topic maps and well-structured taxonomies (Ahmed, 2003).

Pastor-Sanchez et al. (2009) discuss the advantages of thesaurus representation in Simple Knowledge Organization System format, a World Wide Web Consortium standard to promote the use of KOSs in support of the semantic web. They suggest that the conceptual structures of thesauri allow 1) the possibility of establishing lexical relationships adapted to the terminological reality of each language; 2) the indexing of webpages with a thesaurus to present queries without users' having to perform a predictive selection of terms; 3) the development of organization schemes; and, 4) the possibilities of expanding and redefining searches, showing references to documents with content related to that of directly retrieved documents, and suggesting new search terms.

In the context of information retrieval, BS 8723 for *Structured Vocabularies for Information Retrieval* (2005) suggests this:

> It is inappropriate to use the classical definition of taxonomy as the science of classification, or to be concerned with its long-standing adaptation to the classification and naming of organisms. BS8723 deals in general with vocabulary tools designed as retrieval aids, hence the definition of taxonomy used in this standard, as a structured vocabulary using classificatory principles as well as thesaural features, designed as a navigation tool for use with electronic media. The standard also notes that the term taxonomy is used differently.

Therefore, many of the taxonomies that have been used in websites and portals are not used for vocabulary control or do not follow thesaurus construction standards to serve as information retrieval tools. There are practical examples of web-based tools and services that have made use of thesauri for designing their information architecture. The SMETE (Science, Mathematics, Engineering, and Technology Education) Digital Library in the U.S. makes use of a thesaurus developed by the Mathematics Association of America that contains mathematical concepts (Dong and Agogino, 2001).

In the absence of user learning, and with no easy way for users to exploit thesaurus relationships, attention has recently turned to what has come to be called guided navigation. It is one result of the intersection between information architecture and library and information science. As designers of web user experiences, information architects need to find ways to help users, especially online shoppers and corporate employees, navigate through large information spaces containing objects with many potentially searchable attributes (Schwartz, 2008).

Beeson and Chelin (2006) note that if one scans the burgeoning literature on information architecture that is associated with the spread of applications on the web, one finds theories for organizing and searching information, as well as methods for creating metadata, controlled vocabularies, and thesauri—all of which could have come from a textbook on information science.

Almost all the books on information architecture have a chapter on controlled vocabularies and thesauri and the ways in which these tools can be used to properly organize content, as well as to effectively assist users in their information access and retrieval.

1.3 Faceted Search User Interfaces
1.3.1 Facet Analysis

S. R. Ranganathan (1967) proposed the idea of facet analysis, which he used in his faceted Colon Classification scheme. The basic idea was that any component, aspect, or facet of a subject can fit into one of five categories, namely, personality, matter, energy, space, and time.

This technique has been widely used in the design and development of classification schemes and thesauri. The first thesaurus constructed on the principles of facet analysis was *Thesaurofacet*, developed by Jean Aitchison in the 1960s. Examples of thesauri developed on the basis of the facet analysis technique are the AAT and the *ASIS&T Thesaurus of Information Science, Technology, and Librarianship*.

Aitchison et al. (2000) emphasize that faceted classification is useful in thesaurus construction in several ways. First, it provides a tool for the analysis of subject fields and for determining the relationships among concepts. Second, the resulting faceted classification may be used as the systematic display in a thesaurus. Third, facets may be added to terms in existing vocabularies, in order to further define the meaning and role of such terms.

Figure 1.1 shows one of the key facets used by the AAT. As can be seen, the *styles and periods* facet has a rich and detailed hierarchy consisting of sub-facets such as *styles and periods by general area* and *styles and periods by region*. This type of arrangement provides a useful browsing structure for users, who can refine or specify a certain category of style period on the basis of the faceted structure.

Figure 1.2 shows the facet *knowledge and information* and the subfacet *knowledge organization systems* in the *ASIS&T Thesaurus of Information Science, Technology, and Librarianship*. The detailed view provided by this type of faceted structure not only allows users to gain a complete overview of each facet and its scope but also makes browsing and navigating around the thesaurus a more easily understood process.

Application of facet analysis and faceted thesauri has become prevalent among information retrieval user interface designers,

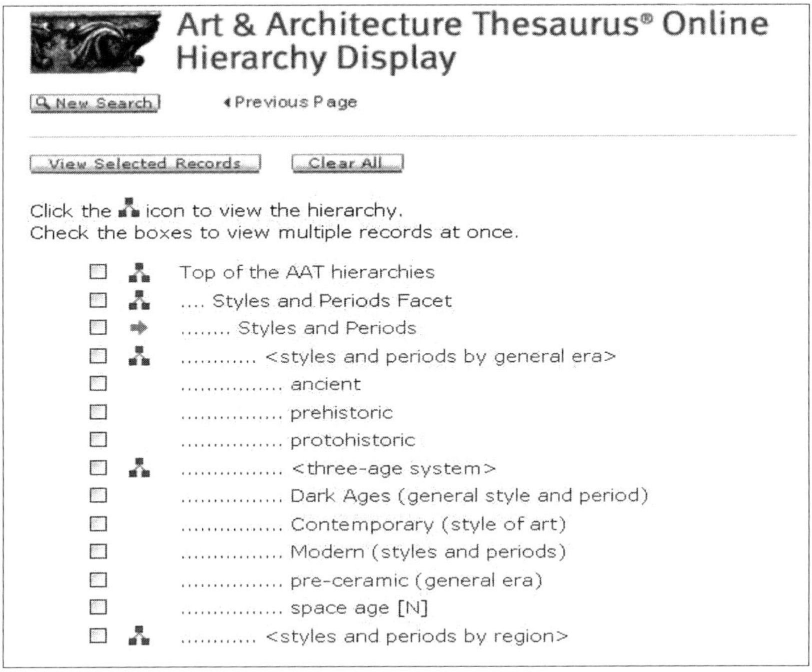

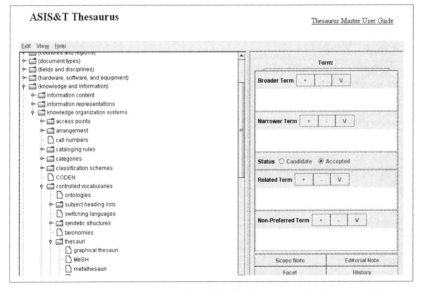

Figure 1.1   Display of the *styles and periods* facet in the Art and Architecture Thesaurus

Figure 1.2   The faceted structure of the *ASIS&T Thesaurus of Information Science, Technology, and Librarianship*

information architects, and web developers of based services. Such applications and web interfaces tend toward a broader view of facets than the traditional library focus on document subjects, incorporating various metadata elements such as commodity price or scalar properties of an object. This can include facets that are essentially pick lists, and there is usually little notion of the semantics of combining facets.

Nonetheless, this simple facet treatment can yield attractive browsing interfaces for websites (Tudhope and Binding, 2008). The FACET (Faceted Access to Cultural hEritage Terminology) project investigated the potential of multifaceted semantic query expansion in controlled vocabulary indexed applications. Query expansion was based on a faceted thesaurus, the AAT. In FACET, such expansion provides an option to include closely related concepts in search. Results are ranked in order of decreasing relevance to the initial query, based on the number of matching query terms and the degree of match between concepts.

1.3.2 Faceted Search

The world of the web is beginning to realize that the tools of facet analysis can build robust, dynamic, mutable, and responsive systems (La Barre, 2004). The term *facet* is widely used in the information science community, but in other disciplines similar concepts are referred to as *attribute, dimension, metadata, property,* or *taxonomy* (Dumais, 2009).

The terms *faceted search, faceted navigation, faceted metadata,* and *faceted browsing* have been used interchangeably, and sometimes loosely, in the literature. In part, this is because of the increasing popularity of integrated searching and browsing in faceted search interfaces. Also called *guided navigation* and *faceted search,* the faceted navigation model leverages metadata fields and values to provide users with visible options for clarifying and refining queries. Faceted navigation is arguably the most significant search innovation of the past decade (Morville and Callender, 2010). It features an integrated, incremental search and browse experience that lets users begin with a classic keyword search and then scan a list of results.

Dumais (2009) outlines the key components of faceted search interfaces and suggests that most systems show the query, the facet structure, the subset of results currently specified, and, sometimes, a

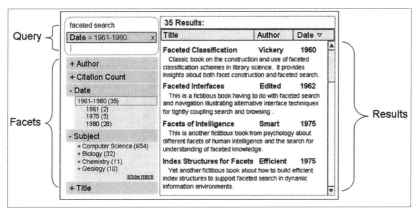

Figure 1.3   Example of a faceted search interface

detailed view of an individual item. Figure 1.3 depicts three main areas of a faceted search interface, namely, query, facets, and results. The interface demonstrates a combined approach to searching and browsing by presenting both the query box and the facets. Each facet can be collapsed and viewed.

One of the early examples of using facet-based user interfaces was HIBROWSE (High Resolution Interface for Database Specific Browsing and Searching), developed by Pollitt et al. (1994). They designed a series of user interfaces for several bibliographical and multilingual databases. An example of such an interface is shown in Figure 1.4; the interface is developed for hotels based on such categories as name, city, number of rooms, rating, and so forth.

In a discussion of user interface design for faceted navigation, Hearst (2008) comments that faceted navigation is a proven technique for supporting exploration and discovery within an information collection. Faceted classification and faceted navigation are now widely used in website search and navigation.

In research on the Flamenco project, Hearst and colleagues (Hearst, 2000; Hearst et al., 2002; Yee et al., 2003; Hearst, 2006) describe the importance of faceted classification systems for website navigation; they have also designed and studied a series of user interfaces to support faceted navigation for everyday users. The overarching design goals of the Flamenco project were to support the following:

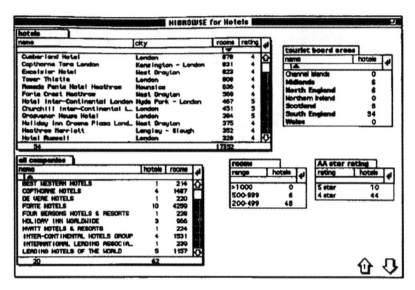

Figure 1.4   HIBROWSE user interface for hotels

- Flexible navigation

- Seamless integration of browsing with directed (keyword) search

- Fluid alternation between refining and expanding

- Avoidance of empty results sets

- User control and understanding at all times

Hearst also notes that another of the Flamenco project's goals was to promote the idea of faceted navigation in online systems, both as an alternative to the hierarchical focus of website structure and in response to the failure of subject searching in online catalogs.

Figure 1.5 shows the Flamenco user interface developed for the University of California–Berkeley Architecture Visual Resources Library, which is organized and represented using such facets as *people, periods, locations, styles,* and *view types.* The interface also allows users to browse and navigate subcategories within each facet.

Based on the idea of faceted search, Cutrell et al. (2006) developed Phlat (Figure 1.6), a user interface to facilitate and improve personal information management (PIM). The interface combines searching and browsing with facets provided as a sorting mechanism.

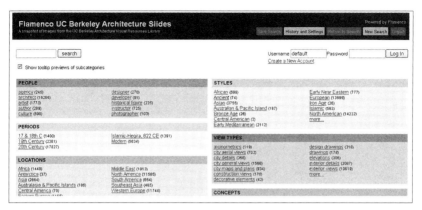

Figure 1.5   Flamenco user interface

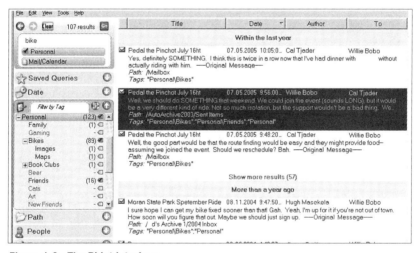

Figure 1.6   The Phlat interface

Several commercial and ecommerce websites make use of faceted browsing and navigation. Two very well-designed examples of faceted navigation are eBay Express and Yelp. In eBay Express (Figure 1.7), a search for *perfume* will provide the user with several facets to navigate, such as *gender and age, fragrance name, brand, condition, type, location,* and *buying format.* Visitors to the website can refine or reformulate their initial query using these facets and sub-facets.

Yelp is a social networking, user review, and local search website that provides location-aware information services in the U.S., Canada, and the U.K. A search for *organic grocery stores* in Edmonton

Figure 1.7   eBay Express

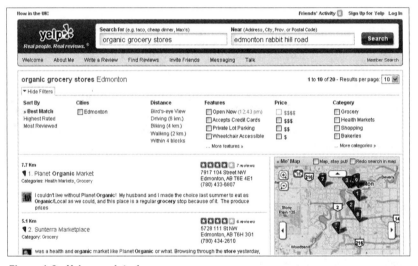

Figure 1.8   Yelp user interface

(Figure 1.8), for example, provides users with the facets *distance, features, price and category, highest rated,* and *most reviewed.*

Online library catalogs have rich metadata, and many have recently started using the metadata to provide faceted navigation of their collections. Faceted navigation enables new ways of and approaches to resource discovery in library catalogs. Figure 1.9 shows a search for *information retrieval* in WorldCat, the world's largest network of library content and services, with the user able to browse and employ various metadata elements such as *author, format, year, audience,* and *language.*

Figure 1.9   Faceted navigation in WorldCat [*Copyright owned by the Online Computer Library Center, Inc., and screenshot used with its permission.*]

Faceted searching, including browsing and navigation, is a promising area now widely used on the web. However, faceted search interfaces are not widely available for general web search as facet values are available only for a small portion of the web. Key determinants of successful application of faceted search methods for web content are 1) understanding which facets are most important to support the varieties of information needs for which people use the web and 2) handling large-scale dynamic collections (Dumais, 2009). Morville and Callender (2010) suggest that faceted navigation is a master search pattern impacting all search and navigation patterns, together with the information architecture as a whole.

1.4 Exploratory Search Interfaces

The term *exploratory search* can be used to describe an information-seeking problem context that is open-ended, persistent, and multi-faceted. It can also describe information-seeking processes that are opportunistic, iterative, and multitactical. In the first sense, exploratory search is commonly used in the context of scientific discovery, learning, and decision making. In the second sense, exploratory tactics are used in all manner of information seeking in order to reflect seeker preferences and experiences as much as their information seeking goal (Marchionini, 2006).

Highly interactive and dynamic user interfaces for exploratory browsing and searching of digital information collections have been the focus of some recent research. White et al. (2006) suggest that in exploratory search, users generally combine querying and browsing strategies to foster learning and investigation. Marchionini (2006) points out that to engage people more fully in the search process and put them in continuous control, researchers are devising highly interactive user interfaces. He proposes that exploratory search consists of "look up," "learn," and "investigate" activities in which examining and comparing results and reformulating queries to discover the boundaries of meaning for key concepts, as well as serendipitous browsing, take place. His view of exploratory search focuses on user interface functionalities that support a combination of browsing and searching, as well as providing the user with a conceptual space for exploration and comprehension of concepts and ideas.

In exploratory search, people usually submit a tentative query to navigate proximal to relevant documents in the collection and then explore the environment to better understand how to exploit it, all the while selectively seeking and passively obtaining cues about their next steps. Examples of exploratory search systems include visualization systems, document clustering and browsing systems, and intelligent content summarization systems (White and Roth, 2009).

Thesauri, as semantic tools and knowledge structures, have the potential to support exploratory searches and can be incorporated into exploratory search interfaces to assist users in the exploration and comprehension of concepts and ideas. As Marchionini (2006) notes, helping searchers to understand data structures and infer relationships among concepts is an important step in exploring and discovering the boundaries of meaning for key concepts. Thesauri, with their rich semantic relations, are capable of facilitating exploratory search activities through allowing the user to form a conceptual map of a particular subject area and to create a context for search and exploration.

Faceted search interfaces combine querying and browsing, allowing people to quickly and flexibly find information based on what they remember about the information they seek. Faceted search interfaces can also help people avoid feelings of being lost in the collection and make it easier for them to explore.

White and Roth (2009) suggest the following set of principles that support exploratory search activities:

- "Support querying and rapid query refinement: Systems must help users formulate queries and adjust queries and views on search results in real time.

- Offer facets and metadata-based result filtering: Systems must allow users to filter and explore results through facet selection and document metadata.

- Leverage search context: Systems must leverage available information about their user, their situation, and their current exploratory search task.

- Offer visualization to support insight and decision making: Systems must present customizable visual representations of the collection being explored in order to support hypothesis generation and trend spotting.

- Support learning and understanding: Systems must help users acquire both knowledge and skills by presenting information in ways amenable to learning, given the user's current knowledge or skill level." (p. 41)

A review of these principles suggests that both thesauri and facets can support some of these exploratory activities through the provision of semantic and conceptual maps of digital information collections. Exploratory search principles may be used to enhance the utility and usefulness of many existing thesauri and faceted classification schemes and structures.

It is interesting to observe the gradual convergence of several lines of current research, namely, exploratory search, faceted search, metadata-based search, and information architecture. All of them share a common aim: to improve and enhance users' access to digital information via similar principles developed over the past four decades. In fact, faceted search interfaces and exploratory search interfaces share similarities to the point that some of the former have also been introduced as the latter.

Figure 1.10 shows mSpace Explorer, a multifaceted, column-based client for exploring large data sets. The mSpace Explorer runs on top of the mSpace framework, an exploratory search system that allows users to choose predefined facets within a broad topic and dynamically modify results in real time. It also assists users in filtering information based on any categories that have been defined as the facets of the mSpace "slice," for example, as shown in the image, categories

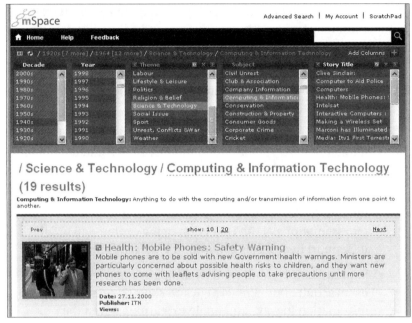

Figure 1.10   mSpace Explorer user interface

such as *year, theme, subject,* and *storyline.* Another feature of this interface lies in its integration of query and browsing.

Another example of an exploratory user interface is Relation Browser, developed by researchers at the University of North Carolina across a series of projects (Zhang and Marchionini, 2005). Figure 1.11 shows an example of the Relation Browser developed for the U.S. Bureau of Labor Statistics (Capra and Marchionini, 2007). It is designed as a tool for understanding relationships between items in a collection and for exploring an information space (i.e., a set of documents). The interface is highly interactive and tightly couples searching and browsing, allowing users to view facets and results at the same time. The results can be dynamically updated and viewed. Users can filter results using such high-level facets as *topic, genre, region,* and *format.* Figure 1.11 shows the user interface features of Relation Browser.

1.5 Dynamic Term Suggestion Systems

Query formulation is a challenging, yet key, stage in the information retrieval process. One of the strategies to engage users in the search

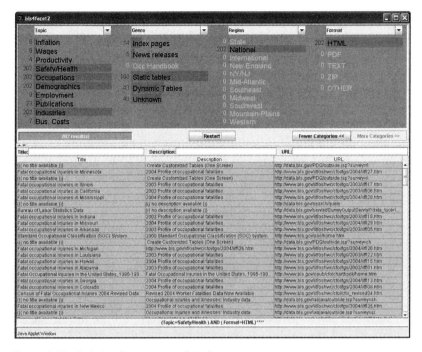

Figure 1.11   Relation Browser user interface

process and support them in formulating better approaches is to suggest search terms. Recently, a number of web search engines and information retrieval systems have incorporated new user interface features that support search term suggestion.

In the literature of search and information retrieval, these features have been called interactive, dynamic, or automated term suggestion mechanisms. These search term suggestion features aim to assist users in query formulation through suggestions of alternative terms and phrases for allowing users to refine or expand their initial search terms.

The advantage of term suggestion is that it helps users to formulate a particular query and, at the same time, form a quick understanding of what the information collection contains on that term or similar terms. As Hearst (2009) notes, the suggestion terms may come from several different sources, including the characteristics of the collection; terms derived from the top-ranked results; a combination of both; a domain-specific, hand-built thesaurus; query logs; or a combination of query logs with navigation or other online behavior.

Recently, numerous search engines, commercial databases, ebusiness websites, and online public access catalogs (OPACs) have started to incorporate term suggestion features into their systems and user interfaces. For example, the Yahoo! Search interface offers search term suggestions as a user starts typing in keywords. Figure 1.12 shows a search for the term *search engine.*

One of the early applications of thesaurus-enhanced interactive term suggestion can be attributed to Schatz et al. (1996), who developed a user interface for the University of Illinois Digital Library Initiative. The interface makes use of the Inspec Thesaurus to suggest terms to the user. Figure 1.13 shows an example of a search for *deductive databases* from the prototype developed by Schatz et al. Displayed are several terms for users to browse through or to select for refinement or reformulation of their initial search.

Other researchers have used mapping and matching techniques to design interactive term suggestion facilities. For instance, Gey et al. (2001) have studied the interactive suggestion to users of subject terms by means of probabilistic mapping between the user's natural language and the technical classification vocabularies. This occurs through a methodology called Entry Vocabulary Indexes. Other researchers have made use of thesauri to suggest terms and query refinement strategies to the user as well.

An interesting and efficient example of incorporating a thesaurus into a search user interface to support interactive term suggestions is the International Atomic Energy Agency (IAEA) digital collection.

Figure 1.12   Yahoo! term suggestion interface [*Reproduced with permission of Yahoo! Inc. ©2011 Yahoo! Inc. YAHOO! and the YAHOO! logo are registered trademarks of Yahoo! Inc.*]

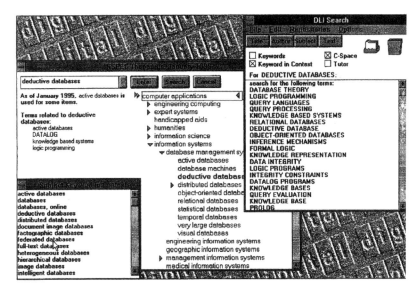

Figure 1.13   Interactive term suggestion interface developed by Schatz et al. (1996)

When a user searches for a term in the collection, the main search page shows the results for the term, and a list of suggested terms for narrowing down the search appears on the right-hand side of the interface. For example, a search for *pollution* retrieves 48,200 results, as indicated in Figure 1.14.

The user can then click on the narrower terms shown to reduce and refine the retrieved results to a more specific set of documents. In this example, if the user decides to narrow down the search using one of the narrower terms, say, *air pollution monitoring*, the number of retrieved results decreases to 3,240. The user can further narrow down the search by choosing another narrower term from the right side of the interface, as shown in Figure 1.15.

Recently, Gray et al. (2010) have developed a system that uses multiple astronomical thesauri to assist users in finding the right term in their search process. As part of the system, Gray et al. created Vocabulary Explorer, which allows users to search and browse the various thesauri. Detailed information about any matched term will be shown in order to help the user identify the right term.

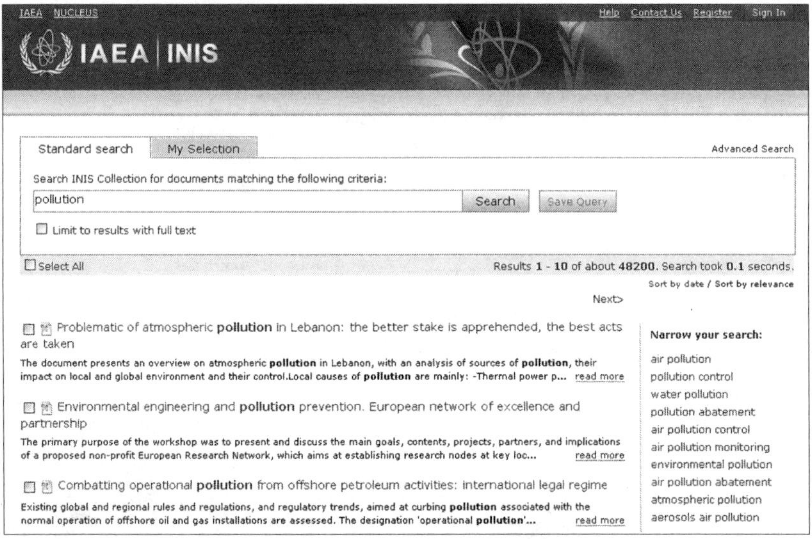

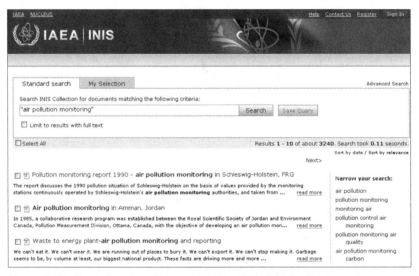

Figure 1.14   IAEA digital collection search term suggestion based on the
International Nuclear Information System Thesaurus

Figure 1.15   Narrowing down the search in the IAEA digital collection using
thesaurus-based term suggestions from the International Nuclear
Information System Thesaurus

1.6 Thesauri and Social Tagging

Social tagging, sometimes referred to as *social bookmarking*, is defined variously as the classification of resources "by the use of informally assigned, user-defined keywords or tags" (Barsky and Purdon, 2006, p. 66) and elsewhere as the classification of resources "using free-text tags, unconstrained and arbitrary values" (Tonkin, 2006). In addition to *social bookmarking*, quasi-synonymous terms for social tagging include *collaborative tagging, folksonomy, folk categorization, communal categorization, ethno-classification, mob indexing,* and *free-text tagging*.

Social tagging emerged in popular practice around 2003, at the same time as social networking websites, and constitutes an important part of the interactive, democratic nature of Web 2.0 because the responsibility for the classification of web resources is placed squarely in the hands of the users. Tonkin (2006) proposes a two-part taxonomy of social tagging systems: "'broad,' meaning that many different users can tag a single resource, or 'narrow,' meaning that a resource is tagged by only one or a few users."

Shiri (2009) provides a comparative examination of a typology of social tagging systems that encompasses social networks, social bookmarking, video blogging and sharing, photo sharing, academic bookmarking, and slide sharing. He notes that some social tagging services, such as Technorati, Flickr, Bubbleshare, YouTube, and MySpaceTV, require users to organize their posted items in predetermined categories imposed by the service (generally anywhere from five to 20 categories). These categories represent a thesaurus-like hierarchical structure and often serve as a complement to tagging activities. For example, a YouTube user posting a video must put it in a category such as entertainment, comedy, or news, as well as describe it with appropriate tags.

A number of studies have discussed the comparison and reconciliation of controlled vocabularies with social tagging and folksonomies. Macgregor and McCulloch (2006) provide a succinct review of early debates about controlled vocabularies and collaborative tagging. Most of the difficulties associated with social tags and folksonomies (e.g., low precision, lack of collocation and consistency) originate from the absence of those properties that have come to characterize controlled vocabularies. Macgregor and McCulloch speculate that, ultimately, the coexistence of controlled vocabularies and collaborative tagging systems will emerge, with each appropriate for use within the following distinct information contexts: formal (e.g., academic tasks, industrial research, corporate knowledge management) and informal (e.g., recreational research, PIM, exploration of exhaustive subject areas prior to formal exploration).

Spiteri (2007) evaluated tags against Section 6 (choice and form of terms) of the NISO guidelines for the construction of controlled vocabularies and found that the folksonomy tags correspond closely to the NISO guidelines pertaining to the types of concepts expressed by the tags, the predominance of single tags, the predominance of nouns, and the use of recognized spelling. She suggests that folksonomies could serve as a very powerful and flexible tool for increasing the user-friendliness and interactivity of public library catalogs.

Hastings et al. (2007) report the findings that various studies have in common on people's image tagging and descriptions: 1) tags assigned to groups of images and individual images differ in terms of their level of abstraction, 2) image tagging specificity and exhaustivity levels differ greatly among individuals, and 3) the accordance between existing controlled vocabularies and tags varies in terms of image attributes.

In a user-centered study of authors and readers of digital collections, Golub et al. (2009) investigated how social tags can be enhanced by the use of controlled vocabularies such as classification schemes and thesauri. Their findings showed the importance of controlled vocabulary suggestions for both indexing and retrieval in order to accomplish several functions: help produce ideas of tags for users, make it easier to find focus for the tagging, ensure consistency, and increase the number of access points in retrieval. The quality of the suggestions from the controlled vocabularies was found to be a key factor.

In a series of studies comparing social tags and controlled vocabularies, Kipp (2010) and Lu and Kipp (2010) concluded that there is continuity between conventional indexing and user tagging, and that this continuity could form the basis for a complementary system of subject access that would enrich conventional indexing and support its continued utility.

These studies suggest that social tagging and controlled vocabularies have their own advantages and disadvantages, but that social tags do not replace the latter; rather, social tags complement controlled vocabularies and provide additional access points for users. To afford better user experiences, information access and retrieval systems should use a combination of controlled vocabularies and social tags in order to create more-inclusive user interfaces. The ways in which combined use of controlled vocabularies and tags can be achieved depend, to a large extent, on the nature of the target audience, on the content and context of the information collection, and on the information search tasks that the system is designed to support.

1.7 Conclusion

This chapter has provided a brief history of information retrieval thesauri, along with the associated standards. Functions, uses, and types of thesauri were introduced. It was noted that the advent of the World Wide Web facilitated much greater use of thesauri on the web and in a variety of search environments.

Developments related to web technologies and web-based services and systems provide an opportunity for the reusing and repurposing of thesauri as networked KOSs.

The information architecture community benefits from various applications of thesauri as searching, browsing, and navigation tools.

Faceted and exploratory search systems and interfaces have adopted thesauri to expand and enhance the search horizon through semantic and conceptual structures embedded in thesauri, thus facilitating the exploration of digital collections and the performance of effective searches.

Thesauri have long been used as search strategy support mechanisms to suggest terms to users in a dynamic and interactive mode, with the goal of encouraging and engaging users in the search process. All of these developments suggest that thesauri have an increasingly major role to play in powering search in the new information environment.

References

Ahmed, K. (2003). Topic map design patterns for information architecture. *XML Europe, Londra 2003*, pp. 5–8. Retrieved from www.techquila.com/tmsinia.html (accessed May 1, 2012).

Aitchison, J., and Dextre Clarke, S. D. (2004). The thesaurus: A historical viewpoint. With a look to the future. *Cataloguing and Classification Quarterly*, 37(3/4), 5–21.

Aitchison, J., Gilchrist, A., and Bawden, D. (2000). *Thesaurus construction and use: A practical manual*, 4th ed. London: Aslib.

Anderson, J. D., and Rowley, F. A. (1991). Building end-user thesauri from full-text. In: Barbara H. Kwasink and Raya Fidel (Eds.), *Advances in classification research (Proceedings of the 2nd ASIS SIG/CR classification research workshop*, pp. 1–13). Medford, NJ: Learned Information.

ANSI/NISO Z39.19: 1993. (1993). *Guidelines for the construction, format, and management of monolingual thesauri.* Bethesda, MD: National Information Standards Organization Press.

ANSI/NISO Z39.19: 2005. (2005). *Guidelines for the construction, format, and management of monolingual controlled vocabularies.* Bethesda, MD: National Information Standards Organization Press.

Barsky, E., and Purdon, M. (2006). Introducing Web 2.0: Social networking and social bookmarking for health librarians. *Journal of the Canadian Health Libraries Association, 27*(3), 65–67.

Bates, M. J. (1986). Subject access in online catalogs: A design model. *Journal of the American Society for Information Science, 37* (6), 357–376.

Beeson, I., and Chelin, J. (2006). Information systems meets information science. *ITALICS, 5*(2). Retrieved from www.ics.heacademy.ac.uk/italics/vol5iss2.htm (accessed May 1, 2012).

Broughton, V. (2006). *Essential thesaurus construction.* London: Facet.

Broughton, V., Hansson, J., Hjørland, B., and López-Huertas, M. J. (2005). Knowledge organization. In: *European curriculum reflections on library and information science*, 133–148. Retrieved from www.webcitation.org/5Vl9HJpm1 (accessed May 1, 2012).

BS 5723: 1987. (1987). *Guide to establishment and development of monolingual thesauri.* London: British Standard Institutions.

BS 6723: 1985. (1985). *Guidelines for the establishment and development of multilingual thesauri.* London: British Standards Institution.

BS 8723: 2005. (2005). *Structured vocabularies for information retrieval: Guide. Part 2. Thesauri.* London: British Standards Institution.

Capra, R., and Marchionini, G. (2007). Faceted browsing, dynamic interfaces, and exploratory search: Experiences and challenges. In: *Workshop on human-computer interaction and information retrieval: Workshop proceedings* (pp. 7–9). Retrieved from projects.csail.mit.edu/hcir/web/hcir07.pdf (accessed May 29, 2012).

Chamis, A. Y. (1991). *Vocabulary control and search strategies in online searching.* New York: Greenwood Press.

Cochrane, P. A. (1992). Indexing and searching thesauri, the Janus or Proteus of information retrieval. In: N. J. Williamson and M. Hudon (Eds.), *Classification research for knowledge organization*, FID, pp. 161–178.

Cutrell, E., Robbins, D. C., Dumais, S. T., and Sarin, R. (2006). Fast, flexible filtering with Phlat: Personal search and organization made easy. In: R. E. Grinter, T. Rodden, P. Aoki, E. Cutrell, R. Geffries, and G. Olson (Eds.), *Proceedings of the SIGCHI conference on human factors in computing systems* (pp. 261–270). Montreal, Canada.

Dextre Clarke, S. D. (2001). Thesaural relationships. In: C. A. Bean and R. Green (Eds.), *Relationships in the organization of knowledge* (pp. 37–52). Boston: Kluwer.

Dextre Clarke, S. D. (2008). The last 50 years of knowledge organization: A journey through my personal archives. *Journal of Information Science*, 34(4), 427–437.

Dong, A., and Agogino, A. M. (2001). Design principles for the information architecture of a SMET Education Digital Library. In: E. Fox and C. Borgman (Eds.), *Proceedings of the ACM/IEEE joint conference on digital libraries 2001* (pp. 314–321). New York: ACM Press.

Dumais, S. (2009). Faceted search. In: L. Liu and M. T. Özsu (Eds.), *Encyclopedia of database systems*. New York: Springer.

Education Resources Information Center. ERIC thesaurus. Retrieved from www.eric.ed.gov/ERICWebPortal/thesaurus/thesaurus.jsp (accessed May 1, 2012).

Garshol, L. M. (2004). Metadata? Thesauri? Taxonomies? Topic maps! Making sense of it all. *Journal of Information Science*, 30(4), 378–391.

Gey, F., Buckland, M., Chen, A., and Larson, R. (2001). Entry vocabulary: A technology to enhance digital object search. In: J. Allan (Ed.), *Proceedings of the first international conference on human language technology* (pp. 91–95). Stroudsburg, PA: ACM Press.

Gilchrist, A. (1971). *The thesaurus in retrieval*. London: Aslib.

Gilchrist, A. (2003). Thesauri, taxonomies, and ontologies: An etymological note. *Journal of Documentation*, 59(1), 7–18.

Golub, K., Jones, C., Lykke Nielsen, M., Matthews, B., Moon, J., Puzon, B., and Tudhope, D. (2009). EnTag: Enhancing social tagging for discovery. In: F. Heath, M. L. Rice-Lively, and R. Furuta (Eds.), *Proceedings of the joint conference on digital libraries (JCDL)* (pp. 163–172). New York: ACM.

Gray, A. J. G., Gray, N., Hall, C. W., and Ounis, I. (2010). Finding the right term: Retrieving and exploring semantic concepts in astronomical vocabularies. *Information Processing and Management*, 46(4), 470–478.

Gruber, T. (2009). Ontology. In: L. Liu and M. T. Özsu (Eds.), *Encyclopedia of database systems*. New York: Springer.

Hastings, S., Neal, D., Rorissa, A., Yoon, J., and Iyer, H. (2007). Social computing, folksonomies, and image tagging: Reports from the research front. Panel presentation. In: *Proceedings of the 2007 American Society for Information Science & Technology 70th annual meeting* (Vol. 45, pp. 1026–1029). Milwaukee, Wisconsin.

Hearst, M. A. (2000). Next generation web search: Setting our sites. *IEEE Data Engineering Bulletin*, 23(3), 38–48.

Hearst, M. A. (2006). Design recommendations for hierarchical faceted search interfaces. In: A. Z. Broder and Y. S. Maarek (Eds.), *Proceedings of the 29th annual international ACM SIGIR conference on research and development in information retrieval (SIGIR'06) workshop on faceted search* (pp. 26–30). Seattle, Washington.

Hearst, M. A. (2008). UIs for faceted navigation: Recent advances and remaining open problems. In: *The workshop on human computer interaction and information retrieval, HCIR 2008*. Redmond, Washington.

Hearst, M. A. (2009). *Search user interfaces*. Cambridge, UK: Cambridge University Press.

Hearst, M. A., English, J., Sinha, R., Swearingen, K., and Yee, K. P. (2002). Finding the flow in web site search. *Communications of the ACM*, 45(9), 42–49.

Hodge, G. (2000). *Systems of knowledge organization for digital libraries: Beyond traditional authority files*. Washington D.C.: Digital Library Federation. Retrieved from www.clir.org/pubs/reports/pub91/contents. html (accessed May 1, 2012).

Information Architecture Institute. (2005). Retrieved from www.iainstitute. org (accessed May 1, 2012).

International Atomic Energy Agency (IAEA). International Nuclear Information System (INIS) Collection. Retrieved from inis.iaea.org/ search/default.aspx (accessed May 1, 2012).

ISO 2788: 1986. (1986). *Guidelines for the establishment and development of monolingual thesauri*. International Organization for Standardization.

ISO 5964: 1985. (1985). *Guidelines for the establishment and development of multilingual thesauri*. International Organization for Standardization.

ISO 25964-1: 2011. (2011). Information and documentation. *Thesauri and interoperability with other vocabularies. Part 1: Thesauri for information retrieval*. International Organization for Standardization.

Kekäläinen, J. and Jarvelin, K. (1998). The impact of query structure and query expansion on retrieval performance. In: W. B. Croft et al. (Eds.), *Proceedings of the Association for Computing Machinery Special Interest Group on Information Retrieval (ACM/SIGIR) 21st annual international ACM SIGIR conference on research and development in information retrieval 98* (pp. 130–137). Melbourne, New York: ACM Press.

Kipp, M. E. I. (2010). Convergence and divergence in tagging systems: An examination of tagging practices over a four year period. In: *Proceedings of the 2010 annual meeting of the American Society for Information Science and Technology*. Pittsburgh, Pennsylvania.(Conference Poster)

Knapp, S. D., Cohen, L. B., and Judes, D. R. (1998). A natural language thesaurus for humanities. *Library Quarterly*, 68 (4), 406–430.

Kristensen, J. (1993). Expanding end-users' query statements for free text searching with a search-aid thesaurus. *Information Processing and Management*, 29 (6), 733–744.

Kristensen, J., and Jarvelin, K. (1990). The effectiveness of a searching thesaurus in free text searching of a full-text database. *International Classification*, 17 (2), 77–84.

La Barre, K. (2004). Adventures in faceted classification: A brave new world or a world of confusion? In: I. C. McIlwaine (Ed.), *Advances in knowledge organization: Knowledge organization and the global information society* (Proceedings of the eighth international ISKO conference; pp. 79–84). Würzburg, Germany: Ergon Verlag.

Lopez-Huertas, M. J. (1997). Thesaurus structure design: A conceptual approach for improved interaction. *Journal of Documentation*, 53 (2), 139–177.

Lu, K., and Kipp, M. E. I. (2010). An experimental study on the retrieval effectiveness of collaborative tags. In: *Proceedings of the 2010 annual meeting of the American Society for Information Science and Technology*. Pittsburgh, Pennsylvania.

Lykke Nielsen, M. (1998). Future thesauri: What kind of conceptual knowledge do searchers need? In: W. M. El Hadi, J. Maniez, and S. Pollitt (Eds.), *Structures and relations in knowledge organization* (Proceedings of the 5th international ISKO conference; pp. 153–160). Würzburg, Germany: Ergon Verlag.

Lykke Nielsen, M. (2001). A framework for work task-based thesaurus design. *Journal of Documentation*, 57 (6), 774-797.

Macgregor, G., and McCulloch, E. (2006). Collaborative tagging as a knowledge organisation and resource discovery tool. *Library Review*, 55(5), 291–300.

Mandala, R., Tokunaga, T., and Tanaka, H. (2000). Query expansion using heterogeneous thesauri. *Information Processing & Management*, 36(3), 361–378.

Marchionini, G. (2006). Exploratory search: From finding to understanding. *Communications of the ACM*, 49(4), 41–46.

McIlwaine, I. C. (2003). Trends in knowledge organization research. *Knowledge Organization*, 30(2), 75–86.

Miller, U. (2003). Thesaurus and new information environment. In: M. Drake and M. N. Maack (Eds.), *Encyclopedia of library and information science*, 2nd ed. Boca Raton: Taylor & Francis Group.

Milstead, J. L. (1998). Use of thesauri in the full-text environment. Retrieved from www.bayside-indexing.com/Milstead/useof.htm (accessed May 1, 2012).

Morville, P., and Callender, J. (2010). *Search patterns*. Sebastopol, CA: O'Reilly.

Morville, P. and Rosenfeld, L. (2007). *Information architecture for the World Wide Web: Designing Large-Scale Web Sites*, 3rd ed. Sebastopol, CA: O'Reilly.

mSpace Explorer. Retrieved from research.mspace.fm/projects/explorer (accessed May 1, 2012).

Networked Knowledge Organization Systems/Services (NKOS). Retrieved from nkos.slis.kent.edu (accessed May 1, 2012).

Olson, H. A. (2007). How we construct subjects: A feminist analysis. *Library Trends*, 56(2), 509–541.

Pastor-Sanchez, J. A., Martinez, F. J., and Rodriguez, J. V. (2009). Advantages of thesaurus representation using the Simple Knowledge Organization System (SKOS) compared with proposed alternatives. *Information Research*, 14(4), paper 422. Retrieved from InformationR.net/ir/14-4/paper422.html (accessed May 1, 2012).

Perez, E. (1982). Text enhancement: Controlled vocabulary vs. free text. *Special Libraries*, 73(July), 183–192.

Piternick, A. (1984). Searching vocabularies: A developing category of online searching tools. *Online Review*, 8(5), 441–449.

Pollitt, A. S., Ellis, G. P., and Smith, M. P. (1994). HIBROWSE for bibliographic databases. *Journal of Information Science*, 20(6), 413–426.

Project ISO 25964. (2012). Thesauri and interoperability with other vocabularies. Retrieved from www.niso.org/workrooms/iso25964 (accessed May 1, 2012).

Ranganathan, S. R. (1967). *Prolegomena to library classification*. New York: Asia Publishing House.

Rosenfeld, L., and Morville, P. (1998). *Information architecture for the World Wide Web: Designing Large-Scale Web Sites*. Sebastopol, CA: O'Reilly.

Saumure, K., and Shiri, A. (2008). Knowledge organization trends: A comparison of the pre- and post-web eras. *Journal of Information Science*, 34(5), 651–666.

Schatz, B. R., Johnson, E. H., and Cochrane, P. A. (1996). Interactive term suggestion for users of digital libraries: Using subject thesauri and co-occurrence lists for information retrieval. In: E. Fox and G. Marchionini (Eds.), *Proceedings of the 1st Association for Computing Machinery international conference on digital libraries* (pp. 126–133). Bethesda, MD: ACM Press.

Schwartz, C. (2008). Thesauri and facets and tags, oh my! A look at three decades in subject analysis. *Library Trends*, 56(4), 830–842.

Shiri, A. (2009). An examination of social tagging interface features and functionalities: An analytical comparison. *Online Information Review*, 33(5), 901–919.

Shiri, A. A., and Revie, C. (2000). Thesauri on the web: Current developments and trends. *Online Information Review*, 24(4), 273–279.

Soergel, D. (1999). The rise of ontolgoies or the reinvention of classification. *Journal of the American Society for Information Science*, 50(12), 1119–1120.

Soergel, D. (2003). Functions of a thesaurus/classification/ontological knowledge base. Retrieved from ontolog.cim3.net/file/work/Ontologizing Ontolog/TaxoThesaurus/SoergelKOSOntologyFunctions2—Dagobert Soergel_20060616.pdf (accessed May 1, 2012).

Spiteri, L. F. (2007). Structure and form of folksonomy tags: The road to the public library catalogue. *Webology*, 4(2), Article 41. Retrieved from www.webology.org/2007/v4n2/a41.html (accessed May 1, 2012).

Tonkin, E. (2006, April 30). Folksonomies: The fall and rise of plain-text tagging. *Ariadne*, (47). Retrieved from www.ariadne.ac.uk/issue47/tonkin (accessed May 1, 2012).

Tudhope, D., and Binding, C. (2008). Faceted thesauri. *Axiomathes*, 18(2), 211–222.

UNISIST (1980). *Guidelines for the establishment and development of multilingual thesauri*, rev. ed. Paris, UNESCO.

UNISIST (1981). *Guidelines for the establishment and development of monolingual thesauri*, 2nd ed. Paris, UNESCO.

U.S. National Library of Medicine. (2011). Medical Subject Headings (MeSH). Retrieved from www.nlm.nih.gov/mesh (accessed May 1, 2012).

Vickery, B. C. (1960). Thesaurus—A new word in documentation. *Journal of Documentation*, 16(4), 181–189.

Wang, Z., Chaudhry, A. S., and Khoo, C. S. (2008). Using classification schemes and thesauri to build an organizational taxonomy for organizing content and aiding navigation. *Journal of Documentation*, 64(6), 842–876.

White, R. W., Kules, B., Drucker, S. M., and Schraefel, M. C. (2006). Supporting exploratory search. *Communications of the ACM*, 49(4), 36–39.

White, R. W., and Roth, R. A. (2009). *Exploratory search: Beyond the query-response paradigm*. San Rafael, CA: Morgan & Claypool.

Williamson, N. (2000). Thesauri in the digital age: Stability and dynamism in their development and use. In: C. Beghtol, L. C. Howarth, and N. Williamson (Eds.), *Proceedings of the sixth international ISKO conference* (pp. 268–274). Germany: Ergon Verlag.

Williamson, N. (2007). Knowledge structures and the internet: Progress and prospects. *Cataloging & Classification Quarterly*, 44(3/4), 329–342.

Wodtke, C., and Govella, A. (2009). *Information architecture: Blueprints for the web*. Berkeley, CA: New Riders.

WorldCat. Retrieved from www.worldcat.org (accessed May 1, 2012).

Yee, K., Swearingen, K., Li, K., and Hearst, M. (2003). Faceted metadata for image search and browsing. In: G. Cockton and G. Korhonen (Eds.), *Proceedings of the ACM conference on human factors in computing systems* (pp. 401–408). New York: ACM Press.

Yelp. Retrieved from www.yelp.com (accessed May 1, 2012).

Zhang, J., and Marchionini, G. (2005). Evaluation and evolution of a browse and search interface: Relation Browser++. In: L. Delcambre and G. Giuliano (Eds.), *Proceedings of the 2005 national conference on digital government research* (pp. 179–188). Marina del Rey, CA: Digital Government Society of North America.

Zhang, X., Strand, L., Fisher, N., Kneip, J., and Ayoub, O. (2002). Information architecture as reflected in classrooms. In: *Proceedings of the American Society for Information Science and Technology annual meeting* (pp. 78–82). Philadelphia, Pennsylvania.

CHAPTER 2

Thesauri in Interactive Information Retrieval

This chapter contextualizes thesauri within interactive information retrieval research. It discusses ways in which interactive information retrieval models have addressed thesauri as a component in the search process. Information interaction is considered as a foundational concept, and the role of thesauri as knowledge and cognitive structures is elaborated.

2.1 What Is Human Information Interaction?

Over the past 15 years, the term *human information interaction* has been widely used in the literatures of information searching, seeking and retrieval, human-computer interaction, and information architecture. This chapter provides an overview of the definitions presented in these various research domains, with the aim of offering a comprehensive perspective on the scope, use, and application of each term. It also discusses and contextualizes thesauri in general and subject access in particular, along with a number of information interaction models.

In 1995, Nahum Gershon coined the term *human information interaction* to denote how human beings interact with, relate to, and process information regardless of the medium connecting the two. Since then, the term has been widely adopted by the traditional information science and retrieval communities (Morville, 2005). A number of researchers have argued that human information interaction is a better phrase than human-computer interaction to represent the complexity of users' interactions with information in a wide variety of settings. Morville (Jones et al., 2006) argues that human-computer interaction approaches are optimal for applications and interfaces in which designers exercise great control over form and function.

Human information interaction approaches are optimal for net-worked, transmedia systems in which control is sacrificed for inter-operability and findability. At the crossroads of ubiquitous computing and the internet, users may find and interact with objects through a variety of devices and interfaces. The context of use is dif-ficult to predict and impossible to control, and so the emphasis shifts from interface to experience and from human-computer interaction to human information interaction.

It should be noted that some researchers (Fidel et al., 2004) have used *human information interaction* as a synonym for human infor-mation behavior with a particular focus on cognitive aspects of inter-action. However, this is a much broader research area. In the current chapter, the focus is on human information interaction within the context of electronic environments in which users interact with digi-tal information systems.

Increasing human participation in the information retrieval process has resulted in new research and development that takes into account the importance of human interaction with information. Marchionini (2004) notes that human interaction with information may be represented as a process in which users interact with both queries and results in a more engaged and dynamic manner and take active roles in the whole information search and retrieval process. In a broader sense, users may interact with a wide range of information-bearing objects such as text, images, videos, and animations, as well as with their representations in various formats, including search terms coming from different sources, tags, annotations, metadata, and so forth.

Figure 2.1, from Marchionini (2004), represents a user with an information need who acts on and interacts with information and its representation. He argues that *information interaction* is a better term than *information retrieval* to reflect the dynamic and engaging nature of human participation in the information-seeking process. He notes that information interaction addresses the ways in which digital information objects and human information seekers interact with, and exert influence on, each other. The new forms of informa-tion objects and new patterns of interaction make the area of human information interaction a necessary and interesting research and development area for both information retrieval and human-computer interaction communities (Marchionini, 2008).

Information interaction is a complex process that integrates aspects of the user, the content, and the system that delivers content

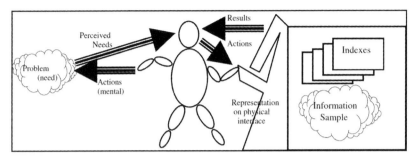

Figure 2.1   User-centered information interaction (Marchionini, 2004)

to the user (Toms, 2002). Users may interact with classes, categories, or terms extracted from classification schemes and thesauri, which may be viewed as pathways to the underlying content.

Toms (2002) proposes a model of information interaction (Figure 2.2) in which a user determines or recognizes a goal for an interaction, selects a category (which may be a menu or a term from an index, a thesaurus, or a taxonomy), and then identifies cues, which can be either hyperlinks in a webpage or cues used by indexers, such as semantic links. The user next reads and extracts information and integrates it with what is already known about a particular piece of information. At the final stage, the user evaluates information in terms of relevance, usefulness, or level of interest.

In information interaction, users are likely to perform several iterations of the process before terminating a session. They initiate the process either by formulating a goal, as in the traditional information-seeking process, or by simply making a decision to examine a body of information. In both cases, a category such as a menu is selected. Toms places particular emphasis in the information interaction process on text as information. With the great variety of information-bearing objects on the web, it is clear that the notion of information interaction should be viewed in a broader spectrum of this variety in information genres and users' interactions with them.

Resmini and Rosati (2010) argue that information architecture can enhance users' interaction experience if semantic elements and structures are incorporated into websites. They propose a cross-context human information interaction model focusing on the principle of findability. The model suggests that semantic support can be provided through thesauri, taxonomies, and classification schemes to improve

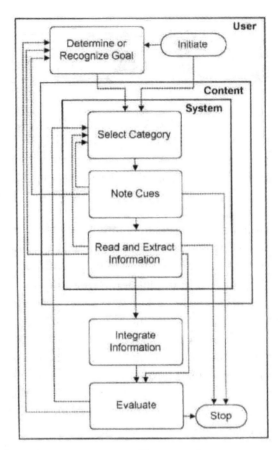

Figure 2.2 Information interaction model (Toms, 2002)

findability and enhance users' interactions with various types of information in a wide array of digital information contexts.

Greenberg (2004) notes that studying the interaction between users and thesauri is a growing trend. Two key factors motivating this growth are 1) intensified research efforts in human-computer interaction and information-seeking behavior and 2) increased public access to thesauri-supported information systems via the web.

2.2 Information-Seeking and Information Retrieval Interaction Models

This section reviews information-seeking and information retrieval interaction models and their implications for search term selection, query formulation, and expansion. Particular attention is given to assessing the extent to which these models have considered the subject approach and, in particular, any thesaural components within their modeling of query formulation and expansion.

The role of a model is to depict the main elements of and relations between objects, which encompass system, process, entity, structure, and idea. Scientific models are characterized by the property of testability. Therefore, models themselves are a subject of examination and critique in terms of how well they depict an object (Saracevic, 1997). Models in the general field of information behavior may be described as frameworks for thinking about a problem: They are statements, often in the form of diagrams, that attempt to describe an information-seeking activity, the causes and the consequences of that activity, or the relationships among stages in an information-seeking behavior model (Wilson, 1999).

The development of most of the models for information retrieval interaction can be traced back to the 1980s and 1990s. During this period, models were proposed to address issues related to understanding the complex nature of human information interaction. Such models have approached the issues from a range of perspectives. *Information retrieval interaction, information-seeking behavior, information-searching behavior,* and *information behavior* are among the terms used to denote the features of these models. As Beaulieu (2000) comments, information seeking, information searching, and information retrieval interaction have traditionally been the concerns of separate research communities having in common the element of interaction. Taken together, these communities provide complementary views of a highly dynamic process.

In a review of information behavior models, Wilson (1999) identifies two major types of models: information-seeking behavior models and information-searching models. He looks at these models from the information behavior perspective involving those activities a person may engage in when identifying his or her own information needs, searching for such information in any way, and using or transferring that information.

This is a more general perspective than that of most information retrieval researchers, who view both information-searching models and information-seeking behavior models as subsets of information retrieval. To examine individual models related to information seeking and searching, and information retrieval, Wilson's categorization is used here to divide models into two groups: information-seeking behavior and information retrieval interaction.

2.2.1 Information-Seeking Behavior Models

Models of information-seeking behavior strive to depict all steps, stages, and efforts that are undertaken by users in interacting with information represented in a wide range of sources regardless of format, coverage, or presentation. This modeling encompasses all situations, tasks, and activities that users deal with, from the instantiation of an information need to information use and retrieval satisfaction. As these models also include generalized descriptions of information-seeking behaviors, only those that make explicit reference to query formulation and the subject approach are examined here.

In his study of the information-seeking patterns of academic social scientists, Ellis (1989) derives a behavioral model with implications for information retrieval system design. The model includes six characteristics, which constitute the principal generic features of the different individual patterns. These features are named *starting, chaining, browsing, differentiating, monitoring,* and *extracting.* Based on this model and a detailed analysis of the social scientists' behavior, Ellis found subject access (i.e., browsing subject terms) to be a common problem in browsing and recommended the adoption of specific features in information retrieval system design. The browsing feature in his model has significant bearing on the subject approach and the use of thesauri for search term selection and query formulation. He suggests that some form of broader and narrower subject description is necessary to provide browsing facilities for retrieval system exploration. His model suggests that it would be useful to provide searchers with the possibility of browsing the hierarchical structure of a thesaurus in order to broaden or narrow a search, as well as to find related terms for inclusion in the search formulation.

Bates's (1989) model of browsing and berrypicking is one of the most-cited search process models. She uses the term *berrypicking* by way of analogy to picking huckleberries or blueberries in a forest, in order to develop a model of evolving query formulation and modification. The model touches on different behavioral, heuristic, and physical aspects of the process that searchers might encounter during online searching. Query and search terms are perceived as dynamic entities varying in part or in whole to satisfy an information need throughout the search process. In considering manual information-seeking behaviors, she identifies various capabilities that users might be interested in using during the search process. She refers to six main strategies users employ: footnote chasing, citation searching, journal run, area scanning, subject searching in bibliographies and abstracting/indexing services, and author searching. The notion of area scanning refers to browsing materials that are physically collocated with materials located earlier in a search.

Two of these strategies, area scanning and subject searching in bibliographies and abstracting/indexing services, are strongly related to the subject approach in the information search process. In area scanning, the focus is on a subject approach to library catalogs, while in subject searching, subject indexes and categories are referred to as information-searching tools. Among the search design features Bates suggests based on her berrypicking model is the provision of capabilities for users to browse general as well as subdivisions of the classification categories used in an abstracting and indexing service.

Kulthau's (1991) model of the information search process is derived from a series of five studies investigating common experiences of users in information-seeking situations. Stages identified in her model are initiation, selection, exploration, formulation, collection, and presentation.

As such, the model depicts the information-seeking process from a user's perspective. Both the selection and formulation stages are similar in nature to the elements of user-system interaction. In Kulthau's model, the selection stage deals mainly with topic selection with an overview of alternative topics that can be compared to the selection of search terms in the interaction process. The formulation stage is seen to be an important aspect of the search process, as the user goes about trying to form a focused perspective on the topic. This stage can also be compared with the formulation of a proper query to find relevant information. These two stages have useful implications for query formulation and reformulation during the search process.

The models discussed so far attempt to explicate human information interaction from a broad range of perspectives covering, in a very general sense, the universe of needs, behaviors, strategies, and information sources and are strongly influenced by social, psychological, and communication theories. The next section provides an overview of information retrieval interaction models and discusses the extent to which they have incorporated thesauri into the search term selection process.

2.2.2 Information Retrieval Interaction Models

Models classed as information retrieval interaction models focus on the nature of the interaction between users and computerized information retrieval systems. The rationale behind these models is to provide a holistic view of all of the components, processes, actions, and steps that are involved in user interaction with an information retrieval system.

A number of information retrieval interaction models have been proposed, some of which have undergone various developmental stages to take into account as many human system interaction dimensions and perspectives as possible. The major models of interest are discussed here: Ingwersen's cognitive model, Belkin's episode model, Saracevic's stratified model, Sutcliffe's process model of information-searching activities, and Vakkari's task-based information retrieval model.

Ingwersen's (1996) cognitive model can be viewed as one of the major information retrieval interaction models concentrating on different cognitive structures affecting information retrieval interaction. It is an extended and completed version of previous cognitive models proposed by Ingwersen (1982, 1992). The model suggests that human cognitive structures are inherent in various stages of information retrieval interaction, with elements that can affect the user's cognitive state while interacting with an information retrieval system, which Ingwersen refers to as "cognitive origins."

The users and their cognitive space are found at the heart of the model, and different cognitive transformations occur between and among the elements depicted in the model (e.g., a user interacting with an intermediary, an intermediary interacting with the information retrieval system). Ingwersen states that a variety of human actors—including system designers and producers, indexing rule constructors, indexers, authors of texts and images, intermediary mechanism designers, and users—all possess cognitive structures that can influence information retrieval interaction. For example, index terms are representations of the human indexer's cognitive structures added to the original information objects, which in turn affect the formulation of the query. Thesauri can be construed as cognitive structures, which interact with other cognitive structures and influence information retrieval interaction in general and query characteristics in particular. Ingwersen also suggests the notion of polyrepresentation to refer to different cognitive structures such as problem statement, information need, and current cognitive state. From the polyrepresentational point of view, thesauri are viewed as one type of representation of information objects, which, when coupled with other types of representation, affect the user's decision making and interaction.

User-thesaurus interaction in this model can be construed as the interaction between cognitive constructs of users and indexers, in which the semantic structure of the thesaurus influences the user's articulation of an information need and well-defined query construction. Figure 2.3 shows that multiple representations of information may cognitively overlap. The thesaurus, in this model, is viewed as one type of cognitive structure that overlaps with other cognitive constructs in the information interaction process. Thesaurus terms are document representations that may overlap with the user's mental model of a particular information retrieval system or document collection.

The episode model of Belkin (1993; Belkin et al., 1995) is another information retrieval interaction model that considers user interaction with texts defined as any information-bearing objects as the central phenomenon of information retrieval. It proposes a number of information-seeking strategies. The principal process for information retrieval in this model is the interaction of user with text in support of a wide range of information-seeking behaviors and related goals relevant to a wide variety of problematic situations. Each information-seeking strategy can be defined as an episode. Belkin points to the useful distinction between *searching* for a given item and *scanning* for interesting items within the information collection. The dimension of "goal" in the interaction implies the intention of a user in dealing with an information retrieval system, which may be learning about some aspect of the resource or selecting useful items for retrieval. The mode of retrieval signifies the extent of the user's knowledge about the location of the item. If the search is for identified items, the retrieval model would be called *retrieval by specification*, because the item has already been specified. If the user does not have a clear idea of the item and finds the item by scanning similar items, the retrieval mode is referred to as *retrieval by recognition*.

Another dimension of the model refers to the two types of information resources with which users interact. The first is information, the item through which the user's need can be met. The second is meta-information sources such as thesauri and classification systems,

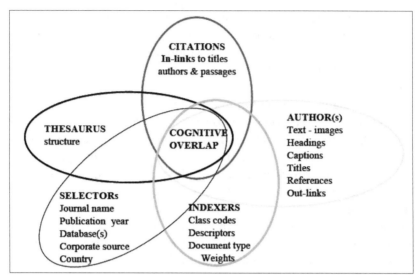

Figure 2.3   Principle of polyrepresentation in academic documents (Larsen et al., 2006)

which may be consulted by users to characterize how information resources have been represented in the information retrieval system. In this model, the use of thesauri is interpreted as one type of information-seeking strategy that can be used in at least eight of the 16 strategies proposed. User interaction with thesauri is viewed as related to various searching and browsing strategies.

The stratified model of information retrieval interaction proposed by Saracevic (1997) attempts to cast light on the complex human system interaction process and its constituent elements. Interaction in this model is conceived as a layered dialogue between the participants, user, and computer through an interface, the main purpose of which is to influence the cognitive state of the user to ensure more effective use of information in connection with the task at hand.

In the user interaction perspective, the model depicts processes such as search term selection derived from different sources for query specification and modification, together with search tactics that occur at the interface level. All such processes are considered to be influenced by a range of cognitive, affective, and situational characteristics of the user. At the cognitive level, users interact with texts and their representations in the information sources. At the affective level, users interact with their intentions and all that is associated with intentionality, such as beliefs, motivation, and feelings. At the situational level, users interact with the given situation or problem that originally produced the information need. In this model, query characteristics are considered to be an important component of the user dimension.

The model views search term selection as a dynamic interactive process, subject to a range of changes and shifts throughout the search process. One of the advantages of Saracevic's model is its extension (Spink and Saracevic, 1997) for search term selection, providing some useful implications for the use of the model in an empirical environment. Within this model, thesauri, index terms, classification schedules, and other sources are viewed as possible sources of term selection during interaction.

Sutcliffe and Ennis (1998) propose a process model of information-searching activities and knowledge sources that models the cognitive tasks involved. Figure 2.4 depicts the activities and tasks that the user may complete in the information search process. Thesauri assist users in a number of search activities. For example, in the articulation of needs, thesauri may be used as a source of search terms. In the query reformulation stage, users may benefit from thesauri as they implement narrowing or broadening strategies. Searches may be narrowed by choosing more specific terms in a hierarchical schema or, alternatively, by reducing synonyms and adding related terms. Searches may be broadened by pursuing the opposite strategies: adding synonyms and removing related terms or substituting more general for more specific terms. One of the functions of a thesaurus in this model is related to the support of users when they possess insufficient domain knowledge. In these circumstances, the system thesaurus may be consulted to acquire more terms and concepts. And finally, the model recognizes the provision of browsing support within an information retrieval system through the use of thesauri, concept maps, metadata dictionaries, and database indexing structures.

Based on a series of longitudinal empirical studies of users, Vakkari (2001) developed a task-based information retrieval model (Figure 2.5). His model highlights the importance of thesauri by including a component called terminological support (such as thesauri) that may impact users' selection of search terms and formulation of queries. He suggests that users need terminological support in order to find appropriate terms for their searches. A search thesaurus is a partial means for doing this. Such tools help people to develop ideas about how to structure a topic and how to express a vague information need in greater detail. Thus equipped with related terms, synonyms, and

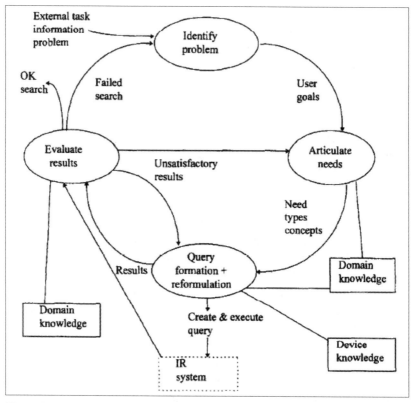

Figure 2.4   Process model of information-searching activities and knowledge sources (Sutcliffe and Ennis, 1998)

narrower terms that are provided by the system, users can reformulate a query using terms with greater differentiating power. This should enable more-relevant information items to be found.

The previously discussed models have elements and activities associated with the use of thesauri in the context of information interaction. Most of the models provide a broad perspective of information search and retrieval interaction. In the following section, several models are reviewed that place particular emphasis on users' interactions with thesauri and associated tasks and activities.

2.3 Thesaurus Interaction Models

One of the early subject-based interaction models is attributed to Bates (1986), who proposed a two-layered interaction model to support

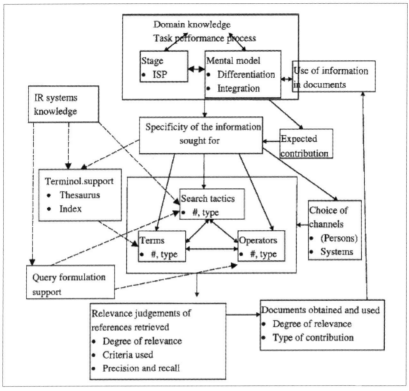

Figure 2.5   A theory of task-based information retrieval process (Vakkari, 2001)

users in formulating queries. She suggests that the system should help searchers "get a feel both for how to interact with the system and for the intellectual world of the system through exploration of vocabulary and relationships between terms. The system provides searchers with links and associations between terms that may be surprising and stimulating of further thought and information seeking" (p. 368). She suggests a front-end system mind whereby an end-user thesaurus with a large entry vocabulary is used to support users' interactions and encourages awareness of other search terms, exploration of unanticipated possibilities, the making of mental associations, and the development of a "feel" for the system. This model depicts an interesting and information-rich user interface that is enhanced with vocabularies and provides easy access to the retrieval system.

In the 2000s, a number of empirical studies of end-user interaction with thesauri gave rise to the development of user-thesaurus interaction

models. A pilot study by Shiri et al. (2002) examined how users interact with and select terms within a thesaurus-enhanced search system. The study focused on the conceptual and physical moves that
users make while browsing or searching within a thesaurus-
enhanced system. The authors propose a Thesaurus Interaction
Impact Matrix to quantitatively evaluate users' interactions with thesaurus terms and to examine users' search term selection behaviors.

Figure 2.6 shows the matrix that categorizes searches based on the
number of initial search terms used and the impact that thesaurus
interaction has on the number of terms selected. The average number of terms viewed for each quadrant of the model is also shown. It
can be seen that those searches with a larger number of terms originally in mind resulted in an average of three times as many terms
being viewed. However, in the case of both the "many" and the "few"
initial terms, the relative numbers of terms eventually selected were
not related to the numbers of terms viewed. In this model, high and
low levels of interaction are assessed through the analysis of terms
browsed and selected compared with retrieved documents reviewed.
The authors suggest that the use of the Thesaurus Interaction Impact
Matrix may aid with the modeling of interaction, browse, and navigation behaviors adopted by different users in their formulation and
expansion of queries.

Lykke Nielsen (2004) evaluated a task-based associative thesaurus
involving users in a pharmaceutical company. Although she did not
attempt to propose a model, the methodology used for the evaluation
of thesaural interaction may be viewed as a model for evaluating
users' interactions with thesauri. She identifies four sub-processes:
problem analysis, query reformulation, conceptual understanding,
and lead-in. Users may take advantage of the semantic map of thesauri for problem analysis, that is, for gaining a clearer understanding
of the problem situation, by exploiting concept definitions, hierarchies, and related concepts. Conceptual understanding implies that
users show how concepts and topics are interrelated from the perspective of the domain. Lead-in refers to synonymous terms that
guide the user from a personal vocabulary to alternative vocabularies. These processes can be viewed as the variety of interactions that
users might have with a thesaurus in order to meet an information
need. The study also identifies three types of thesaurus moves,
described as thesaurus look-up before searching, thesaurus look-up
during searching, and thesaurus browsing. The study does not, however, provide specific interactive instances of thesaural browsing.

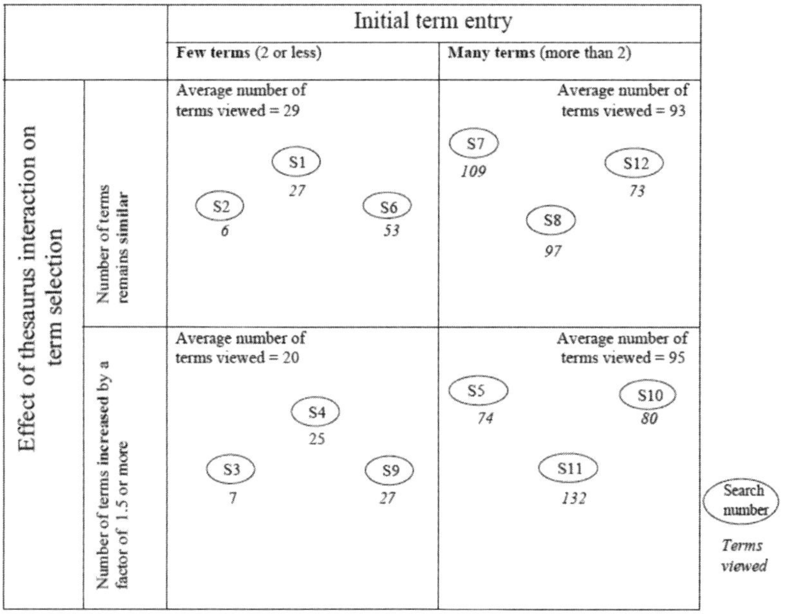

		Initial term entry	
		Few terms (2 or less)	**Many terms** (more than 2)

Figure 2.6   Thesaurus Interaction Impact Matrix (Shiri et al., 2002)

Drawing on an empirical study, Blocks et al. (2006) developed a thesaurus-based search model depicting six stages in the interaction process, starting with a concept or free text term submitted by the user to the system (Figure 2.7). Based on this information, the system retrieves controlled terms that could potentially represent the concept or a set of candidate terms. The model implies that the user will then be able to select terms for query formulation. The system retrieves records matching the query and presents them as results to the searchers. The model defines a *record* as the set of results retrieved by the query. A record consists of a number of different aspects, with controlled indexing terms (or metadata) being the most important in the context of this model. Other elements might include a textual description, a photograph, information on the location of the item represented by the record, and so forth. Users may want to reformulate or expand their queries based on the evaluation of a record and may iteratively repeat query formulation or reformulation steps. Finally, the record or records can be added to the broader collection of relevant records.

The model provides a detailed account of various decisions made throughout the interaction process. However, it focuses only on how a user term or concept can be guided to assist in the query formulation process and does not provide interaction instances in which users may have the opportunity to browse thesaurus terms and their semantic relations to formulate or expand queries.

Beaulieu (2000) discusses the notion of interaction and interactivity, pointing to the importance of individual interactive tasks and their influence on the search and retrieval process. She notes that the interaction within a particular task could affect the actual progression to the next step or task and have an impact on the way the successive steps are taken:

> The selection of a particular information source may influence the choice of query terms and in turn determine the search strategy to be adopted (i.e., a keyword search or browsing a thesaurus). In fact, the steps themselves may not necessarily be clearly demarcated. Browsing a thesaurus, for instance, may be associated with query formulation in

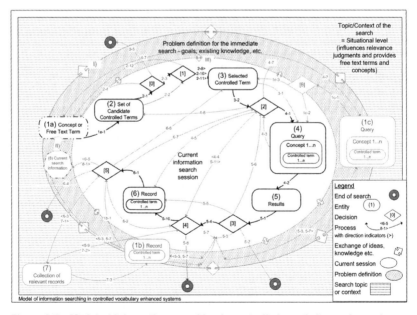

Figure 2.7   Model of information searching in controlled vocabulary enhanced systems (Blocks et al., 2006)

some cases and with the actual search execution in another. (p. 436)

From this statement, it is evident that various layers and levels of interaction in thesaurus-based searching and browsing can be identified that may influence users' query formulation and reformulation strategies.

2.4 Conclusion

This chapter discusses the concept of information interaction as a basis for interactive information retrieval. A number of information-seeking and information-searching models are introduced to explore and identify those interaction elements and processes relevant to research in thesaurus-aided search term selection for query formulation and expansion. These models include some general recommendations to incorporate subject tools such as thesauri and classification schedules in retrieval systems in order to support the information-seeking process.

In contrast, more specific implications are found in information retrieval interaction models for search term selection, query formulation, and the role of thesauri. This is because these information retrieval interaction models depict the specific interaction of users with computerized retrieval systems. Ingwersen's (1996) model conceptualizes thesauri, index terms, and users as cognitive structures, which constitute the interaction elements that affect the whole information retrieval process.

Thesauri are perceived as supportive tools for browsing and searching within the episodic model of information-seeking strategy (Belkin, 1993). Elucidated in the stratified interaction model (Saracevic, 1997) are query characteristics, search term selection, and the sources of search terms (such as thesauri), together with shifts and changes in the query formulation process.

The main focus of thesaurus interaction models is on the ways in which users interact directly with thesauri while conducting searches. These models, however, provide little information as to how thesaurus browsing and navigation can be modeled to provide insight into users' selection of specific thesaurus terms and relationships. The next chapter extends this analysis.

References

Bates, M. J. (1986). Subject access in online catalogs: A design model. *Journal of the American Society for Information Science*, 37(6), 357–376.

Bates, M. J. (1989). The design of browsing and berrypicking techniques for online search interface. *Online Review*, 13(5), 407–431.

Beaulieu, M. (2000). Interaction in information searching and retrieval. *Journal of Documentation*, 56(4), 431–439.

Belkin, N. J. (1993). Interaction with texts: Information retrieval as information-seeking behaviour. *Information retrieval von der Modellierung zur Anwendung* (First Conference of the Gesellschaft fur Informatik Fachgruppe Information Retrieval)(pp. 55–66). Universitaetsverlag Konstanz, Germany.

Belkin, N. J., Cool, C., Stein, A., and Thiel, U. (1995). Cases, scripts and information-seeking strategies: On the design of interactive information retrieval systems. *Expert Systems and Applications*, 9(3), 379–395.

Blocks, J., Cunliffe, D., and Tudhope, D. (2006). A reference model for user-system interaction in thesaurus-based searching. *Journal of the American Society for Information Science and Technology*, 57(12), 1655–1665.

Ellis, D. (1989). A behavioural approach to information retrieval system design. *Journal of Documentation*, 45(3), 171–212.

Fidel, R., Mark Pejtersen, A., Cleal, B., and Bruce, H. (2004). A multidimensional approach to the study of human information interaction: A case study of collaborative information retrieval. *Journal of American Society of Information Science and Technology*, 55(11), 939–953.

Greenberg, J. (2004). User comprehension and searching with information retrieval thesauri. *Cataloging & Classification Quarterly*, 37(3/4), 103–120.

Ingwersen, P. (1982). Search procedures in the library analysed from cognitive point of view. *Journal of Documentation*, 38(3), 165–191.

Ingwersen, P. (1992). *Information retrieval interaction*. London: Taylor Graham.

Ingwersen, P. (1996). Cognitive perspectives of information retrieval interaction: Elements of a cognitive IR theory. *Journal of Documentation*, 52(1), 3–50.

Jones, W., Pirolli, P., Card, S. K., Fidel, R., Gershon, N., Morville, P., Nardi, B., and Russell, D. M. (2006). It's about the information stupid!: Why we need a separate field of human-information interaction. In: *Conference on human factors in computing systems*, Montreal, Quebec, Canada (pp. 65–68). New York: ACM Press.

Kulthau, C. C. (1991). Inside the search process: Information seeking from the user's perspective. *Journal of the American Society for Information Science*, 42(5), 361–371.

Larsen, B., Ingwersen, P., and Kekäläinen, J. (2006) The polyrepresentation continuum in IR. In: I. Ruthven (Ed.), *IIiX: Proceedings of the 1st international conference on information interaction in context* (pp. 88–96), October 18–20, 2006, Copenhagen, Denmark. New York: ACM Press.

Lykke Nielsen, M. (2004). Task-based evaluation of associative thesaurus in real-life environment. *Proceedings of the American Society for Information Science and Technology*, 41(1), 437–447.

Marchionini, G. (2004). From information retrieval to information interaction. In: S. McDonald and J. Tait (Eds.), *Advances in information retrieval* (pp. 1–11). New York: Springer-Verlag.

Marchionini, G. (2008). Human-information interaction research and development. *Library and Information Science Research*, 30(3), 165–174.

Morville, P. (2005). *Ambient findability*. Sebastopol, CA: O'Reilly.

Resmini, A., and Rosati, L. (2010). The semantic environment: Heuristics for a cross-context human–information interaction model. In: E. Dubois, P. Gray, and L. Nigay (Eds.), *The engineering of mixed reality systems* (pp. 79–99).

Saracevic, T. (1997). The stratified model of information retrieval interaction: Extension and applications. In: C. Schwartz and M. Rorvig (Eds.), *ASIS'97: Proceedings of the American Society for Information Science* (pp. 313–327). Silver Spring, Maryland: ASIS.

Shiri, A. A., Revie, C., and Chowdhury, G. (2002). Assessing the impact of user interaction with thesaural knowledge structures: A quantitative analysis framework. In: *Challenges in knowledge representation and organization for the 21st century: Integration of knowledge across boundaries. Proceedings of the 7th International Society for Knowledge Organization (ISKO) Conference* (pp. 517–526). Würzburg, Germany: Ergon Verlag.

Spink, A., and Saracevic, T. (1997). Interaction in information retrieval: Selection and effectiveness of search terms. *Journal of the American Society for Information Science*, 48(8), 741–761.

Sutcliffe, A., and Ennis, M. (1998). Towards a cognitive theory of information retrieval. *Interacting with Computers*, 10(3), 321–351.

Toms, E. G. (2002). Information interaction: Providing a framework for information architecture. *Journal of the American Society for Information Science and Technology*, 53(10), 855–862.

Vakkari, P. (2001). Changes in search tactics and relevance judgments when preparing a research proposal: A summary of the findings of a longitudinal study. *Information Retrieval* 4(3–4), 295–310.

Wilson, T. D. (1999). Models in information behaviour research. *Journal of Documentation*, 55(3), 249–270.

CHAPTER 3

User-Centered Approach to the Evaluation of Thesauri: Query Formulation and Expansion

This chapter documents and analyzes research into the use of thesauri as sources of search terms for various categories of users. In particular, it examines the use of thesauri for query formulation and query expansion and the methodological frameworks on which related studies have been conducted.

3.1 Thesaurus-Assisted Search Term Selection and Query Expansion: A Review of User-Centered Studies

This section reviews the application of domain-specific thesauri in the search and retrieval process, focusing on studies that adopt a user-centered approach. It surveys the methodologies and results from empirical studies undertaken on the use of thesauri as sources of term selection for query formulation and expansion during the search process. It summarizes the ways in which domain-specific thesauri from different disciplines have been used by various types of users and how these tools aid users in the selection of search terms.

The review consists of two sections: studies on thesaurus-aided search term selection and studies dealing with query expansion using thesauri. Both sections are illustrated with case studies that have adopted a user-centered approach. (An earlier version of this literature review appears in Shiri et al., 2002.)

The selection of search terms for query formulation and expansion is a challenging task within the information search and retrieval process. Two general approaches have been adopted in studies of search term selection: system centered and user centered. The system-centered approach is represented by work on algorithms and evaluation based on the traditional information retrieval model. The traditional model fundamentally ignores users and their interaction with the system.

In contrast, the user-centered approach focuses on the cognitive, interactive, and contextual aspects of information retrieval, and considers users, use, situations, context, and interaction with the system (Saracevic, 1999). The user-centered approach has been developed to address a range of poorly understood issues relating to behavioral and cognitive aspects of the information retrieval process. Spink (1994a) and Spink and Saracevic (1997) have emphasized the need for further research into the user-centered approach to search term selection and query expansion, in order to improve the use of and interaction with information retrieval systems. This approach is concerned with the ways in which users of information retrieval systems select their search terms for formulating and/or expanding their queries. It also considers factors and variables that cognitively and behaviorally affect the user's decision making in the search term selection process.

Knowledge structures in general and domain- or subject-specific thesauri in particular are potential sources of search terms for query formulation and expansion. Several studies have evaluated the use of thesauri by different types of users. While all of these studies have adopted user-oriented approaches, their treatment of the use of thesauri, types of users, and methodologies varies.

The main objective of this review is to survey and critique the methodological issues and main findings of a relatively comprehensive set of user-centered studies on thesaurus-aided search term selection and query expansion. Two criteria were considered in defining the scope of the review. First, the review focuses on studies that have treated thesauri as sources of term selection and query expansion. Second, since there are different types of thesauri, only studies that have applied or evaluated domain-specific, manually constructed thesauri with standard relationships (hierarchical, equivalence, and associative) are addressed. Thus, for example, studies that have evaluated the role of automatically constructed thesauri in search term selection and query expansion are excluded.

There are two reasons for choosing manually constructed thesauri for the present research. The first reason is that this type of thesaurus represents semantic relationships defined by humans and involves an intellectually reliable set of terms and relationships. The second reason, based on previous research (Fidel, 1991b; Beaulieu, 1997;

Greenberg, 2001b), is that manually constructed thesauri were found to be beneficial to the search term selection and query expansion process.

This review is structured into two major sections. The first deals with the use of thesauri for search term selection. The second is concerned with the application of thesauri for query expansion purposes to improve search results.

3.2 Approaches to Search Term Selection

The selection of search terms for query formulation and expansion within the information retrieval process has been studied from a range of perspectives. Spink and Saracevic (1997) identify two general types of research into search term selection, namely, algorithmic and human.

The focus of the algorithmic approach is on developing and evaluating different types of algorithms for selecting, weighting, and/or ranking search terms in order to improve information retrieval in the process of query formulation or expansion. Examples of this type of research are numerous: Spark Jones, 1979; Van Rijsbergen et al., 1981; Salton and Buckley, 1988; Robertson, 1990; Efthimiadis, 1993; Magennis and Van Rijsbergen, 1997; and Robertson et al., 1997. Much of the research documented in the Text REtrieval Conference (TREC) proceedings is of this type as well.

The human approach, in contrast, is concerned with studying and evaluating the ways in which users choose terms for formulating, expanding, or modifying their queries during the search process. It involves cognitive and behavioral models and issues that affect the selection of search terms by users. Research of this type focuses on user-centered variables, such as those relating to information needs, user intentions, personal characteristics, and different user information-seeking profiles, and investigates their relationships to term selection in the search process.

3.3 Sources of Search Term Selection

A number of sources for search term selection in query formulation and expansion have been suggested in the literature. For instance, Fidel (1991a) analyzes search term selection based on two types of source, free-text descriptors and controlled vocabulary descriptors.

Efthimiadis (1996) categorizes sources for term selection in query expansion into two types: those based on the relevance-feedback process and those that use some form of knowledge structure. Such structures can be either collection dependent (corpus based) or collection independent, such as thesauri and dictionaries.

Spink and Saracevic (1997) identify five sources of search terms in a study investigating source effectiveness during mediated online searching. These sources are the question statement, user interaction with the intermediary, the thesaurus, the human intermediary, and term relevance feedback (TRF). In these studies and those reviewed in the following sections, thesauri are recognized as tools suited to the provision of search terms at either the query formulation or the query expansion phase of the information retrieval process.

3.4 Thesaurus-Aided Search Term Selection: User Studies

This section focuses on studies that have investigated information searching behaviors, tactics, and strategies to better understand term selection and the ways in which thesauri are utilized by users during the term selection phase of searching.

In a discussion of search strategy, Bates (1979) defines four categories of search tactics, two of which are relevant in the present context: search formulation tactics and term tactics. *Search formulation tactics* refers to the process of designing or redesigning the search formulation and the ways in which information request and query elements are analyzed. This process includes making the search formulation precise, broad, or specific. Bates's category of *term tactics* relates to the selection and revision of specific terms within the context of search formulation. Such tactics focus on moving upward, downward, or sideways within a hierarchical structure in order to find broader or narrower terms during the term selection process. The goal of these tactics is to capture the complexity of the human search term selection process and the sophisticated decision-making effort involved.

Several studies have investigated search term strategies and users' behavior in term selection in a wide variety of disciplines, backgrounds, and environments. Although thesauri were treated differently in some of these studies, all of those selected for discussion later in this chapter considered or evaluated thesauri as search term sources. These studies can be categorized according to the user population involved:

- Professional searchers only
- Professional searchers and end users in a mediated environment
- Both professionals and novices (comparisons of their search behavior)
- End users only

3.4.1 Search Term Selection Behavior of Professional Searchers

Although the investigation of the searching behavior of professional online searchers is a well-developed research theme, several of the key studies concerned with thesaural use were initiated by Fidel. In an early investigation of the behavior of five experienced searchers in search formulation, reformulation, and term selection, Fidel (1984) identified two styles of information-searching behaviors, which she named the *operationalist* and the *conceptualist*. Both styles involve the use of thesauri and the ways in which searchers cognitively process terms in a request and translate them into queries accepted by the retrieval system.

In the operationalist style, searchers try to formulate a query by identifying the related descriptors for each component of the request. They look for such descriptors and check their categories and locations in the hierarchical structure in order not only to find permitted entry terms but also to gain a better understanding of the request. In situations in which they cannot find a descriptor to represent a concept, they search using the free-text mode.

In contrast, conceptualist searching focuses on the structure of the vocabulary for conceptual analysis of the request and query formulation. These searchers look for relationships between the facets of the request and the structure of the controlled vocabulary. They tend to use free-text terms for the initial search formulation in cases in which they are confident there is no controlled way to express the concept or in which the terms are very specific and well-defined and very little has been written about the subject.

In another study, Fidel (1986) observed the online searching behavior of eight searchers in order to provide a set of rules for search term selection by an intermediary expert system. The search keys selected by the searchers and the reasons for choosing these terms were examined. Using this evidence, Fidel developed a *selection routine* that details the conditions for selecting search keys from both free-text and controlled vocabularies. The selection routine describes different conditions under which searchers try to map a search term to a descriptor in the thesaurus or controlled vocabulary, and other conditions that lead to a decision to use the term as a free-text key. Mapping to such a descriptor can be carried out through an exact match or a partial match, or the key might be mapped to a broader descriptor or to narrower terms.

By analyzing the patterns of selection routine, Fidel illustrates the significance of decisions made during search key selection to the success of a search. Her model also shows that a "good" search term is a single-meaning term that can be mapped to a descriptor, while a term is "not adequate" if it is a common term and/or cannot be mapped to a descriptor. She points out the lack of a general typology of requests to support the selection of different ways of choosing terms and suggests that more investigation should be undertaken into searching behavior in order to reveal the conditions under which the user chooses each of the term selection options. One of Fidel's contributions with her selection routine approach is identifying the problematic points in the search term selection process and providing guidelines for research into the searching behavior of online searchers.

In a larger investigation of the search term selection process, Fidel (1991a) studied 47 professional online searchers performing job-related searches. Two distinct types of search keys were compared: words used in free-text searching, and descriptors taken from a controlled vocabulary. In the first part of the study, built on her previous research into the validation and expansion of a search term selection routine (Fidel, 1986), she defined *single-meaning terms* as those that are good for free-text searching and *common terms* as those that are not.

To develop a formal model of search term selection, different conditions for selecting a term were identified, such as whether a common or a single-meaning term can be mapped to a descriptor and, if it can, whether the term is an exact or a partial match. Different strategies for choosing broader, narrower, or synonymous terms were identified.

Searchers who participated in the study were asked to provide reasons for the selection of search keys. Three categories of reasons were identified: request related, database related, and searcher related. Request-related reasons involved the characteristics of the requests; database-related reasons were associated with facilities and characteristics of the databases used by the searchers, such as their use of thesauri or other features; and searcher-related reasons were associated with individual searching behaviors and habits of the searchers. These factors influenced the ways in which searchers chose free-text or thesaurus descriptors. For instance, if a request was very specific, the searcher would tend to use free-text terms. Also, if a database did not have a thesaurus, the searcher would be more inclined to enter free-text terms.

In the second part of the study, Fidel (1991b) observed how the 47 professional searchers used descriptors and text words as search terms. She identified a number of variables for measuring the factors affecting the selection of search keys, including institutional setting, subject area, databases used, number of search keys, number of moves, ratio of free-text keys to total number of keys, and thesaurus neglect ratio. The results showed that of the 3,200 search keys selected, half were descriptors and half were free-text terms. In an analysis of all the search terms used, it was revealed that searchers consulted a thesaurus for 75 percent of the case selections. Characteristics of databases, thesauri, and requests were the major factors affecting search key selection.

One of the main results of this part of the study was that searchers used a thesaurus when it was of satisfactory quality and easily available to them. In contrast, the absence of a thesaurus tended to increase the number of search keys and the number of moves in a search, thus increasing the effort necessary to perform a search. Fidel also suggests that database designers and search-system vendors should encourage the use of thesauri by designing easy-to-use, flexible thesauri, particularly as reliable sources of synonyms.

The third part of Fidel's study (1991c) explored the searching styles of the professional searchers specifically in relation to their modification of search strategies. She identified different moves for increasing and reducing the size of retrieved sets, as well as various moves to increase both recall and precision with regard to the operationalist and conceptualist searching models created earlier (Fidel, 1984). She states that the association between the number of search keys and the total number of moves is a significant pattern in online searching behavior. It was revealed that the searchers who made more moves were likely to use more search keys than were searchers making fewer moves. On average, searchers selected 13 keys per search, but the average number of keys per searcher varied greatly, ranging from just under three to almost 70. The results also demonstrated that the average number of keys per search is typical for a searcher and that a person's searching style will thus determine how extensive the person's use of terms will be. Fidel found that searchers considered recall to be the most important factor in selecting search keys, as well as in when they modify search strategies.

3.4.2 Search Term Selection Behavior of Professional Searchers and End Users in a Mediated Environment

Studies considered in this section examine the search term selection and interaction behavior of professional searchers and end users in a mediated retrieval environment.

Saracevic et al. (1988) conducted a large-scale experimental study to characterize the elements involved in information seeking and retrieving, particularly from the cognitive and human decision-making perspective. They observed the selection of search terms by different searchers for the same questions on five main variables: user, question, searcher, search, and items retrieved. Forty users, 39 searchers, and 40 questions constituted the experimental environment, and different techniques, such as questionnaires, interviews, transaction logs, and videotape, were used for data collection.

The researchers made a significant effort to explore the different cognitive structures involved in the information retrieval interaction process by examining the following elements: users, intermediaries (searchers), information retrieval systems, questions, and their interplay. To analyze and evaluate all of the variables influencing the search and retrieval process, they defined four sources of search terms: 1) terms derived from an oral statement about the problem recorded by the user, but without any reference to the written question; 2) terms extracted from the recorded oral statement and the written question submitted by the user; 3) terms from the written question, using only the words in the question as search terms but without any further elaboration; and 4) terms derived from the written question, together with terms from an appropriate thesaurus for elaboration.

The results indicated that searches based on the user's written question plus the use of a thesaurus were rated as the second-best searches in terms of recall and precision, outperformed only by the relatively intensive approach that used oral and written user statements. The research demonstrated that given the same question, professional searchers tend to select a few common terms and a considerable number of terms that are different. Searches based on different search term selection sources produced a significant difference in recall but no significant difference in precision. While end users were involved in the research, the primary focus of this study was on the process of search term selection by professional searchers and the ways in which they evaluated the search requests and selected terms based on the four search-term sources noted previously.

In a study by Spink and Saracevic (1997) that investigated the selection and effectiveness of search terms, the searches were again performed by professional searchers, but end users played an active role in selecting search terms during online sessions. The data consisted of the interactions of 40 faculty and doctoral students with four professional searchers as they searched 40 questions provided by the participants. The main data-gathering techniques were interviews, questionnaires, and transaction logs, together with video recording. The variables defined in the study were user satisfaction rating; search outcome variables, including number of relevant and nonrelevant items retrieved and precision measures; search process variables, including number of cycles and moves; and user characteristics such as domain knowledge. The researchers identified and classified the following five sources of search terms:

- "Question statements: Search terms derived from the user's written request

- User interaction: Search terms suggested by the user prior to and/or during the online search but not included in the user's question statement

- Thesaurus: Search terms derived from a thesaurus associated with the database

- Intermediary: Search terms suggested by the search professional prior to and/or during the online search

- TRF: Search terms suggested either by the user or the professional searcher, taken from the retrieved items identified by the user as relevant" (p. 741)

The authors evaluated the effectiveness of each source and its contribution to search results. Question statements and interaction with the user were responsible for 38 percent and 23 percent of the selected terms, respectively, with thesauri contributing an additional 19 percent of the terms. A further 11 percent of the search terms came from TRF, while professional searchers were responsible for the remaining 9 percent. In addition to supplying the largest proportion of terms, question statements were the most productive in terms of retrieving relevant items. User-interaction terms were slightly less effective, with around 50 percent resulting in relevant retrieved items.

Terms derived from thesauri were less effective again, a fact that led Spink and Saracevic (1997) to conclude that thesaurus terms are most effective when combined with user terms in search statements. This finding emphasizes the significance of interaction between users' terms and the terms taken from a thesaurus. Although thesauri were one of the sources of terms used during the search process, the interactions between end users and thesauri were not examined in this investigation.

In addition to the previously discussed studies, several others have explored the interaction in a mediated environment between users, professional searchers, and information retrieval systems. These studies considered the process of search term selection in less detail and did not specifically examine thesauri as sources of term selection (Spink, 1996; Spink et al., 1996; Spink et al., 2002).

3.4.3 Search Term Selection Behavior of Professional and Novice Searchers Compared

To compare search term selection and information searching behavior with users' different levels of experience, a number of studies have employed professional and novice searchers. In an investigation of the behaviors associated with the process of online bibliographic searching using ONTAP, a subset of the ERIC database, Fenichel (1981) examined the differences among five groups of searchers with different levels of online searching experience. The main variables studied were environmental, searcher, search process, and search outcome. Variables associated with the search process were the number of commands used, free-text and thesaurus terms chosen, sets viewed, cycles, search modifications, and connect time.

The results showed that all five groups used more thesaurus terms than free-text terms. The most experienced group used a significantly higher proportion of descriptors taken from the thesaurus than did the other groups. In addition, searchers with ERIC experience used significantly more thesaurus terms than did those without such experience. The study showed that having experience of databases equipped with thesauri affects the ways in which a searcher selects terms. However, the finding that novice searchers also make use of thesauri indicates the importance of recognizing that thesauri can be useful sources of search terms for users with varying levels of experience.

Hsieh-Yee (1993) investigated the effects of subject knowledge and search experience on novice and experienced searchers' use of search tactics in online searches. Using transaction logs, onsite observation, and think-aloud techniques, she studied the online searching processes of 33 professional and 30 novice searchers. Based on previous search tactics, she defined a number of variables related to search term selection, such as use of the searcher's own terms, the searcher's reliance on the thesaurus structure, offline term selection efforts, online usage of search terms, inclusion of similar concepts and synonyms, and the searcher's combination of terms. To evaluate the effect of subject knowledge, the study used two familiar and two unfamiliar questions for both novice and professional searchers to consider.

The results showed that when searching a topic of which searchers had some knowledge, experienced searchers included more synonyms and tried more combinations of search terms than did novice searchers. Experienced searchers looked to the thesaurus for term suggestion and tended to formulate a more comprehensive search, while novice searchers tended to rely on their own terms. Novice searchers consulted the thesaurus much less frequently than did experienced searchers. Although the use of the thesaurus as a term selection tactic was considered in this study, the interaction of searchers with the thesaurus interface was not examined.

In a study of differences in search term selection between the most and the least consistent searchers, Iivonen (1995) evaluated the inconsistencies among 32 research participants, consisting of 24 experienced searchers and eight undergraduate students in information studies. They were given the option of using both descriptors from a thesaurus and free-text terms to perform specified search tasks. Three factors relating to the terminological style of the searchers were identified: the number of search terms per search request, the number of search terms per search concept, and the proportion of descriptors among search terms.

The results suggested that as the number of search terms increases, term consistency is adversely affected. However, increasing the proportion of descriptors leads to improved term consistency. Those searchers who chose only a few search terms per request and per search concept and attempted to ensure that these terms were controlled vocabulary descriptors achieved higher intersearcher consistency than the average. These results are in line with prior expectations in that, by selecting from the controlled vocabulary, the searcher has already limited the number of potential search terms. The study also found that differences in the searchers' experience resulted in the use of different terminological styles.

Based on an empirical study of searchers during the pre-online stage, Iivonen and Sonnenwald (1998) proposed a cognitive model of the search term selection process. Once again, their study population was 24 professional searchers with backgrounds in special, university, and public libraries, together with eight students. Each searcher was presented with 12 requests to formulate query statements prior to the search process. Searchers used a Finnish database to select descriptors but also had the option to incorporate free-text terms into their queries.

The study revealed six different sources of term selection, referred to by the researchers as six *discourses*. By discourse, they meant a specific way of thinking and talking about a certain topic within a community. These six discourses, which constituted the elements of their proposed model, were controlled vocabularies, documents and domain, indexing practice, the client's search request, databases, and prior search experience. The discourse of documents and domain refers to the titles and abstracts of records, representing the way a topic is discussed within a community of authors and publishers. Indexing practice relates to a searcher's perception of indexing rules and the practices adopted by indexers in the use of particular terms and concepts. Database discourse refers generally to the content and structure of a database and specifically implies knowledge of the subject categories and fields available in a given database.

The study revealed that all but two of the searchers used controlled vocabularies. Regardless of the searcher's background, the only discourse that was frequently cited as a source of search terms was the controlled vocabulary. This illustrates the strong influence that the discourse of controlled vocabularies exerts on professional searchers. Controlled vocabularies provide a mechanism to describe a topic and to aid navigation by showing the relationships between topics.

The results of this study illustrate the multidimensionality and the complexity of the search term selection process and provide insights into the ways searchers navigate different discourses. The study suggested that further research was needed to fully identify and validate the characteristics of each discourse and to explore those aspects that facilitate the search term selection process.

3.4.4 Search Term Selection Behavior of End Users Searching Independently

While a number of studies have investigated end-user searching behavior, few of them have focused on search term selection. Among those that consider discipline-oriented search terminology are the investigations of Bates et al. (1993) and Siegfried et al. (1993), which provide insights into the search terms used by humanities scholars as end users. Their work examined the search techniques, queries, and search terms of 27 scholars searching Dialog databases. The researchers defined three major terminological categories in order to identify the vocabulary used by humanities researchers, namely, type of search need, such as works of an author or works on a subject; bibliographic features, such as date or form of publication; and types of subject, including individuals, geographic locations, date, or period. While there were cases of using controlled vocabulary descriptors during search formulation, the study did not examine how and to what extent the searchers chose such descriptors or their impact on search term use.

The results of this research showed that the terminology used by humanities researchers was remarkably different from the vocabulary used in other fields, as were aspects of the information seeking and online searching behavior. The humanities scholars searched for more named individuals, geographical terms, chronological terms, and discipline terms. This finding has significant implications for developing thesauri and online search aids in the humanities, suggesting that thesauri developed for the humanities should incorporate more comprehensive sets of geographic and chronological terms, as well as proper names.

Sutcliffe et al. (2000) investigated end-user behavior in a study of the performance of 17 medical students searching the Medline database. The participants were categorized as expert or novice searchers on the basis of their knowledge of the search system. Search performance, query pattern, search strategy, query construction, term use, and system facility usage were the variables studied. The study found that more than 80 percent of the expert searchers used the thesaurus or term suggestion facilities in order to explore concepts. However, no reference was made to how the participants interacted with the thesaurus or what difference this made to search term selection. Expert searchers used more terms in their queries, constructed more complex queries, performed more iterations, and used more system facilities. Novices, in contrast, used simple queries and fewer search terms; they made less use of system facilities and carried out fewer search iterations.

The research concluded that although there were behavioral differences between novice and expert searchers, no simple correlations were found between behavior and performance. A number of usability problems with the system thesaurus and term suggestion facilities were identified. Suggestions were made about how to enhance access to alternative terms and how to reduce the effort required to use the thesaurus or other term suggestion facilities.

Vakkari (2000, 2001) investigated changes in search term usage and tactics among 11 students involved in producing a research proposal as part of their master's thesis. Using survey questionnaires, interviews, the think-aloud technique, and transaction logs, he studied the search behavior of students as they performed this task. He examined the number and types of search terms and tactics used by the students in relation to their prior knowledge of topics, and he analyzed different types of new terms introduced by the students and classified the terms as broader, narrower, related, or synonymous.

The results demonstrated that a growing focus and clearer understanding of the task led students to choose narrower and synonymous terms, to discard broader terms from their search formulation, and to use simpler search tactics. Vakkari suggests that, for novices in a domain, structured terminological support would not only improve search results by encouraging the use of an increased number of narrower terms but might also support searchers in "deconstructing" the topic and interrelating its constituent parts.

A number of studies of end-user behavior in different environments have commented on the specific issue of term selection with regard to information retrieval interfaces (Marchionini et al., 1991; Meadow et al., 1995; Brajnik et al., 1996). For example, Belkin et al. (2001) report the use and effectiveness of term suggestion facilities for supporting end users in an interactive and relevance-feedback environment.

Another line of investigation adopted by researchers has been to study the search term selection patterns of children as end users engaged in information seeking and retrieval behavior (Marchionini, 1989; Solomon, 1993). While these studies have not evaluated thesauri as sources of term selection, results nevertheless indicate the need to incorporate thesauri and terminological support in the information retrieval interface in order to facilitate query formulation by children.

Other research has examined search term use among end users of web search engines (Spink et al., 1999; Spink et al., 2000; Jansen et al., 2000; Spink et al., 2001). These studies have investigated a number of variables related to search terms used by the public, including the number and types of search terms, the number of terms per query, search term subject categorization, search term frequencies, co-occurrences, search strategies, and tactics. Results reveal that most people use few search terms, view few webpages, and rarely employ advanced search features such as Boolean operators or relevance feedback.

In a thorough review of studies that have investigated web search behavior of both children and adults in a wide variety of environments, Hsieh-Yee (2001) points out that web search behavior researchers have drawn on earlier work about online search behavior and studied such variables as search terms, search reformulation, search patterns, tactical moves, search time, and types of search task. This finding reflects researchers' awareness of the importance of examining users in their information context and exhibits rigor in design.

3.4.5 Summary of Search Term Selection Research

This section summarizes the key characteristics of the major search term selection studies discussed previously. These studies have involved a variety of research populations. Nine studies investigated the search behavior of professional searchers, two of which compared professional searchers with novice users. Three investigations focused on the search term selection patterns of end users. Table 3.1 summarizes the major studies that have adopted a user-based approach to thesaurus-assisted search term selection.

These studies encompassed a wide range of databases from different disciplines, with six studies using databases from the broad area of health and medical science and six others drawing on social science,

Table 3.1   Major studies that have adopted a user-based approach to thesaurus-assisted search term selection

Author	Research population	Subject domain	Data collection techniques	Variables	Sources of search terms
Fenichel (1981)	Professional searchers and LIS students	Education	Questionnaire, search transcriptions	Search, searcher, search outcome, environmental	Thesaurus terms and free-text terms
Fidel (1984)	Professional searchers	Health sciences	Observation, interview, think-aloud, search protocol	Exploratory study – no specific variables reported	Thesaurus terms and free-text terms
Fidel (1986)	Professional searchers	Life sciences	Observation, interview, think-aloud, search protocol	Exploratory study – no specific variables reported	Thesaurus terms and free-text terms
Saracevic et al. (1988)	Professional searchers and end users	Medicine, sciences, social sciences, the humanities	Videorecorded interview, questionnaire, search records	Users, questions, searchers, searches, retrieved items	Oral and written problem statement, thesaurus
Fidel (1991b)	Professional searchers	Medicine, sciences, social sciences	Observation, interview, think-aloud, search protocol	Text–word ratio, thesaurus neglect ratio, search keys, moves, subject area, environment	Thesaurus terms and free-text terms
Bates et al. (1993)	End users	The humanities	Transaction logs, interview	Database, search features, commands, terms and vocabulary	Free-text statements and term relevance feedback
Hsieh-Yee (1993)	Experienced and novice searchers	Education	Transaction logs, think-aloud, observe	Search experience, subject knowledge, search tactics	Thesaurus terms and free-text terms
Iivonen (1995)	Professional searchers	Social sciences	Interview	Education, experience, environment, search term selection and strategy	Thesaurus terms and free-text terms
Spink and Saracevic (1997)	Professional searchers and end users	Medicine, social science, physical sciences, the humanities	Transaction logs, videorecorded interview	Search terminology, user characteristics, user satisfaction, search process and outcome	Questions, user interaction, searcher, thesaurus, term relevance feedback
Iivonen and Sonnenwald (1998)	Professional searchers	Social sciences	Interview	Exploratory study – no specific variables reported	Thesaurus, domain and docs, indexing practice, search request, database, search experience
Sutcliffe et al. (2000)	End users	Medicine	Audio-video recording, think-aloud	Query terms, query syntax, search strategies and effectiveness	Thesaurus terms and free-text terms
Vakkari (2001)	End users	Library and information science	Transaction logs, think-aloud, interview, questionnaire	Knowledge of the topic, number and types of search terms, operators and tactics used	Free-text
Lykke Nielsen et al. (2004)	End users	Pharmacology	Questionnaire, logging, relevance assessments, structured observation and interviews	Thesaurus terms, query formulation, conceptual understanding, search performance and search interaction	Search problem, thesaurus terms, retrieved records

humanities, and library and information science databases for their investigations.

The variables identified in the search term selection studies can be classified as follows:

- Searcher characteristics, encompassing search experience, education, subject knowledge, and satisfaction

- Search characteristics, including search strategy, search tactics, and search commands

- Search term characteristics, including free-text terms and thesaurus terms

- Search results characteristics, such as relevance and effectiveness

Research focusing on user-centered approaches to search term selection demonstrates the complexity and importance of human decision making in the information retrieval process. There is a growing interest in the cognitive and behavioral aspects of users' search term selection and the factors affecting that process, including variables such as the user's initial request, search experience, environment, and domain knowledge, together with different types of user-system interaction.

Because the search process in general and search term selection in particular involve a range of cognitive and behavioral characteristics, most studies have employed a combination of data gathering techniques to provide sufficient qualitative, as well as quantitative, data. The qualitative techniques derive mainly from disciplines within the social sciences, human-computer interaction, and psychology. Data gathering tools used in these studies have included questionnaires (pre-search, during-the-search, and post-search), interviews (both audio- and videotaped), the think-aloud technique, transaction logging, and observation.

Most of the studies reviewed previously have considered, in varying degrees of detail, the role and influence of thesauri as one source for term selection. While some studies regarded thesauri as marginal or peripheral tools, others treated them as substantial sources of terms that users could take advantage of during online searching, with the format and presentation of thesauri appearing to affect their use. Most of the thesauri used by searchers in these studies were in printed format and were thus considered to be external sources. However, even in the research in which thesauri were available in electronic format, no specific attempt was made to examine and evaluate the user-thesaurus interaction as part of the term selection process.

Most of the studies reviewed have focused on the term selection behavior of professional searchers. Those studies dealing specifically with end users gave little attention to the role of thesauri as aids to search term selection. Rather, their results are limited to suggestions of methods to facilitate the use of thesauri by end users during the online search process. For instance, Fenichel (1981) suggests the need for facilities such as hierarchical display of descriptors or "exploding" options to include all narrower terms of a descriptor, while Hsieh-Yee (1993) proposes that front-end software could incorporate features that encourage searchers to actively survey alternative search terms. Vakkari (2000) points to the need for system-provided synonyms and narrower terms as means of facilitating search term selection and query reformulation.

Lykke Nielsen (2004) carried out a user-based evaluation of two types of thesauri, the first type developed using literature-based techniques and the second type created using word association tests. She used a combination of qualitative and quantitative data gathering tools, consisting of questionnaires, logging, relevance assessments, structured observation, and interviews.

Analysis showed that the test thesauri were primarily used for lead-in and for query formulation, with most searchers (86 percent) consulting the thesaurus either before or while searching. The analysis also showed that 21 percent of the associative thesaurus terms were unique, compared with 17 percent of the terms selected from the literature-based thesaurus. Thus, both types of test thesauri offered unique terms.

Results revealed that the numbers of preferred terms, broader terms, and related terms were similar. However, there were differences between types of thesaurus terms. The percentage of narrower terms was higher for the word association thesaurus, while the percentage of synonyms was higher for the literature-based thesaurus. Study participants were most satisfied with thesaural support to find precise terms, synonyms, and related terms. They were willing to explore the thesaurus and interact with the content, and they selected terms knowingly and consciously.

As the number of electronic thesauri attached to information retrieval systems has grown in recent years, several interface features and facilities have been developed to aid users in the selection of search terms. However, very little research has explored ways end users interact with these types of interfaces or into the ways in which these integrated thesauri affect search term selection (Jones et al., 1995; Beaulieu, 1997; Blocks et al., 2002).

Further research is required to shed light on the search term selection behavior of various end-user communities who make use of information retrieval systems with thesaural and other terminological support for improving search performance. This research should not only address thesauri as term sources but also evaluate the impact of different types of user interfaces for providing thesaurus-aided search facilities.

3.5 Query Expansion

Query expansion is defined as a stage of the information retrieval process during which a user's initial query statement is enhanced by additional search terms in order to improve retrieval performance. As studies began to address specific stages of the search process, the application of thesauri in this expansion and reformulation became an area of increasing interest. Query expansion is based on the recognition that initial query formulation does not always reflect the exact information need and request of the user; a query may often be enhanced by the addition of search terms in a manner that results in improved information retrieval.

Three types of query expansion are discussed in the literature, namely, manual, automatic, and interactive, which is also known as *semiautomatic, user mediated,* or *user assisted.* These three approaches use different sources of search terms and a variety of expansion techniques. Beaulieu and Robertson (1996) argue that the distinction between manual and interactive methods of query formulation is problematic since both involve human intervention. The difference is that the manual approach does not include any consultation of the collection, while in the interactive approach, the query is modified through a feedback process. In both cases, however, assistance can be sought from other sources, including a dictionary or thesaurus.

Spink (1994b) comments that extensive research has been carried out on both automatic and semiautomatic query expansion techniques. Automatic techniques exploit the text of a user's question and/or retrieved documents found to be relevant by the user, thus functioning as input to techniques for deriving a set of search terms to retrieve additional relevant documents.

In interactive query expansion, users are responsible for selecting from candidate search terms suggested by the retrieval system. Several studies have been conducted on interactive query expansion to reach a variety of goals: to evaluate the ranking algorithms based on users' relevance judgment of candidate search terms (Efthimiadis, 1993; Efthimiadis, 1995), to study user interaction through graphical user interfaces (Beaulieu et al., 1995; Beaulieu, 1997), and to investigate simulated users' term selection within the context of interactive query expansion (Harman, 1988; Magennis and Van Rijsbergen, 1997).

The human approach to query expansion research "investigates the user's representation of their question and whatever tools, e.g. thesaurus or experiences they use to extract or modify a set of search terms during query expansion" (Spink, 1994a, p. 81). This approach stresses the importance of decision making, as well as of the behavioral and cognitive characteristics of users, in reformulating and expanding their search statements.

3.5.1 Query Expansion Using Thesauri

Several studies have reported the construction and use of different types of thesauri as aids to the query expansion process. In general, thesauri within information retrieval systems belong to one of three main types: standard manually constructed thesauri, searching thesauri, and automatically constructed thesauri.

Standard thesauri with hierarchical, equivalence, and associative relationships have been widely used for search term selection and query expansion purposes. Much of the research in this area has focused on comparing the performance and effectiveness of controlled vocabularies versus free-text terms in information retrieval (Markey et al., 1980; Perez, 1982; Svenonius, 1986; Dubois, 1987; Cousins, 1992; Rowley, 1994; Muddamalle, 1998). These types of thesauri have also been incorporated as knowledge bases or interface components in several prototype expert and intelligent systems to assist users in the process of search term selection and query expansion (Efthimiadis, 1996).

Searching thesauri, also referred to as end-user thesauri, are defined as a category of thesauri enhanced with a large number of entry terms that are synonyms, quasi synonyms, or term variants that assist end users in finding alternative terms to add to their search queries (Perez, 1982; Piternick, 1984; Bates, 1986; Cochrane, 1992). A number of searching thesauri have been designed and developed (Anderson and Rowley, 1991; Lopez-Huertas, 1997; Knapp et al., 1998; Lykke Nielsen, 2001) and evaluated in query expansion research (Kristensen and Jarvelin, 1990; Kristensen, 1993; Kekäläinen and Jarvelin, 1998).

The design and testing of several types of automatically constructed thesauri has also been extensively reported in the literature. Several researchers have constructed thesauri based on co-occurrence in order to evaluate the performance of thesaurus-based query expansion (Qiu and Frei, 1993; Schutze and Pedersen, 1997). Using a laboratory environment and the TREC test collections, these studies resulted in a slight improvement in retrieval performance.

General-purpose thesauri such as WordNet have also been evaluated in the query expansion process but have demonstrated little difference in retrieval effectiveness (Voorhees, 1994). Thesauri constructed automatically via a linguistic approach have also demonstrated a marginal improvement in retrieval performance (Jing and Croft, 1994). Combining different types of thesauri for query expansion has shown better retrieval results than using only one type of thesaurus (Mandala et al., 1999). Recently, researchers have created a large association thesaurus based on the Wikipedia free encyclopedia. The thesaurus interface is live and operational but has not been subject to any user-based evaluation (Nakayama et al., 2008).

Automatically constructed thesauri have also been evaluated in user-oriented environments (Chen and Dhar, 1991; Chen et al., 1995; Chen and Ng, 1997). In addition, some researchers have found that the integration of automatically and manually constructed thesauri has a positive effect on the query expansion process (Chen and Ng, 1995; Schatz et al., 1996; Chen et al., 1998; Ding et al., 2000).

The research reviewed in the following section focuses on those studies that have investigated thesaurus-based query expansion using standard domain-specific thesauri in a user-oriented environment.

3.5.2 Thesaurus-Aided Query Expansion: User-Centered Studies

Research on user-assisted query expansion with domain-specific thesauri can be divided into three categories based on the extent to which users are involved in the search and retrieval process:

- Users are involved only in providing requests and relevance judgments.

- User involvement is mediated by professional searchers.

- Users operate in an interactive environment.

The following sections review studies conducted in each of these categories.

3.5.2.1 Users Involved Only in Providing Requests and Relevance Judgments

In the studies reported in this section, users were not involved in the actual search process; rather, searches were typically performed by professional searchers, who also carried out any thesaurus-aided query expansion. In one such study, Kristensen and Jarvelin (1990) examined the effectiveness of a small searching thesaurus, with 328 terms, on recall and precision in a full-text database. The test environment was an operational database with around 34,000 newspaper articles relating to economic issues, and the queries were elicited from five journalists, who performed relevance judgments. Each query was searched in three distinct modes: basic search, synonym search, and related term search. The basic search included only the journalists' initial query statements.

It was found that expanding original queries with synonyms from the searching thesaurus significantly increased the number of new relevant records. Query expansion using related terms also increased the recall rate but led to a marked decline in precision. This indicates that related terms can be used as query expansion terms if high recall is required. The authors concluded that a searching thesaurus can improve results in free-text searching of a full-text database.

Kristensen (1993) investigated the effects of the searching thesaurus on recall and precision in a full-text database using an expanded set of five distinct search modes: basic search, synonym search, narrower term search, related term search, and union of all these searches. The test environment consisted of an operational database of 227,000 newspaper articles, a test thesaurus of 1,573 terms, and 30 queries elicited from journalists. The author carried out all modes of search, with relevance judgments again being supplied by the journalists.

She concluded that the effect of a search-aid thesaurus was substantial and that retrieval results were improved. While the union search resulted in a 10 percent decrease in precision compared with the basic search, twice as many relevant documents were found. Each of the three expanded search modes retrieved several unique articles, but the expansions using synonyms and related terms performed better in terms of relevance than those using the narrower terms. The findings showed that a searching thesaurus was clearly a recall-enhancing tool, and the author suggests that the active involvement of end users in the term selection process could further enhance the levels of precision.

3.5.2.2 User Involvement Mediated by Professional Searchers

To evaluate thesaurus-aided query expansion in a more user-oriented setting, some researchers have studied the selection by users of search terms for query expansion in mediated search environments. Spink (1994a), for instance, examined the selection and effectiveness of search term sources while observing user-based query expansion in order to provide guidelines for information retrieval system enhancement. She collected the users' written question statements and pre-online interviews, as well as the search logs created during online interaction between 40 users and professional searchers.

The study identified five different sources of term selection for query expansion: user question statement, user interaction (suggested by a user during interaction with the intermediary or the online search), intermediary, thesaurus, and TRF based on terms extracted by users after examination of retrieved documents. Spink also evaluated the effectiveness of these sources in retrieving relevant items with a special focus on TRF.

Results showed that the thesaurus was rated as the third most effective source of search terms, after the user's question statement and user interaction with the intermediary. The TRF search terms were more effective in retrieving relevant items than were search terms suggested by the professional searchers or terms selected from the thesaurus. TRF terms that proved effective in retrieving relevant records were largely selected from the title and descriptor fields of the records viewed. This finding suggests that descriptors, which are normally terms in the thesaurus, contributed significantly to the retrieval of relevant records.

The study concluded that the most effective sources of search terms for query expansion were users' written question statements, terms derived during the interaction between users and professional searchers, and terms selected from the title and descriptor fields of the retrieved records. At the same time, however, because end users did not have any direct interaction with the thesaurus as a main source of term selection, the value of thesaurus-based terms may have been underestimated.

Greenberg (2001a, 2001b) investigated the effectiveness of different thesaural relationships for automatic and interactive query expansion in an operational environment. She explored how end-user search terms can be mapped to a thesaurus and, if there are additional thesaurus terms representing some type of semantic relationship, which terms are good candidates for interactive and automatic query expansion. The test environment consisted of the ProQuest controlled vocabulary, ABI/INFORM (a business periodical database), and 42 queries obtained from business administration students. Data were collected from user profile questionnaires, relevance judgments, and a post-evaluation questionnaire. In the evaluation of automatic query expansion using thesauri, different query treatments were examined in terms of the sources used to expand the query. Greenberg included the participants' initial search statement and five treatments involving the thesaurus: mapped, narrower, broader, related, and synonymous terms. In the interactive query expansion process, the participants were presented with lists of thesaurus terms related to their initial queries and asked to select search terms that they thought would have been useful. In both the automatic and interactive cases, Greenberg developed the search strategy and performed all searches, while end users were mainly responsible for providing real information requests, together with relevance judgments.

The findings suggest that synonyms and narrower terms yield more precise results and are good candidates for automatic query expansion because they increase recall with a minimum loss in precision. The results also show that all semantic relationships increase recall if applied in automatic query expansion. If precision is required, narrower terms can be good candidates for interactive query expansion. Related terms are better candidates for interactive query expansion than for automatic query expansion. The results also demonstrate that when end users select terms via interactive query expansion, they can have a significant impact on the precision of the results. This study confirms that semantic relationships in standard thesauri can have a positive influence on retrieval performance and can be used as sources for query expansion.

3.5.2.3 Users Operating in an Interactive Environment

The research reviewed in the previous two sections covers studies with only partial user involvement in thesaurus-aided search term selection for query expansion. A few studies have investigated selection behavior by end users in an interactive environment. Jones et al. (1995), for instance, investigated user interaction behavior with a thesaurus as a source of query expansion terms in order to identify strong patterns for possible rule- or weight-based systems for term expansion and to compare the effectiveness of queries enhanced by thesaural use with that of the original query terms. The experimental environment within which the users' thesaurus navigation and term selection behavior was recorded consisted of three elements: the Inspec Thesaurus, 39 users with real information needs, and the Okapi ranked output information retrieval system. The interface was designed in such a way that, following the entry of the original query, users were shown exact or partially matched thesaurus terms and encouraged to browse and select thesaurus terms for expansion. The focus of the study was on the performance of thesaurus terms in relevant retrieval, which was determined by examining the number and types of terms seen and selected by users.

The analysis showed that the majority of terms retrieved by thesaurus navigation came through the association relationship, perhaps reflecting the fact that Inspec has more associative links than hierarchical ones. However, based on the users' relevance judgments based on only author, title, and journal, there were no significant differences in the results generated by original queries compared with those generated by the selected thesaurus terms.

The study also evaluated the retrieval performance of hybrid searches, which included both the original and the controlled terms. The hybrid search retrieved more records than the original search did, although it did not show a marked improvement in overall performance. Jones et al. (1995) conclude that thesaurus-based query expansion may increase recall and uncover additional relevant documents but will not improve queries that are already quite fully specified. They also suggest that users obtain good results if they have a large number of terms from which to select and, since users' choices of terms will vary, it is not feasible to design a generic automatic expansion procedure. Rather, tools should be provided to aid the end user in thesaurus navigation. User feedback also indicates that thesaurus navigation is a useful and informative activity and that important issues in determining the degree of enhancement to the query expansion process are thesaural depth and coverage and user interface quality.

Beaulieu (1997) reported on experiments conducted to evaluate different interfaces supporting query expansion, again based on the Okapi search engine. The experiments were carried out with both an online library catalog and the Inspec database and thesaurus. Data gathering consisted of observation, talk-aloud, online pre-search, and post-search questionnaires, together with transaction logs. Three types of interfaces supporting automatic and interactive query expansion were tested by examination of user interaction behavior. Thesauri were used in different ways within the interface design as tools for supporting interactive query expansion.

The results showed that both the explicit and the implicit use of a thesaurus (i.e., interactive and automatic query expansion, respectively) can be beneficial. It was found that the overall number and specific presentation of candidate terms for query expansion was important. For instance, the way in which thesaural terms and document-extracted terms were displayed had an effect on the ultimate set of search terms selected by the user. The study also suggested that the different cognitive styles adopted by users when seeking information were an important issue in designing interfaces that could effectively support query expansion.

Sihvonen and Vakkari (2004) examined how experts and novices in pedagogics expanded queries supported by the ERIC thesaurus while carrying out easy and difficult search tasks. The study population consisted of the expert group, consisting of 15 undergraduates in pedagogy, and the novice group, 15 students with no previous academic study in the field. The system used was the ERIC database with ERIC Wizard interface and thesaurus. The data-gathering techniques were recorded search logs and pre- and post-search interviews.

Results revealed that both groups used more thesaurus terms than their own terms in reformulation, especially with the difficult task. About two-thirds of the expansion terms originated from the thesaurus. With the easy task, novices used proportionately more thesaurus terms, whereas this was the case for experts only with the difficult task. In both tasks, experts navigated more intensively in the thesaurus than did novices, entering more of their own terms and seeing more terms. However, experts selected fewer terms in the easy task than novices did and about equal numbers of terms in the difficult task. Both user groups selected related terms most frequently in both tasks. In the difficult task, both groups also frequently picked system-suggested terms.

A major finding was that the increase in search effectiveness was associated with the number and type of thesaurus terms used in expansion by experts but not by novices. The authors conclude that sufficient familiarity with the search topic is a vital condition for benefiting from a thesaurus in query expansion and thereby improving search results.

Tudhope et al. (2006) developed a thesaurus-based query expansion system using the Art and Architecture Thesaurus. Their system provides a matching function whereby users' terms can be matched to the thesaurus terms and an expanded list of thesaurus terms can be shown to the user. Users select any number of terms to add to their initial search terms and are able to browse thesaurus terms and relationships. A formative evaluation of the system was carried out on a pilot system. Data gathering included transcripts of think-aloud sessions, screen capture videos, and log files of interactions such as query runs, thesaurus browsing, and records viewed. There were 20 sessions totaling 22 hours of recorded data (not including training time), and they involved 23 selected users, the vast majority of whom were museum-related contacts in various U.K. institutions, including catalogers, collections management staff, and curators.

Findings were that users vary in the time they are willing to spend in browsing a thesaurus, and the distinctions between hierarchies or node label arrays can sometimes be confusing for people who are not subject experts. This suggests that the application of semantic expansion to hypertext browsing of a thesaurus may be useful in interfaces in which thesaurus content is made available but details of thesaural structure are hidden.

Shiri and Revie (2006) reported an investigation of the query expansion behavior of end users interacting with a thesaurus-enhanced search system on the web. They recruited two user groups, academic staff and postgraduate students. Data were collected from 90 searches performed by 30 users using the Ovid interface to the Centre for Agricultural Bioscience (CAB) Abstracts database. Data-gathering techniques included questionnaires, screen-capturing software, and interviews. Variables studied were search-topic and search-term characteristics, number and types of expanded queries, usefulness of thesaurus terms, and behavioral differences between academic staff and postgraduate students in their interactions.

Results showed that users expanded 68 (76 percent) of the 90 searches and that narrower and related terms, taken together, constituted approximately 60 percent of the query-expansion terms selected by users. On average, users selected 2.2 additional terms from the thesaurus in expanding their queries. In addition, in 87 percent of these cases, the additional terms provided by the thesaurus were useful.

Other key findings were that 1) academic staff chose more narrow and synonymous terms than did postgraduate students, who generally selected broader and related terms; 2) topic complexity affected users' interaction with the thesaurus, in that complex topics required more query expansion and search term selection; 3) users' prior search experience with a topic appeared to have a significant effect on their selection and evaluation of thesaurus terms; and 4) users were unaware of the terms at the beginning of the search in 50 percent of those searches in which additional terms were suggested from the thesaurus, an observation particularly noticeable in the case of the postgraduate students.

Tang et al. (2009) evaluated the search characteristics, querying behavior, and search performance of 44 health and biomedical graduate students. They compared two different interfaces, the PubMed standard interface and an experimental interface that would suggest terms and facets based on the Medical Subject Headings (MeSH) Thesaurus. Users were asked to carry out two search tasks based on genuine information needs. The study used pre- and post-search questionnaires, screen capture software, and Lickert-type scale questions.

It was found that users tended to employ more terms to expand their queries when they used the experimental thesaurus-enhanced interface. They were also more satisfied with the experimental interface when "goodness of the query" was measured on the basis of users' new or revisited searches. Also, users found the experimental interface more useful for their new searches. This indicates that users with no prior experience with the search topic find the suggested terms from the MeSH Thesaurus more useful than those generated by the PubMed standard interface.

3.5.3 Summary of Thesaurus-Aided Query Expansion Research

Table 3.2 provides an overview of some key characteristics of the query expansion studies discussed in this chapter that have considered the

Table 3.2   Key studies that have considered the role of users in thesaurus-based query expansion

Author(s)	Research population	Subject domain	Database	Thesaurus
Kristensen and Jarvelin (1990)	End users	Economics	Finnish newspaper articles	In-house search-aid thesaurus
Kristensen (1993)	End users	Economics	Newspaper articles	In-house search-aid thesaurus
Spink (1994a)	Professional searchers and end users	Various subjects	Dialog bibliographic	Not specified
Jones et al. (1995)	End users	Computer, electronics, information science	Inspec	Inspec
Beaulieu (1997)	End users	Computer, electronics, information science	Inspec	Inspec
Greenberg (2001b)	End users	Business	ABI/Inform	ProQuest controlled vocabulary
Sihvonen and Vakkari (2004)	End users	Pedagogy	ERIC	ERIC thesaurus
Tudhope et al. (2006)	Cataloguers, collections management staff and curators	Museum	National Museum of Science and Industry's collections	Art and Architecture Thesaurus
Shiri and Revie (2006)	End users	Life and veterinary sciences	CAB Abstracts	CAB Thesaurus
Tang et al. (2009)	End users	Health and biomedical sciences	PubMed	MeSH

role of users in thesaurus-based query expansion. Two of the studies adopted a laboratory experiment approach, in which end users were involved only in providing search requests and relevance judgments (Kristensen and Jarvelin, 1990; Kristensen, 1993). In six studies, end users' search behavior was examined in an operational setting (Jones et al., 1995; Beaulieu, 1997; Sihvonen and Vakkari, 2004; Tudhope et al., 2006; Shiri and Revie, 2006; Tang et al., 2009). The remaining pair of query expansion studies considered a mediated environment in which professional searchers interacted with end users (Spink, 1994a; Greenberg, 2001b). Disciplinary coverage was varied, with three investigations using economic and business databases, two involving computer and information science databases, and the other covering a range of subject domains.

The results of these studies demonstrate the usefulness of thesauri in terms of both providing users with alternative search terms for query expansion and improving retrieval performance. Interactive query expansion research (Beaulieu, 1997) shows that user interface design can play a major role in encouraging the use of thesauri as query expansion term sources. This finding has implications for the design and evaluation of interfaces enhanced with thesauri to support query expansion.

Efthimiadis (2000) suggests that during query expansion, a thesaurus could be used to display the relationships of the selected terms to other terms. This could be achieved, for example, by displaying the hierarchical tree to which a term belongs (as in the Inspec or MeSH tree displays) or by presenting broader, narrower, or related terms on screen for users to browse and make selections from.

As end-user searching becomes more prevalent, research on user-thesaurus interaction within the context of the information searching process is also needed to evaluate the ways in which various end-user communities use and interact with thesauri and how this affects their term selection for query expansion. Such research must take into account the user's attitudes and cognitive aspects of the search process and the mechanisms by which the user may select terms, issues little investigated in the reviewed literature.

Research also suggests that the coverage and richness of thesauri play a significant role in their contribution to users' term selection for query expansion (Fidel, 1992; Jones et al., 1995). Given that few domain-specific thesauri have been evaluated in terms of their coverage and performance for query expansion, research needs to be carried out to evaluate thesaurus-aided query expansion in a range of subject domains.

In addition to the research reviewed previously, recent studies have investigated user queries submitted to several different search engines and digital libraries. To determine the value of thesauri in supporting query formulation and expansion, these studies have compared user query terms with standard thesauri. Shiri and Chambers (2008), for example, investigated users' query terms as revealed by transaction log analysis of a nanoscience and technology digital library and assessed the extent to which the search terms had exact or partial match equivalents in two thesauri attached to the Inspec and Compendex databases.

They found that the Compendex thesaurus had exact matches for 49 percent of users' search terms, compared with 37 percent exact matches offered by Inspec. The exact and partial match types indicate that the Compendex thesaurus provides, in general, better coverage for nanoscience and technology user terms than Inspec does. However, because of the differences in coverage of these two thesauri, the authors concluded that both thesauri should be used in order to effectively support users' query formulation and expansion behaviors.

Poikonen and Vakkari (2009) examined the differences between expressions used by lay persons and professionals in nutrition-related questions and answers and the degree to which General Finnish Ontology (GFO) and a medical thesaurus (FinMeSH) cover these expressions.

They found that the vocabularies of lay persons and professionals were quite similar. All term types expressed in both questions and answers matched better with FinMeSH than with GFO. There were some differences in coverage of the thesauri between patients' terms and physicians' terms, with FinMeSH covering 60 percent of synonyms used by physicians but only 38 percent of synonyms used by patients.

Using transaction log analysis, Huurnink et al. (2010) studied queries submitted to an audiovisual archive by media professionals. They evaluated user query terms and compared them with the thesaurus called the GTAA, the Dutch acronym for Common Thesaurus for Audiovisual Archives. They found that 44 percent of the queries contained thesaurus terms, the most common types consisting of proper names of people, places, and events. Together, these accounted for 70 percent of the identified thesaurus terms submitted to the archive.

3.6 Conclusion

This chapter reviews user-centered studies of search term selection and query expansion and, in particular, the use of domain-specific thesauri as sources of term selection. The studies surveyed were classified according to the type of user involved, with most of the search term selection studies focused on the behavior of professional searchers. This was attributable to the studies' having been carried out at a time when mediated online searching was common practice. In addition, most information retrieval systems did not have integrated online thesauri, and so professional searchers were the main users of these tools. Research demonstrates that user characteristics, including cognitive and behavioral factors, are important in analyzing end-user search term selection.

Query expansion studies, in contrast, have been more concerned with the end user, although in some cases end users were not involved in the actual search process. The focus of some of the thesaurus-based query expansion research has been on retrieval performance rather than on the search process and its cognitive aspects. These studies demonstrate that thesauri have the potential for improving retrieval performance and can be used for both automatic and interactive query expansion. In particular, user-centered studies carried out in the 2000s revealed that users with varying degrees of familiarity with a search topic found terms suggested by thesauri useful and relevant to their information need.

Two major trends in modern information retrieval justify additional end-user research into thesaurus-assisted search term selection and query expansion. First, search is now a natural and regular part of users' lives, and the web provides a wider range of search systems and services to allow information search and discovery across a broad range of topics, disciplines, domains, and databases.

To provide better systems, research is needed that explores the behavior and attitudes of different types of searchers who access thesaurus-enhanced information retrieval systems. Searcher behavior incorporates both cognitive and physical aspects, such as, respectively, the ways in which users relate thesaurus terms to their search topics and the ways in which specific interface features are used. Also important are affective characteristics, principally the attitudes of users, including subjective issues of satisfaction with a result set and its relevance, and motivation to use features provided by a given thesaurus.

The second trend in modern information retrieval is the incorporation of thesauri by a growing number of commercial databases, content management systems, digital libraries, and subject gateways into search interfaces in an attempt to encourage users to enhance their queries (Shiri et al., 2002; Shiri and Molberg, 2005).

These developments open avenues for more research, both into the usability and usefulness of these systems and into the extent to which they assist end users in selecting search terms and expanding queries. Focused investigation into searchers' interactions with web-based thesauri will extend our knowledge of user behavior and provide guidance for the design and implementation of better searching systems.

References

Anderson, J. D., and Rowley, F. A. (1991). Building end-user thesauri from full-text. In: B. H. Kwasink and R. Fidel (Eds.), *Advances in classification research: Proceedings of the 2nd ASIS SIG/CR classification research workshop* (pp. 1–13). Medford, NJ: Learned Information.

Bates, M. J. (1979). Information search tactics. *Journal of the American Society for Information Science*, 30(4), 205–214.

Bates, M. J. (1986). Subject access in online catalogs: A design model. *Journal of the American Society for Information Science*, 37(6), 357–376.

Bates, M. J., Wilde, D. N., and Siegfried, S. L. (1993). An analysis of search terminology used by humanities searchers: The Getty online searching project report No 1. *Library Quarterly*, 63(1), 1–39.

Beaulieu, M. (1997). Experiments of interfaces to support query expansion. *Journal of Documentation*, 53(1), 8–19.

Beaulieu, M., Fieldhouse, M., and Do, T. (1995). An evaluation of interactive query expansion in an online library catalogue with a graphical user interface. *Journal of Documentation*, 51(3), 225–243.

Beaulieu, M., and Robertson, S. (1996). Evaluating interactive systems in TREC. *Journal of the American Society for Information Science*, 47(1), 85–94.

Belkin, N. J., Cool, C., Kelly, D., Lin, S., Park, S., Carballo, J. P., and Sikora, C. (2001). Iterative exploration, design and evaluation of support for query reformulation in interactive information retrieval. *Information Processing and Management*, 37(3), 403–434.

Blocks, D., Binding, C., Cunliffe, D., and Tudhope, D. (2002). Qualitative evaluation of thesaurus-based retrieval. In: M. Agosti and C. Thanos (Eds.), *Proceedings of 6th european conference on research and advanced technology for digital libraries* (Lecture notes in computer science, pp. 346–361). Rome, Italy, 16–18 September 2002. Berlin: Springer.

Brajnik, G., Mizzaro, S., and Tasso, C. (1996). Evaluating user interfaces to information retrieval systems: A case study on user support. In: H. P. Frei, D. Harman, P. Schauble, and R. Wilkinson (Eds.), *Proceedings of the 19th annual international ACM/SIGIR conference on research and development in information retrieval* (pp. 128–136). New York: ACM Press.

Chen, H., and Dhar, V. (1991). Cognitive process as a basis for intelligent retrieval systems design. *Information Processing and Management*, 27(7), 405–432.

Chen, H., Martinez, J., Kirchhoff, T., Ng, D., and Schatz, B. R. (1998). Alleviating search uncertainty through concept associations: Automatic indexing, co-occurrence analysis, and parallel computing. *Journal of the American Society for Information Science*, 49(3), 206–216.

Chen, H., and Ng, T. (1995). An algorithmic approach to concept exploration in a large knowledge network (automatic thesaurus consultation): Symbolic branch-and-Bound search vs. connectionist Hopfield net activation. *Journal of the American Society for Information Science*, 46(5), 348–369.

Chen, H., and Ng, T. D. (1997). A concept space approach to addressing the vocabulary problem in scientific information retrieval: An experiment on the worm community system. *Journal of the American Society for Information Science*, 48(1), 17–31.

Chen, H., Schatz, B., Yim, T., and Fye, D. (1995). Automatic thesaurus generation for an electronic community system. *Journal of the American Society for Information Science*, 46(3), 175–193.

Cochrane, P. A. (1992). Indexing and searching thesauri, the Janus or Proteus of information retrieval. In: N. J. Williamson and M. Hudon (Eds.), *Classification research for knowledge organization* (pp. 161–178). Amsterdam: Elsevier Science Publishers.

Cousins, S. A. (1992). Enhancing access to OPACs: Controlled vs natural language. *Journal of Documentation*, 48(3), 291–309.

Ding, Y., Chowdhury, G. G., and Foo, S. (2000). Incorporating the results of co-word analyses to increase search variety for information retrieval. *Journal of Information Science*, 26(6), 429–451.

Dubois, C. P. R. (1987). Free text vs controlled vocabulary: A reassessment. *Online Review*, 11(4), 243–253.

Efthimiadis, E. N. (1993). A user-centred evaluation of ranking algorithms for interactive query expansion. In: Korfhage et al. (Eds.), *Proceedings of the 16th annual international conference on research and development in information retrieval of the Association for Computing Machinery Special Interest Group on Information Retrieval (ACM/SIGIR)*, pp. 146–159. New York: ACM.

Efthimiadis, E. N. (1995). User choices: A new yardstick for the evaluation of ranking algorithms for interactive query expansion. *Information Processing and Management*, 31(4), 605–620.

Efthimiadis, E. N. (1996). Query expansion. In: M. E. Williams (Ed.), *Annual Review of Information Science and Technology* (pp. 121–187). Medford, NJ: Information Today.

Efthimiadis, E. N. (2000). Interactive query expansion: A user-based evaluation in a relevance feedback environment. *Journal of the American Society for Information Science*, 51 (11), 989–1003.

Fenichel, C. H. (1981). Online searching: Measures that discriminate among users with different types of experiences. *Journal of the American Society for Information Science*, 32(1), 23–32.

Fidel, R. (1984). Online searching styles: A case-study-based model of searching behaviour. *Journal of the American Society for Information Science*, 35(4), 211–221.

Fidel, R. (1986). Towards expert systems for selection of search keys. *Journal of the American Society for Information Science*, 37(1), 37–44.

Fidel, R. (1991a). Searcher's selection of search keys: I. The selection routine. *Journal of the American Society for Information Science*, 42(7), 490–500.

Fidel, R. (1991b). Searchers' selection of search keys: II. Controlled vocabulary or free-text searching. *Journal of the American Society for Information Science*, 42(7), 501–514.

Fidel, R. (1991c). Searchers' selection of search keys: III. Searching styles. *Journal of the American Society for Information Science*, 42(7), 515–527.

Fidel, R. (1992). Who needs controlled vocabulary? *Special Libraries*, 83(1), 1–9.

Greenberg, J. (2001a). Automatic query expansion via lexical-semantic relationships. *Journal of the American Society for Information Science and Technology*, 52(5), 402–415.

Greenberg, J. (2001b). Optimal query expansion (QE) processing methods with semantically encoded structures thesauri terminology. *Journal of the American Society for Information Science and Technology*, 52(6), 487–498.

Harman, D. K. (1988). Toward interactive query expansion. In: Y. Chiaramella (Ed.), *Proceedings of the Association for Computing Machinery Special Interest Group on Information Retrieval (ACM/SIGIR) 11th International Conference on Research and Development in Information Retrieval* (pp. 321–331). Grenoble, France: Presses Universitaires de Grenoble.

Hsieh-Yee, I. (1993). Effects of search experience and subject knowledge on the search tactics of novice and experienced searchers. *Journal of the American Society for Information Science*, 44(3), 161–174.

Hsieh-Yee, I. (2001). Research on web search behavior. *Library & Information Science Research*, 23(2), 167–185.

Huurnink, B., Hollink, L., Heuvel, W. V. D., and Rijke, M. D. (2010). Search behavior of media professionals at an audiovisual archive: A transaction log analysis. *Journal of the American Society for Information Science and Technology*, 61(6), 1180–1197.

Iivonen, M. (1995). Searchers and searchers: Differences between the most and least consistent searchers. In: E. Fox, P. Ingwersen, and R. Fidel (Eds.), *Proceedings of the 18th Annual International ACM SIGIR Conference on research and development in information retrieval of the Association for Computing Machinery Special Interest Group on Information Retrieval* (pp. 149–157). New York: ACM.

Iivonen, M., and Sonnenwald, D. H. (1998). From translation to navigation of different discourses: A model of search term selection during pre-online stage of the search process. *Journal of the American Society for Information Science*, 49(4), 312–326.

Jansen, B. J., Spink, A., and Saracevic, T. (2000). Real life, real users, real needs: A study and analysis of user queries on the web. *Information Processing and Management*, 36(2), 207–227.

Jing, Y., and Croft, W. B. (1994). The association thesaurus for information retrieval. Proceedings of *RIAO '94: Intelligent multimedia information retrieval systems and management* (pp. 146–160). Paris: CID.

Jones, S., Gatford, M., Hancock-Beaulieu, M., Robertson, S. E., Walker, W., and Secker, J. (1995). Interactive thesaurus navigation: Intelligence rules ok? *Journal of the American Society for Information Science*, 46(1), 52–59.

Kekäläinen, J., and Jarvelin, K. (1998). The impact of query structure and query expansion on retrieval performance. In: W. B. Croft et al. (Eds.), *Proceedings of the Association for Computing Machinery Special Interest Group on Information Retrieval (ACM/SIGIR) 21st annual international ACM SIGIR conference on research and development in information retrieval 98* (pp. 130–137). New York: ACM Press.

Knapp, S. D., Cohen, L. B., and Judes, D. R. (1998). A natural language thesaurus for humanities. *Library Quarterly*, 68(4), 406–430.

Kristensen, J. (1993). Expanding end-users' query statements for free text searching with a search-aid thesaurus. *Information Processing and Management*, 29(6), 733–744.

Kristensen, J., and Jarvelin, K. (1990). The effectiveness of a searching thesaurus in free text searching of a full-text database. *International Classification*, 17(2), 77–84.

Lopez-Huertas, M. J. (1997). Thesaurus structure design: A conceptual approach for improved interaction. *Journal of Documentation*, 53(2), 139–177.

Lykke Nielsen, M. (2001). A framework for work task-based thesaurus design. *Journal of Documentation*, 57(6), 774–797.

Lykke Nielsen, M. (2004). Task-based evaluation of associative thesaurus in real-life environment. In: L. Schamber and C. L. Barry (Eds.), *Proceedings of the 67th ASIS&T annual meeting* (pp. 437–447). Medford, NJ: Information Today.

Magennis, M., and Van Rijsbergen, C. J. (1997). The potential and actual effectiveness of interactive query expansion. In: *Proceedings of the Association for Computing Machinery Special Interest Group on Information Retrieval (ACM/SIGIR) 20th annual international conference on research and development in information retrieval* (pp. 324–332). New York: ACM Press.

Mandala, R., Tokunaga, T., and Tanaka, H. (1999). Combining multiple evidence from different types of thesaurus for query expansion. In: *Proceedings of the Association for Computing Machinery Special Interest Group on Information Retrieval (ACM/SIGIR) 22nd annual international conference on research and development in information retrieval* (pp. 191–197). New York: ACM Press.

Marchionini, G. (1989). Information-seeking strategies of novices using a full-text electronic encyclopaedia. *Journal of the American Society for Information Science*, 40 (1), 54–66.

Marchionini, G., Meadow, C., Dwiggins, S., Lin, X., Wang, J., and Yuan, W. (1991). A study of user interaction with information retrieval interfaces: progress report. *Canadian Journal of Information Science*, 16(4), 42–59.

Markey, K., Atherton, P., and Newton, C. (1980). An analysis of controlled and free-text search statements in online searches. *Online Review*, 4(3), 225–236.

Meadow, C., Wang, J., and Yuan, W. (1995). A study of user performance and attitudes with information retrieval interfaces. *Journal of the American Society for Information Science*, 46(7), 490–505.

Muddamalle, M. R. (1998). Natural language versus controlled vocabulary in information retrieval: A case study in soil mechanics. *Journal of the American Society for Information Science*, 49(10), 881–887.

Nakayama, K., Hara, T., and Nishio, S. (2008). A search engine for browsing the Wikipedia thesaurus. In: *Proceedings of international conference on database systems for advanced applications (DASFAA) demonstration track* (pp. 690–693). Berlin: Springer-Verlag.

Perez, E. (1982). Text enhancement: Controlled vocabulary vs. free text. *Special Libraries*, 73(July), 183–192.

Piternick, A. (1984). Searching vocabularies: A developing category of online searching tools. *Online Review*, 8(5), 441–449.

Poikonen, T., and Vakkari, P. (2009). Lay persons' and professionals' nutrition-related vocabularies and their matching to a general and a specific thesaurus. *Journal of Information Science*, 35(2), 232–243.

Qiu, Y., and Frei, H. P. (1993). Concept-based query expansion. In: *Proceedings of the Association for Computing Machinery Special Interest Group on Information Retrieval (ACM/SIGIR) 16th international ACM SIGIR conference on research and development in information retrieval* (pp. 160–169). New York: ACM Press.

Robertson, S. E. (1990). On term selection for query expansion. *Journal of Documentation*, 46(4), 359–364.

Robertson, S. E., Walker, S., and Beaulieu, M. (1997). Laboratory experiments with Okapi: Participation in the TREC programme. *Journal of Documentation*, 53(1), 20–32.

Rowley, J. (1994). The controlled versus natural indexing languages debate revisited: A perspective on information retrieval practice and research. *Journal of Information Science*, 20(2), 108–119.

Salton, G., and Buckley, C. (1988). Term-weighting approaches in automatic text retrieval. *Information Processing and Management*, 24(5), 513–523.

Saracevic, T. (1999). Information science. *Journal of the American Society for Information Science*, 50(12), 1051–1063.

Saracevic, T., Kantor, P., Chamis, A. Y., and Trivison, D. (1988). A study of information seeking and retrieving. I. Background and methodology. *Journal of the American Society for Information Science*, 39(3), 161–176.

Schatz, B. R., Johnson, E. H., and Cochrane, P. A. (1996). Interactive term suggestion for users of digital libraries: Using subject thesauri and co-occurrence lists for information retrieval. In: *Proceedings of the 1st Association for Computing Machinery international conference on digital libraries* (pp. 126–133). Bethesda, MD: ACM Press.

Schutze, H., and Pedersen, J. (1997). A co-occurrence-based thesaurus and two applications to information retrieval. *Information Processing and Management*, 33(3), 307–318.

Shiri, A., and Chambers, T. (2008). Information retrieval from digital libraries: Assessing the potential utility of thesauri in supporting users' search behavior in an interdisciplinary domain. In: C. Arsenault and J. Tennis (Eds.), *Proceedings of the 10th International conference of the International Society for Knowledge Organization (ISKO)*. Würzburg, Germany: Ergon Verlag.

Shiri, A., and Molberg, K. (2005). Interfaces to knowledge organization systems in Canadian digital library collections. *Online Information Review*, 29(6), 604–620.

Shiri, A. A., Revie, C., and Chowdhury, G. (2002). Thesaurus-enhanced search interfaces. *Journal of Information Science*, 28(2), 111–122.

Shiri, A., and Revie, C. (2006). Query expansion behaviour within a thesaurus-enhanced search environment: A user-centered evaluation. *Journal of the American Society for Information Science and Technology*, 57(4), 462–478.

Siegfried, S., Bates, M. J., and Wilde, D. N. (1993). A profile of end-user searching behaviour by humanities scholars: The Getty online searching project report No 2. *Journal of the American Society for Information Science*, 44(5), 273–291.

Sihvonen, A., and Vakkari, P. (2004). Subject knowledge improves interactive query expansion assisted by a thesaurus. *Journal of Documentation*, 60(6), 673–690.

Solomon, P. (1993). Children's information retrieval behaviour: A case analysis of an OPAC. *Journal of the American Society for Information Science*, 44 (5), 245–264.

Spark Jones, K. (1979). Search term relevance weighting given little relevance information. *Journal of Documentation*, 35(1), 30–48.

Spink, A. (1994a). Term relevance feedback and query expansion: Relation to design. In: W. B. Croft and C. J. Van Rijsbergen (Eds.), *Proceedings of the Association for Computing Machinery Special Interest Group on Information Retrieval (ACM/SIGIR) 17th annual international conference on research and development in information retrieval* (pp. 81–90). Berlin: Springer-Verlag.

Spink, A. (1994b). Term relevance feedback and mediated database searching: Implications for information retrieval practice and systems design. *Information Processing and Management*, 31(2), 161–171.

Spink, A. (1996). Multiple search sessions model of end-user behaviour: An exploratory study. *Journal of the American Society for Information Science*, 47(8), 603–609.

Spink, A., Goodrum, A., Robins, D., and Wu, M. (1996). Elicitations during information retrieval: Implications for IR system design. In: *Proceedings of the Association for Computing Machinery Special Interest Group on Information Retrieval (ACM/SIGIR) 19th annual international conference on research and development in information retrieval* (pp. 120–127). New York: ACM Press.

Spink, A., and Saracevic, T. (1997). Interaction in information retrieval: Selection and effectiveness of search terms. *Journal of the American Society for Information Science*, 48(8), 741–761.

Spink, A., Bateman, J., and Jansen, B. J. (1999). Searching the web: A survey of Excite users. *Internet Research: Electronic Networking Applications and Policy*, 9(2), 117–128.

Spink, A., Jansen, B. J., and Ozmultu, H. C. (2000). Use of query reformulation and relevance feedback by Excite users. *Internet Research: Electronic Networking Applications and Policy*, 10(4), 317–328.

Spink, A., Wolfram, D., Jansen, B. J., and Saracevic, T. (2001). Searching the web: The public and their queries. *Journal of the American Society for Information Science and Technology*, 52 (3), 226–234.

Spink, A., Wilson, T. D., Ford, N., Foster, A., and Ellis, D. (2002). Information seeking and mediated searching study. Part 3. Successive searching. *Journal of the American Society for Information Science and Technology*, 53(9), 716–727.

Sutcliffe, A. G., Ennis, M., and Watkinson, S. J. (2000). Empirical studies of end-user information searching. *Journal of the American Society for Information Science*, 51(13), 1211–1231.

Svenonius, E. (1986). Unanswered questions in the design of controlled vocabularies. *Journal of the American Society for Information Science*, 37(5), 331–340.

Tang, M., Wu, W., and Hung, B. (2009). Evaluating a metadata-based term suggestion interface for PubMed with real users with real requests. In: *Proceedings of the American Society for Information Science and Technology annual meeting 2009*. Vancouver, BC, Canada.

Tudhope, D., Binding, C., Blocks, D., and Cunliffe, D. (2006). Query expansion via conceptual distance in thesaurus indexed collections. *Journal of Documentation*, 62(4), 509–533.

Vakkari, P. (2000). Cognition and changes of search terms and tactics during task performance: A longitudinal case study. In: *Proceedings of RIAO 2000, content-based multimedia information access RIAO conference* (pp. 894–907). Paris: C.I.D.

Vakkari, P. (2001). A theory of the task-based information retrieval process: A summary and generalisation of a longitudinal study. *Journal of Documentation*, 57(1), 44–60.

Van Rijsbergen, C. J., Harper, D. J., and Porter, M. F. (1981). The selection of good search terms. *Information Processing and Management*, 17(2), 77–91.

Voorhees, E. M. (1994). Query expansion using lexical-semantic relations. In: W. B. Croft and C. J. Van Rijsbergen (Eds.), *Proceedings of the Association for Computing Machinery Special Interest Group on Information Retrieval (ACM/SIGIR), 17th annual international conference on research and development in information retrieval* (pp. 61–69). Berlin: Springer-Verlag.

CHAPTER 4

Thesauri in Web-Based Search Systems

This chapter examines examples of new information environments on the web that have incorporated thesauri into their search and browsing user interfaces. Examples are numerous of services that have made use of thesauri to support users in exploring, browsing, searching, and retrieving information: digital libraries, portals, subject gateways, open archives, and linked data repositories.

The various approaches and features that have been adopted for performing thesaurus-based searching and browsing in these new environments are discussed, and their advantages and disadvantages are highlighted. Given the increasing number of web-based information retrieval and resource discovery systems, services that do not provide thesaurus-based user interface features and functionalities are omitted from this discussion.

The increasing number of knowledge organization systems on the web, combined with the rapid growth of digital library collections in different subject areas, languages, and formats, have provided unprecedented opportunities to bring order to the chaos of web information search and retrieval. An early review by Shiri and Revie (2000) of thesauri applications in digital libraries, subject gateways, and digital archives examines the ways in which thesauri have been used for information organization and retrieval on the web. Some of the broad thesauri applications that they point out are in metadata, website or page indexing, web-accessible databases, and web search engines.

Hodge (2000) suggests that one of the benefits of the internet, the web, and digital libraries is the degree to which resources can be made available to broader audiences. Current technology facilitates the connection of disparate knowledge communities at the network level. However, resource discovery and functional accessibility require that web content and its organization be comprehensible to these communities. Through the provision of alternate subject access, additional modes of understanding, multilingual access, and supplementary terms for expanding free-text searching, knowledge organization systems can facilitate discovery and comprehension by these disparate communities and allow them to interact in new ways.

Hodge observes that thesauri and other types of knowledge organization systems perform functions that enhance the digital library. She points out the advantages of thesauri in creating meta- and multilingual subject access and in assisting users with search expansion through synonyms. Thesauri can be useful for linking a digital library's resources to other information and resources and for filtering or ranking the information obtained. Smrz et al. (2003) also discuss the importance of thesauri in digital libraries and suggest they can be valuable for a wide range of purposes in digital libraries, including the structuring and classification of digital data, query expansion, and the visualization of retrieved information.

Focusing on the application of thesauri in digital libraries, Shiri (2003) notes that digital library researchers operating in different contexts have investigated the potential of these tools for a variety of purposes. He suggests several applications:

- Use of thesauri and classification systems for cross-browsing and cross-searching disparate digital collections

- Creation of ontologies using existing thesauri

- Development of classification systems and specialized controlled vocabularies to provide a general knowledge-representation facility for digital collections with a diverse range of materials

- Use of taxonomies to provide unified and organized access to different digital repositories through description of different layers of the digital collections

Soergel (2002) identifies the following functions of a thesaurus in the context of a digital library:

- To support the learning and assimilating of information

- To assist researchers and practitioners with problem clarification

- To support information retrieval

- To provide knowledge-based support for end-user searching

- To support meaningful information display

- To provide a tool for indexing

- To facilitate the combination of multiple databases or unified access to multiple databases

- To support document processing after retrieval

4.1 Thesauri in Digital Libraries

The most encompassing and the most widely used and referenced definition of the term *digital library* is provided by the Digital Library Federation (Waters, 1998):

> [A] digital library is an organization that provides the resources, including the specialized staff, to select, structure, offer intellectual access to, interpret, distribute, preserve the integrity of, and ensure the persistence over time of collections of digital works so that they are readily and economically available for use by a defined community or set of communities.

Many digital libraries have made use of thesauri for information organization, representation, and retrieval, but far fewer have incorporated thesauri into their search user interfaces. In a study of knowledge organization systems in North American digital library collections, Shiri and Chase-Kruszewski (2009) found that at least 26 digital library collections make use of thesauri in their search user interfaces. This section describes a number of digital library user interfaces enhanced with thesauri for the purposes of searching, browsing, and navigation.

One of the early projects focusing on integrating thesauri into search user interfaces was carried out by Schatz et al. (1996) who used the Inspec Thesaurus to develop a rich user interface. The aim was to support multiple information-seeking strategies through an interface with dynamic term suggestion functionalities.

The middle of the interface displays a hierarchical view of the term *deductive databases*, showing its context and structure (see Figure 1.13 earlier in this book). All of the thesaurus terms are hypertextual, and when a user clicks on a term, details of the term are provided. More specifically, when the thesaurus browser displays the entry for a thesaurus term, appropriate parts of the hierarchy are automatically expanded, and the term is displayed in boldface to clearly show where it occurs, while at the same time leaving other parts of the hierarchy unexpanded. Within the interface, users are able to drag and drop terms for searching or to initiate a browsing session. The interface incorporates the co-occurrence terms drawn from the database and combines them with thesaurus terms to enhance the variability of terms.

Figure 1.13 shows multiple views of the thesaurus terms and co-occurrence terms, with deductive databases shown midway, the bottom left box showing keywords in context, and the top right box displaying co-occurrence terms.

Gordon and Domeshek (1998) describe Déjà Vu, a relatively new user interface for retrieval in digital libraries. It makes use of the Library of Congress Thesaurus for Graphic Materials. Figure 4.1 shows the user interface, divided into upper and lower sections. The top section organizes and displays the thesaurus subject terms, and allows users to browse through these terms to locate those of interest. At any given time, there is one subject term, the Focus term, which is displayed near the upper left corner of that section. All the other lists in the top section contain subject terms that are related to the Focus term in some way. The left side of the top section contains lists for all the standard thesaurus relationships, including broader, narrower, and related terms, as well as notes attached by thesaurus developers to the Focus term.

The right side of this section of the interface displays the Packages associated with the Focus term. Packages group together terms based on library users' best understanding of how corresponding concepts are represented and organized in their minds. Figure 4.1 shows an example of a Package, entitled *Flying on a passenger airplane*, which appears because one of its member terms, *airplanes*, is the current Focus term. In Déjà Vu, each Package is represented and displayed as a simple structure consisting of a distinguishing textual title and a list of thesaurus terms. The list of thesaurus terms is divided into a set of labeled sub-lists, which categorize the terms by the roles they play in the Package. In the example, these sub-lists are labeled *events, places,*

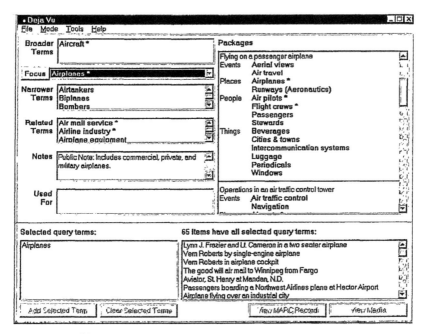

Figure 4.1   Déjà Vu search user interface

people, and *things*. The Packages provide a faceted view of the thesaurus terms related to the query submitted by the user. The bottom section of the display provides users with a way of directly accessing digital materials indexed by terms presented in the top section; the example shows that 65 items have all selected query terms.

Paynter and Witten (2001) describe an interface called Phind, which combines a browsing hierarchy constructed from the full text of a document collection with a completely different hierarchy supplied by a standard subject thesaurus.

The AGROVOC is a multilingual thesaurus for agricultural information systems that was developed by the Food and Agriculture Organization of the United Nations to provide subject control for the AGRIS agricultural bibliographic database and the Current Agricultural Research Information System database of agricultural research projects, known as CARIS.

Users can examine the phrases in the document collection, and the phrases give access to the actual documents containing them. Users can also look at the thesaurus terms, which are tagged with information indicating how often and in which documents they occur. Thesaurus entries suggest new relationships and new terms to search. Users can switch smoothly between document phrases and thesaurus phrases. The result is a combined hierarchical browser based on both thesaurus phrases and all phrases that occur in the document collection.

For a given search term, entries from the thesaurus that include the term are displayed first, followed by the phrases from the document containing the term, and then by the document itself. The first 10 items on each of these three displays appear immediately, and more can be obtained by clicking the Get More links.

In the example shown in Figure 4.2, the user has performed a search for *tools*. The first result is a Use entry from the thesaurus; the results below are phrases from the document collection. The Use entry recommends that the term *equipment* be substituted for *tools* in the query (and also states that it occurs 1,548 times in 599 documents). The user clicks on *equipment*, and a list of narrower terms is displayed in the bottom pane, which displays thesaurus links. The user has expanded the thesaurus list to 40 terms by clicking the Get More Thesaurus Links bar; in fact, there are 184 thesaurus links (terms) for *equipment*, describing a diverse range of equipment. In fact, the vast majority of these thesaurus links would not be found by the phrase browser because neither *tools* nor *equipment* is included.

Using the AGROVOC thesaurus, McKay et al. (2004) developed a user interface for the Greenstone digital library in order to encourage thesaurus-based browsing and searching. The interface has a Thesaurus tab to support exploration of the thesaurus structure itself.

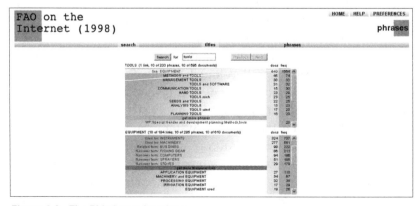

Figure 4.2   The Phind user interface

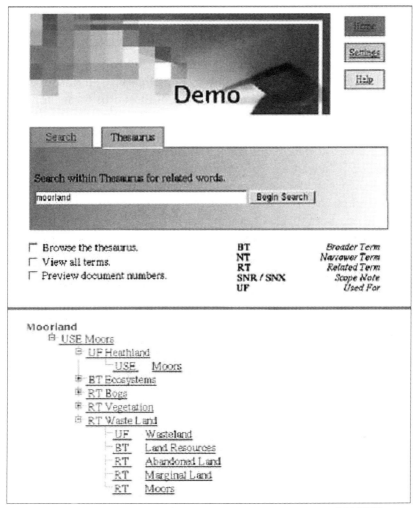

Figure 4.3   Thesaurus-enhanced Greenstone search interface using AGROVOC
Thesaurus

Figure 4.3 shows a search for the term *moorland* and its hierarchy in the thesaurus. Users have three options on this interface, namely, Browse the Thesaurus, View All Terms, or Preview Document Numbers. Child nodes in the hierarchy can be hidden or expanded in the conventional manner by clicking on the plus and minus icons of the parent term. The user can quickly focus on a specific portion of the thesaurus through Search Within Thesaurus for Related Words.

The AGROVOC thesaurus-enhanced search interface also displays a selection of thesaurus terms labeled as Quicklist. This list is similar to many suggested term features currently found on search systems on the web. Ticking a Quicklist term adds it to the terms in the search box. The Quicklist terms are in a broader-, narrower-, and/or related-term relationship with the query. If more than one query term is present, then the Quicklist contains up to three thesaurus terms for each query term; this limits the total number of thesaurus terms appearing on the search page. For example, a search for the term *animals* brings up six related terms, and users can view more related terms through the Show Remaining Related Terms For hyperlink.

One of the advantages of this interface lies in how it combines the results display with a set of additional terms. Users are able to modify and add terms to their initial query by using any or all of the terms shown, or alternatively they can explore additional related terms from within the thesaurus.

The International Development Research Centre (IDRC) digital library uses the Organization for Economic Cooperation and Development Macrothesaurus for Information Processing in the Field of Economic and Social Development. The subject search option allows users to browse and choose a term for searching.

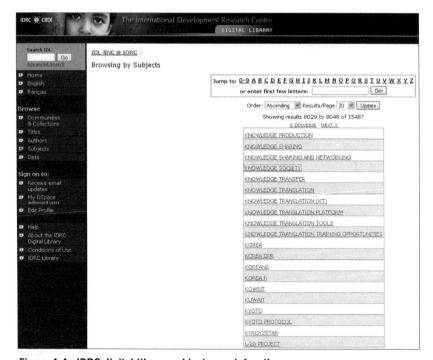

Figure 4.4   IDRC digital library subject search function

Figure 4.4 shows the subject search feature of the IDRC digital library user interface.

The browsing option is very limited in that it shows terms alphabetically only, with the user required to click on each letter to get an overview of the terms beginning with a given letter. The interface does not provide users with the semantic details of the selected term; rather it retrieves a list of documents described as using the term.

The Prairie Postcards Collection at the University of Alberta contains more than 14,000 postcards depicting various aspects of life on the Canadian Prairies from the late 19th through the mid 20th century. The collection uses the Library of Congress Thesaurus for Graphical Materials and provides a browsing interface for exploring

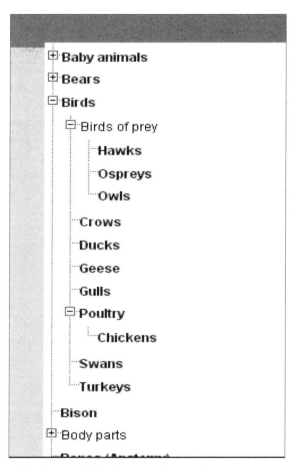

Figure 4.5   Prairie Postcard Collection browsing interface

the content of the Digital Postcards collection. Figure 4.5 shows the browsing view of the content of the collection.

The interface allows users to browse and drill three levels down the hierarchy. Once a term is selected, a list of images is presented, and users have access to a list of subject terms assigned to each image. These subject terms can be selected by users for further query reformulation.

Dalmau et al. (2005) report the design of a user interface for the Charles W. Cushman Online Photo Collection as part of the Indiana University Digital Library Program, which takes advantage of two thesauri, Getty's Thesaurus of Geographic Names and the Library of Congress's Thesaurus for Graphic Materials (TGM). The interface provides a browse and search feature that integrates existing descriptions and controlled vocabularies as core parts of the discovery functionality. The main browse access points into the Cushman Collection are Year, Genre, Subject, and Location. Users can browse these categories either individually or in combination (known as *faceted browsing*). Categories with inherent hierarchical structures, such as subject and location, allow navigation down the hierarchy once the facet is added during browsing.

Figure 4.6 shows a subject browsing option for *aquatic animals.* The user is able to view the retrieved images, as well as a list of browsing suggestions that are presented in a faceted manner. Users can reformulate or narrow their search using the suggested subject terms.

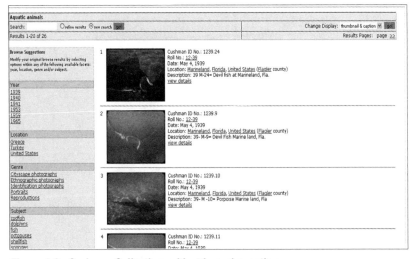

Figure 4.6   Cushman Collection subject browsing option

The user interface also takes advantage of the semantic structure of the TGM to suggest alternative terms for searching. If a user's topical search term finds a match in the thesaurus, the results page provides search suggestions so that the user can broaden or refine a result set based on the TGM structure. These search suggestions assist users in reformulating their queries in context by allowing for topical term-for-term replacement. For instance, if, as shown in Figure 4.7, a user queries for *gardens and California,* narrower related term suggestions will be offered (for example, *botanical gardens* and *Japanese gardens*) and broader term suggestions (for example, *facilities*).

Another interesting function of the interface is that it performs two automatic procedures: mapping of lead-in terms to authorized terms and retrieval of all narrower terms. An example of lead-in mapping is a search for *cars,* which is not an authorized term in the TGM, but the interface provides the user with results by mapping the query to the preferred term *automobiles.* An example of narrower term retrieval is a query for images of *sports,* which would display images relating to specific sports, such as baseball and basketball.

The ERIC thesaurus is one of the long-standing and most widely used thesauri available today. It is currently being used by the ERIC Library. The digital library website provides a Search & Browse the Thesaurus feature that allows users to employ the thesaurus for query formulation. The thesaurus interface has an alphabetical browsing option and a faceted type of browsing feature that facilitates user browsing of the thesaurus by category. Availability of thesaurus terms at various stages of the search process is a key characteristic of a superior thesaurus-enhanced user interface.

Figure 4.7   A search for *gardens and California* in the Cushman Collection

For instance, choosing the term *faculty advisers* permits a user to view details of the term and start an ERIC search, as shown in Figure 4.8. The selected term will appear in the Advanced Search box, where users can add other terms or decide to carry out a free-text search with the thesaurus term. Finally, once the records containing the selected term(s) are retrieved, the interface shows additional semantically

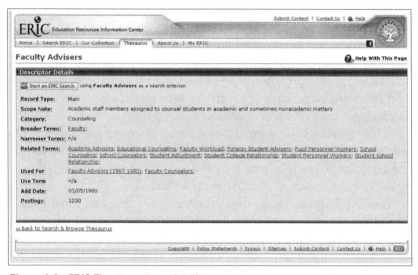

Figure 4.8   ERIC Thesaurus term details

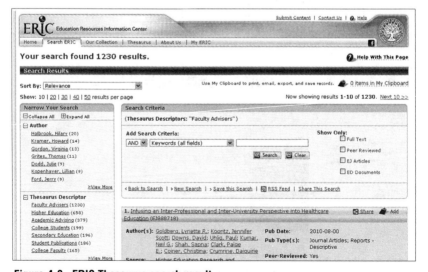

Figure 4.9   ERIC Thesaurus search result

related thesaurus descriptors for possible query reformulation, as shown in Figure 4.9.

The American Society for Information Science and Technology (ASIS&T) Digital Library is a very good example of a digital library that uses a thesaurus for browsing a digital collection. The library uses the *ASIS&T Thesaurus of Information Science, Technology, and Librarianship*, a well-developed faceted thesaurus (Redmond-Neal and Hlava, 2005). Figure 4.10 shows the high-level facets of the *ASIS&T Thesaurus* for browsing. Unlike many thesaurus-based user interfaces, in which the number after a term refers to the number of documents indexed via that term, the ASIS&T Digital Library interface displays the number of specific terms under each facet. This feature may cause confusion for users and is a usability issue.

Users are then able to drill down and browse through each facet to look at more-specific terms. Figure 4.11 shows the term *knowledge organization systems* under the main facet *knowledge and information* in the thesaurus, along with its narrower terms. The related terms and the scope note for the facets appear to the left side of the term.

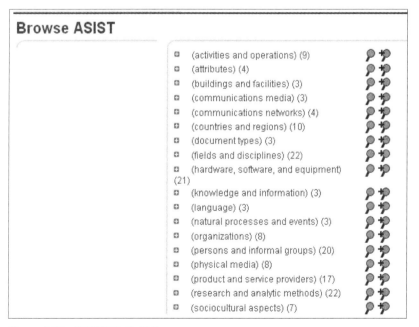

Figure 4.10   ASIS&T Digital Library

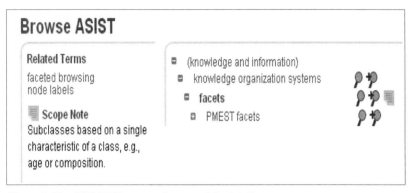

Figure 4.11   *ASIS&T Thesaurus* terms and its details

Figure 4.12   Search result display in ASIS&T Digital Library

On clicking on the magnifying glass icon to the right side of each thesaurus term, the user sees a list of documents (Figure 4.12). However, the thesaurus browsing feature is not available at the search result display interface. It should also be noted that the Digital Library on the Wiley InterScience platform provides a browsing-based interface, and there is no search feature available for exploring within the thesaurus.

The Art Collection, part of the Our Future Our Past digital library (Heritage Community Foundation), provides limited access to the terms from its Art and Architecture Thesaurus to support query formulation. As can be seen in Figure 4.13, the subject search field is designed to allow access to thesaurus terms. If the user clicks on the Browse tab, a small window pops up that shows an alphabetical list of thesaurus terms, along with the number of images indexed with each term. Clicking on the term in the pop-up window inserts the term into the search box. Users can then choose multiple terms in the subject search bar to be included in their search statement. One of the main issues with this interface is the limited view of the thesaurus terms within a small pop-up window. In addition, users are unable to see any term relationships or additional thesaural functionalities, such as hierarchical view.

4.2 Thesauri in Subject Gateways and Portals

Koch (2000) defines subject gateways as "internet-based services which support systematic resource discovery" (p. 26). These gateways

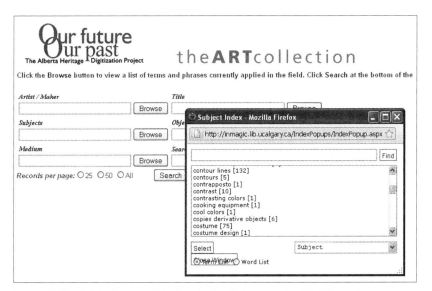

Figure 4.13   Subject search interface in Our Future Our Past Art Collection

provide links to resources (documents, objects, or services) that are predominantly accessible through the internet. Browsing access to the resources by means of a subject structure is an important feature. Subject access through some kinds of knowledge structures such as thesauri and classification systems is one of the significant features of good-quality subject gateways. Such quality-controlled subject gateways have established procedures for selection and content description of webpages; they also use thesauri for careful and consistent resource description. Well-known examples of subject gateways were developed as part of the Electronic Libraries Programme in the U.K. Intute is the hub of several subject gateways, some of which use thesauri for searching and browsing.

Intute: Medicine (including dentistry) provides free access to high-quality resources on the internet. Each resource has been evaluated and categorized by subject specialists based at British universities. The system makes use of the Medical Subject Headings (MeSH) Thesaurus, which is part of PubMed Central, for indexing and retrieval of web documents, so users can browse a list of MeSH terms, as shown in Figure 4.14. The number of documents indexed by each term is shown. It should be noted that, although users can browse the list of terms and click on each term to get access to the documents, the interface does not accommodate any features to display semantic relations between or among terms.

To support users' searching, the system provides a More Details option for each record, through which a user is able to view other thesaurus terms assigned to the document. This feature, shown in Figure 4.15, allows users to employ other thesaurus terms for searching.

Both Intute: Veterinary Medicine and Intute: Agriculture subject gateways make use of the Centre for Agricultural Bioscience (CAB) International Thesaurus for browsing. The thesaurus is used as a tool for indexing and retrieval of information in the CAB Abstracts Database. Intute: Nursing, Midwifery and Allied Health uses both MeSH terms and Royal College of Nursing thesaurus terms. The interface design for all these gateways is similar to that for Intute: Medicine.

AustLit: The Australian Literature Resource (University of Queensland) is an Australian subject gateway that offers an interesting approach to thesaurus-based search support. It uses a collection of thesauri containing 26,000 terms. On entering a search term, the user is provided with the place of the term in the thesaurus structure, making it easy to contextualize the search term, along with a link to

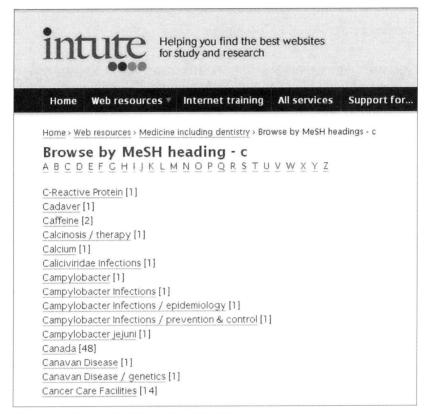

Figure 4.14 Intute: Medicine's list of MeSH terms

get access to the documents indexed by the given term. In the screen-shot captured in Figure 4.16, the user has entered *prose poetry*, and the interface shows its context. This type of interface makes use of the hierarchical structure of the thesaurus to provide more information for search clarification.

WebLaw.edu.au (State Library of New South Wales) is a subject gateway to Australian legal resources that draws on the WebLaw Thesaurus. Used by the New South Wales Attorney General's Lawzone project, it is a two-level list of subject headings with particular emphasis on plain English legal information. The thesaurus provides a simple hierarchical overview of terms for browsing. This type of the-saurus display lends itself to small rather than large thesauri, as it would be challenging to show several facets of the latter within one screen.

Figure 4.15   More Details option in Intute Subject Gateway

One of the long-standing and more successful examples of thesaurus-enhanced user interfaces is the MeSH Thesaurus, mentioned earlier. The PubMed Central repository uses the MeSH Thesaurus for sophisticated searching. The system carries out intelligent matching between the user's terms and those of the thesaurus. The advantage of this type of thesaurus-based searching lies in its automatic redirection of the user's term to a term that is acceptable by the archive to retrieve highly relevant articles. For instance, a search for *skin cancer* suggests *skin neoplasm,* along with subheadings for further specification of the search, and shows the context of the search term in the MeSH hierarchy. Figures 4.17 and 4.18 show how the MeSH Thesaurus supports a user's search.

An effective approach to the integration of thesauri for enhancing searching and browsing can be found in MediaSleuth (National Information Center for Educational Media), a comprehensive web-based database on audiovisual materials developed by Access Innovations. The interface takes advantage of the semantic and conceptual structure of the National Information Center for Educational Media Thesaurus to provide a semantically rich search functionality. It allows a number of thesaurus-based capabilities,

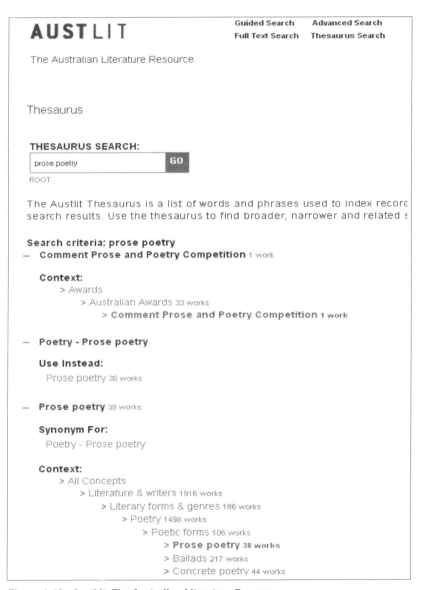

Figure 4.16   AustLit: The Australian Literature Resource

including thesaurus-based autocompletion of terms entered by the user term suggestions for broadening and narrowing the search, and an easy-to-use browsing structure for exploring the content of the database.

**Figure 4.17   A search for *skin cancer* in the PubMed Central MeSH Thesaurus
[*Courtesy of U.S. National Library of Medicine*]**

**Figure 4.18   Hierarchy in the PubMed Central MeSH Thesaurus search feature
[*Courtesy of U.S. National Library of Medicine*]**

Figure 4.19 shows how the interface provides browsing and searching support. On the left side at the top, categories are presented for browsing. For example, if the category *family and consumer sciences* is selected, more specific categories are provided, such as *clothing and dress*, *consumer education*, and *cookery*. If the user selects *cookery*, not only are the results shown on the right pane, but a list of narrower terms close to the result list also appears so that the user can narrow the search using such terms as *baking, boiling*, or *frying*.

The interface provides an information-rich environment for query formulation and reformulation without being cluttered or confusing.

Figure 4.19   Browsing the facets of *family and consumer sciences* in the MediaSleuth search user interface

Also, when a user wants to carry out a search, the interface displays a dynamic list of preferred and synonymous thesaurus term suggestions that may match the initial search term. Let's consider an example of a search for the term *cognitive*. As the user enters this term, terms such as *cognitive development*, *cognitive processes*, and *cognitive psychology* are suggested, along with a non-preferred term, *cognitive style*. If there are no results for the non-preferred term, the interface instructs the searcher to use a preferred term, in this case, *cognitive processes*.

One of the key advantages of this interface lies in its integration of searching and browsing with results display. This approach to user interface design allows seamless access to the semantic structure of the thesaurus and the search results and facilitates query formulation and reformulation.

Glasgow Health Information Gateway is a central gateway to quality online health information and learning resources developed by the Greater Glasgow and Clyde National Health Service Board. This subject gateway makes use of the MeSH Thesaurus to offer a number of thesaurus-enhanced functionalities. The user undertakes browsing and searching based on the terms and high-level facets of the MeSH Thesaurus. Users can choose to browse the collections of documents using either alphabetical or hierarchical (Figure 4.20) options.

In the alphabetical arrangement, each term is displayed, along with the number of documents indexed by that term. An alphabetical

Figure 4.20   Glasgow Health Information hierarchical browsing interface

navigation bar appears at the top to allow users to quickly choose terms based on the first letter of the term.

In the hierarchical browsing mode, users are shown the top 15 high-level MeSH facets, whereby they can browse and drill down the hierarchy to see narrower terms for each facet.

Figure 4.20 shows how users can easily make use of plus and minus signs to expand and collapse the high-level facets. The hierarchy can be explored to a maximum of three levels. To display the last level, users click on an arrow sign before the terms appearing at the lowest hierarchy level. Users can then choose a particular term and retrieve the results.

The Glasgow Health Information Gateway interface also provides a subject search facility whereby users can combine up to three thesaurus terms using the Boolean operators AND and OR. For term selection, three drop-down lists of subject terms are shown to the user. In addition, users can limit their searches using additional metadata elements such as *audience, document type*, and *sector*.

The portal Social Care Online (Social Care Institute for Excellence) is the U.K.'s largest collection of information on social work and social care. It makes effective use of thesauri for browsing and navigation.

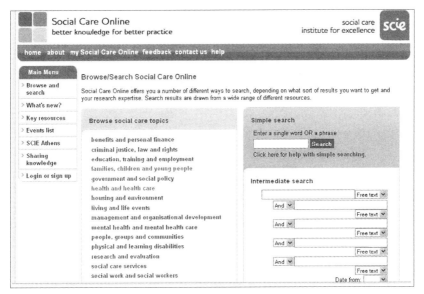

Figure 4.21   Social Care Online browsing interface

The browsing option provides users with 15 high-level facets, as can be seen in Figure 4.21.

Clicking on a high-level facet provides a list of narrower terms under the facet, along with the number of indexed documents using the term (Figure 4.22). Users can drill down the hierarchy by clicking on the plus sign. They can then click on a hyperlinked term to retrieve documents, or if they want to choose more than one term to search, they can tick the boxes next to each term to select them. This selection will result in the selected terms appearing in the pink box on the right side of the interface; the box functions as a search term pool for conducting multiterm searches. As can be seen in Figure 4.22, the default Boolean operator for combining the selected term is AND, but users can change it to other Boolean operators if they desire.

In addition to the display of selected terms in the pink box, if any of the selected terms have related terms or notes, those will appear in the pink box under the Combine Topics box. In Figure 4.22, the terms *emotions*, *happiness*, and *parental attitudes* are selected, having appeared in the Combine Topics box. Also, the term *parents* appears at the bottom with a tick box that users can select.

This type of design provides an interesting and effective use of thesaurus terms to support the user's term selection. Another interesting

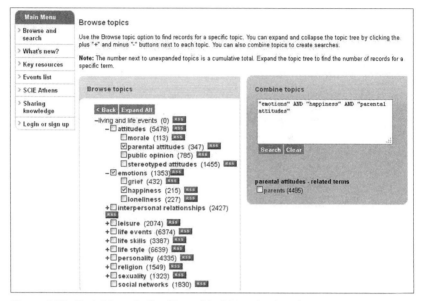

Figure 4.22   Social Care Online hierarchical browsing interface

and useful feature of the browsing functionality is the Expand All and Collapse All features, which permit a user to quickly display or hide narrower terms within the hierarchy. The Find a Topic feature allows the user to search within thesaurus terms and displays the same hierarchical structure to allow for browsing. Even better would be seamless access both to retrieved documents and to the hierarchy of thesaurus terms so that users are able to switch more easily between the thesaurus and the retrieved documents.

4.3 Thesauri in Digital Archives

Several digital and open archives currently use thesauri for browsing and searching. Fenton (2010), for example, in a discussion of controlled vocabularies and thesauri in British online finding aids, notes that the main three controlled vocabularies used by U.K. archives are Library of Congress Subject Headings, the UNESCO thesaurus, and the U.K.'s Archival Thesaurus (UKAT).

A well-known example of open archives is the U.K.'s UK Data Archive, which makes use of the Humanities and Social Science Electronic Thesaurus (HASSET). Entering a search term (consisting of one or more words) into the HASSET interface results in either a

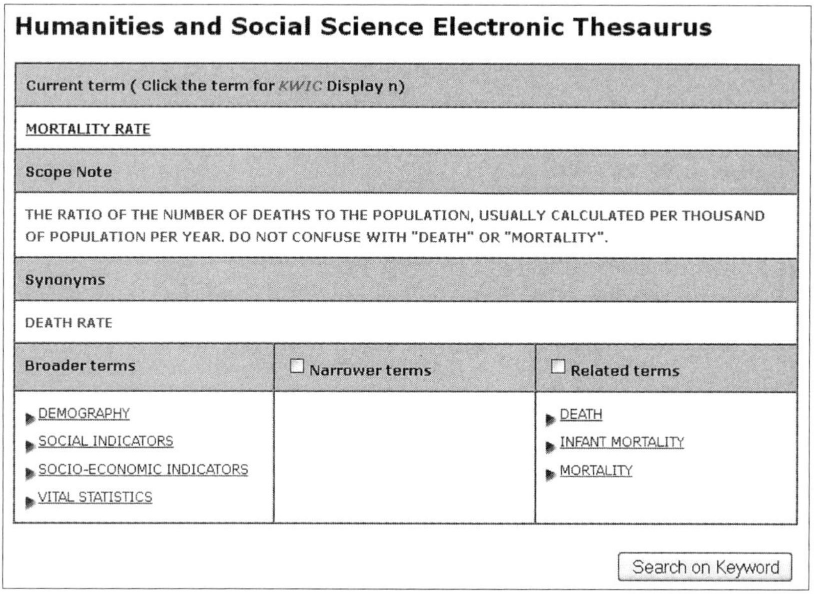

Humanities and Social Science Electronic Thesaurus

Current term (Click the term for *KWIC* Display n)

MORTALITY RATE

Scope Note

THE RATIO OF THE NUMBER OF DEATHS TO THE POPULATION, USUALLY CALCULATED PER THOUSAND OF POPULATION PER YEAR. DO NOT CONFUSE WITH "DEATH" OR "MORTALITY".

Synonyms

DEATH RATE

Broader terms	☐ Narrower terms	☐ Related terms
▸ DEMOGRAPHY ▸ SOCIAL INDICATORS ▸ SOCIO-ECONOMIC INDICATORS ▸ VITAL STATISTICS		▸ DEATH ▸ INFANT MORTALITY ▸ MORTALITY

Search on Keyword

Figure 4.23   UK Data Archive HASSET Thesaurus search [*Reproduced with permission of the UK Data Archive at the University of Essex*]

match with the word in the thesaurus or, if there is no exact match, a listing of partial matches. Figure 4.23 shows a search for *mortality rate*, with the thesaurus presenting a scope note as well as synonymous, broader, narrower, and related terms. Cross referencing to synonyms suggests alternative terms and provides links to other conceptually related terms. Note that users are able to browse broader terms or include narrower or related terms in their search along with the original query term.

In addition, users may choose to see the context of the term *mortality rate* in a Keyword in Context (KWIC) list of terms. This allows users to see the concept space and possibly terms that they may not have thought of at the beginning of their search.

In addition to a KWIC display, the hierarchical view of the thesaurus is available for browsing. Figure 4.24 illustrates how, on clicking on a term in the hierarchy, users are shown the details of the term, along with its broader, narrower, and related terms. Once a user chooses to search the collection by using the thesaurus term, a list of results will appear, but there is no access at the result presentation interface. Users will have to return to the initial page to get access to the thesaurus terms.

Hierarchical Display

Select a term from the list below to view that term in the HASSET thesaurus.

DEMOGRAPHY
¦..DEMOGRAPHIC STATISTICS
¦   :..CENSUS DATA
¦   :..VITAL STATISTICS
¦   :..BIRTH RATE
¦   :..CAUSES OF DEATH
¦   :..DIVORCE RATE
¦   :..FERTILITY
¦   :..MARRIAGE RATE
¦   :..MORBIDITY
¦   :..MORTALITY
¦   :..INFANT MORTALITY
¦   :..MATERNAL MORTALITY
¦   :..MORTALITY RATE
¦   :..NATALITY
¦   :..ILLEGITIMATE BIRTHS
¦   :..NUMBER OF DIVORCES
¦   :..NUPTIALITY
¦   :..SURVIVAL RATE
¦..POPULATION DISTRIBUTION
¦   :..AGE DISTRIBUTION
¦   :..POPULATION DENSITY
¦..POPULATION DYNAMICS
¦   :..AGEING POPULATION
¦   :..POPULATION DECREASE
¦   :..POPULATION INCREASE
¦   :..POPULATION PROBLEMS
¦   :..OVERPOPULATION
¦..POPULATION PROJECTION
¦   :..LIFE EXPECTANCY

Figure 4.24   UK Data Archive HASSET Thesaurus hierarchical display [*Reproduced with permission of the UK Data Archive at the University of Essex*]

Archives in London and M25 Area (AIM25) is a permanent web-accessible database of descriptions of the archives and manuscript collections of more than 100 of London's higher education institutions, learned societies, cultural organizations, and City livery companies. The collection makes use of a number of thesauri, including the UNESCO, MeSH, and UKAT. Thesaurus terms are available

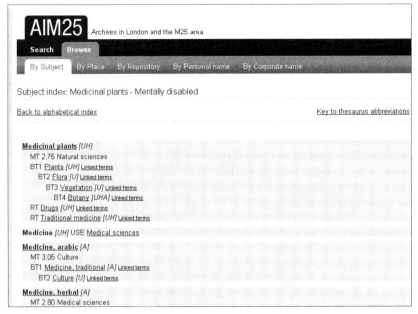

Figure 4.25   AIM25 Thesaurus browsing interface

through the Browse option, with standard thesaurus notations for broader terms, narrower terms, and related terms.

Figure 4.25 shows the term *medicinal plants* and its associated terms from the various thesauri. When a user clicks on a term, documents indexed by that term will be shown. This type of display is useful for indexers and information professionals but can be difficult for general users who are not familiar with these notations.

One of the interesting user interface features of AIM25 is that when the results of a search are displayed, a list is provided of Related Subject Search terms derived from the thesauri. This list allows users to modify, expand, or reformulate their search terms.

4.4 Thesauri in Linked Data Repositories

The term *linked data* is closely related to the notion of the semantic web. Heath et al. (2009) note that linked data is "simply about using the web to create typed links between data from different sources" (p. 2). These linked data sources may be as diverse as databases maintained by two organizations in different geographical locations, or they may simply be two or more heterogeneous systems within one organization that historically have not easily interoperated at the data level.

Technically speaking, *linked data* refers to "data published on the web in such a way that it is machine-readable; its meaning is explicitly defined; it is linked to other external data sets; and it can in turn be linked to from external data sets" (p. 2). The Linking Open Data project is the most well-known example of interlinking various large, open-data sources, such as data about geographic locations, people, companies, books, scientific publications, films, music, television and radio programs, genes, proteins, drugs, clinical trials, online communities, statistical data, census results, and reviews.

Berners-Lee (2006) outlines a set of "rules" for publishing data on the web in such a way that all published data become part of a single global data space:

1. Use uniform resource identifiers (URIs) as names for things.

2. Use HTTP URIs so that people can look up those names.

3. When someone looks up a URI, provide useful information, using the standards (RDF, SPARQL).

4. Include links to other URIs, so that users can discover more things.

These have become known as the *linked data principles*. They provide a basic recipe for publishing and connecting data via the infrastructure of the web while at the same time adhering to its architecture and standards. Heath et al. (2009) note that in order to increase the utility of linked data sources, several types of metadata should be used. General and domain-specific controlled vocabularies such as ontologies and thesauri are particularly useful tools for interlinking and connecting various data sources and for supporting meaningful and organized access to linked data sources.

The Simple Knowledge Organization System (SKOS) is a standard developed by the World Wide Web Consortium to build a bridge between the world of knowledge organization systems—including thesauri, classifications, subject headings, taxonomies, and folksonomies—and the linked data community, with the goal of bringing benefits to both. Libraries, museums, newspapers, government portals, enterprises, social networking applications, and other communities that manage large collections of books, historical artifacts, news reports, business glossaries, blog entries, and other items can now use SKOS to leverage the power of linked data. The standard makes use of the Resource Description Framework (RDF), which facilitates the encoding of information for sharing and interoperability across various computer applications. Currently, a number of thesauri have been encoded based on SKOS and can be used within the context of linked data sources.

The European Environment Information and Observation Network hosts a GEneral Multilingual Environmental Thesaurus (GEMET) linked data service in 28 languages using SKOS. For instance, if a search is conducted for *apiculture* in GEMET, it provides details of the term, including broader and narrower terms, together with its equivalent in other languages (Figure 4.26). The thesaurus terms are linked with other data sources, namely, Wikipedia and AGROVOC, a multilingual agricultural thesaurus developed and maintained by the Food and Agriculture Organization of the United Nations. Users can click on the Wikipedia link to retrieve the Wikipedia article on apiculture.

Building on the notions of SKOS and linked open data sources, Schandl and Blumauer (2010) developed a tool called PoolParty, which creates and maintains multilingual SKOS-based thesauri. The tool facilitates various commercial applications of thesauri, such as semantic search engines, recommender systems, auto-completion services, and faceted browsing. It provides several different features to support thesauri in different languages and to connect them to

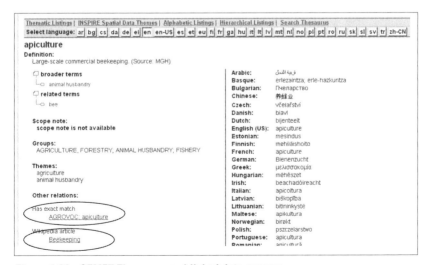

Figure 4.26   GEMET Thesaurus and linked data sources

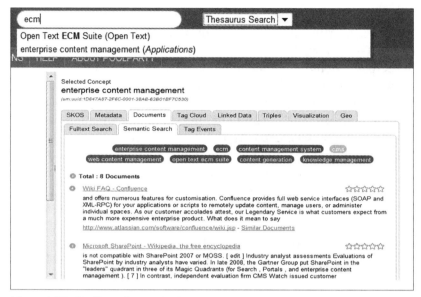

Figure 4.27   PoolParty Search Assistant User Interface

linked data sources. Thesaurus-aided search features include query expansion, faceted and visual browsing, and auto-completion of user terms. Figure 4.27 shows these features via the Thesaurus Search option at the top right side of the interface. Users are presented with recommendations for improving their search, and the selected term is searched across linked data sources such as wikis.

The application offers a moderated search function through which a user can create more-complex queries and modify or add terms to the initial query by using various thesaurus terms. Figure 4.28 shows details of a search for *Protestantism OR Pentecostalism*, in which users are provided a number of broader, narrower, and related terms that can be selected to search across linked data sources.

Examples of thesauri encoded using the SKOS standard include the following:

- The Common Audiovisual Archives Thesaurus, developed by the Netherlands Institute for Sound and Vision

- The Library of Congress's TGM is encoded in SKOS in order to create access to linked data sources

- The MeSH Thesaurus

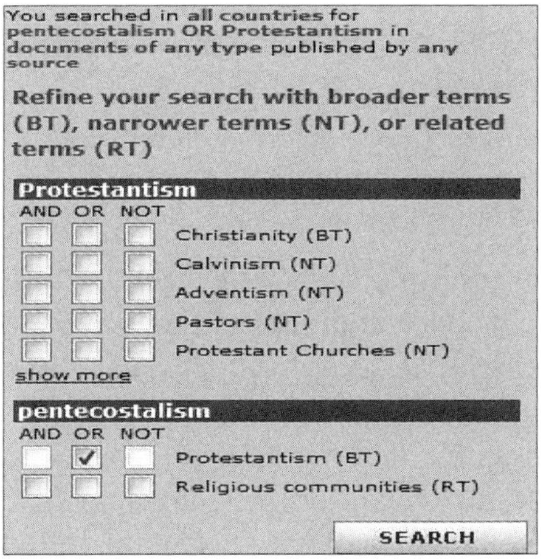

Figure 4.28 Moderated Search feature in PoolParty

- The Standard Thesaurus Wirtschaf (STW) Thesaurus for Economics: Thesaurus for economics and business economics in English and German, maintained by the German National Library of Economics

- EuroVoc, the Multilingual Thesaurus of the European Union

- UKAT

Application of the previously mentioned thesauri in linked data sources is at various stages of development, but most of them do not at present have an operational search user interface. Nonetheless, the SKOS standard provides a consistent approach for federation and mapping of several thesauri to be used in linked data sources. Details of mapping and integrating thesauri for searching and browsing are discussed in Chapter 7.

4.5 Conclusion

This chapter discusses thesauri as one type of knowledge organization system and their application in new information environments. It explains some of the ways in which thesauri are used to provide search and browsing interfaces to support information access. The following examples of thesaural use in these new information environments are discussed:

- Digital libraries

- Subject gateways

- Digital and open archives

- Linked data sources

Some of these projects, such as Déjà Vu, ERIC, the Cushman Online Photo Collection, and Greenstone have incorporated thesauri into their search interfaces to support users at various stages of the search and interaction process (McKay et al., 2004). These interfaces integrate thesauri into both query formulation and result presentation displays in order to encourage user interaction with the thesaurus and to allow switching between the retrieved documents and thesaurus terms for further specification or modification of search terms.

Other user interfaces, such as HASSET and the ASIS&T Digital Library, focus more on presenting the thesaurus browsing interface for users and do not provide an integrated thesaurus and results display interface. Once users are provided with a list of retrieved items, the thesaurus is no longer available for further interaction. The SKOS, an increasingly popular World Wide Web Consortium standard, provides a web-compliant, effective, and consistent approach to thesaural use in a wide range of web applications and services. The chapter presents examples of thesauri encoded in SKOS-based search systems that have made use of thesauri in their search interfaces.

References

Access Innovations, Inc. Retrieved from www.accessinn.com/index.html (accessed June 1, 2012).

AIM25: Archives of London and M25 Area. Retrieved from www.aim25.ac.uk/index.stm (accessed June 1, 2012).

American Society for Information Science and Technology. ASIS&T Digital Library and Thesaurus. Retrieved from onlinelibrary.wiley.com/asist?context Term=%28fields%20and%20disciplines%29 (accessed June 1, 2012).

Berners-Lee, T. (2006). Linked data. Retrieved from www.w3.org/Design Issues/LinkedData.html (accessed July 23, 2011).

Dalmau, M., Floyd, R., Jiao, D., and Riley, J. (2005). Integrating thesaurus relationships into search and browse in an online photograph collection. *Library Hi Tech*, 23(3), 425–452.

Education Resources Information Center. ERIC thesaurus. Retrieved from www.eric.ed.gov/ERICWebPortal/thesaurus/thesaurus.jsp (accessed June 1, 2012).

European Environment Information and Observation Network. *EIONET GEMET thesaurus*. Retrieved from www.eionet.europa.eu/gemet (accessed July 25, 2012).

Fenton, C. (2010). Use of controlled vocabulary and thesauri in UK online finding aids. *Journal of the Society of Archivists*, 31(2), 187–205.

Gordon, A., and Domeshek, E. A. (1998). Déjà Vu: A knowledge-rich interface for retrieval in digital libraries. In: *Proceedings of the 1998 international conference on intelligent user interfaces* (pp. 127–134). New York: ACM Press.

Greater Glasgow and Clyde National Health Service Board. Glasgow health information. Retrieved from www.ghi.org.uk/index.asp (accessed June 1, 2012).

Heath, T., Hepp, M., and Bizer, C. (2009). Linked data: The story so far. *International Journal on Semantic Web and Information Systems*, 5(3), 1–22.

Heritage Community Foundation. Alberta heritage digitization project: Our future our past: The art collection. Retrieved from inmagic.lib.ucalgary.ca/dbtw-wpd/nam/Eng/eng_nam.html (accessed June 1, 2012).

Hodge, G. (2000). *Systems of knowledge organization for digital libraries: Beyond traditional authority files*. Washington, D.C.: Digital Library Federation. Retrieved from www.clir.org/pubs/reports/pub91/contents.html (accessed April 12, 2011).

International Development Research Centre. Digital library. Retrieved from idl-bnc.idrc.ca/dspace/ (accessed June 1, 2012).

Koch, T. (2000). Quality-controlled subject gateways: Definitions, typologies, empirical overview. *Online Information Review*, 24(1), 24–34.

McKay, D., Preeti, S., Hunt, R., and Cunninghum, S. J. (2004). Enhanced browsing in digital libraries: Three new approaches to browsing in Greenstone. *International Journal on Digital Libraries*, 4(4), 283–297.

National Information Center for Educational Media. MediaSleuth. Retrieved from http://www.mediasleuth.com/MediaSleuthSearcher/navtree/ index.jsp (accessed June 1, 2012).

Paynter, G. W., & Witten, I. H. (2001). A combined phrase and thesaurus browser for large document collections. In: *Proceedings of the 5th European conference on research and advanced technology for digital libraries* (pp. 25–36). Berlin: Springer.

Redmond-Neal, A., and Hlava, M. M. K. (Eds.). (2005). *ASIS&T thesaurus of information science, technology, and librarianship*, 3rd ed. Medford, NJ: Information Today.

Schandl, T., and Blumauer, A. (2010). PoolParty: SKOS thesaurus management utilizing linked data. *The semantic web: Research and applications* (Lecture notes in computer science, 6089), 421–425.

Schatz, B. R., Johnson, E. H., and Cochrane, P. A. (1996). Interactive term suggestion for users of digital libraries: Using subject thesauri and co-occurrence lists for information retrieval. In: *Proceedings of the 1st Association for Computing Machinery international conference on digital libraries* (pp. 126–133). Bethesda, MD: ACM Press.

Shiri, A. (2003). Digital library research: Current developments and trends. *Library Review*, 52(5), 198–202.

Shiri, A., and Chase-Kruszewski, S. (2009). Knowledge organisation systems in North American digital library collections. *Program: Electronic Library and Information Systems*, 43(2), 121–139.

Shiri, A. A., and Revie, C. (2000). Thesauri on the web: Current developments and trends. *Online Information Review*, 24(4), 273–279.

Smrz, P., Sinopalnikova, A. and Povolný, M. (2003). Thesauri and ontologies in digital libraries. In: *Proceedings of the 5th Russian conference on digital libraries* (pp. 14–17). Saint-Petersburg, Russia: Saint-Petersburg State University Published Press.

Social Care Institute for Excellence. Social care online. Retrieved from www.scie-socialcareonline.org.uk/default.asp (accessed June 1, 2012).

Soergel, D. (2002). Thesauri and ontologies in digital libraries tutorial. In: *European conference on digital libraries*. Rome, Italy. Retrieved from www.dsoergel.com/cv/B63_rome.pdf (accessed June 13, 2012).

State Library of New South Wales. Legal Information Access Centre (LIAC). WebLaw thesaurus. Retrieved from www.weblaw.edu.au/info_thesaurus. phtml (accessed June 13, 2012).

UK Data Archive. Humanities and Social Sciences Electronic Thesaurus (HASSET). Retrieved from www.esds.ac.uk/search/hassetSearch.asp (accessed June 1, 2012).

University of Queensland. AustLit:Ausralian Literature Resource. Retrieved from www.austlit.edu.au (accessed June 1, 2012).

Waters, D. J. (1998). What are digital libraries? *CLIR Issues*, 4, July/August. Retrieved from www.clir.org/pubs/issues/issues04.html#dlf (accessed June 13, 2012).

World Wide Web Consortium (W3C). Simple knowledge organization standard (SKOS). Retrieved from www.w3.org/2004/02/skos (accessed June 1, 2012).

CHAPTER 5

Thesaurus-Based Search and Browsing Functionalities in New Thesaurus Construction Standards

This chapter discusses the rationale for incorporating thesauri into search user interfaces and reviews the evolution of efforts encouraging the use of knowledge organization systems, such as thesauri, to support information retrieval on the web. It examines the specific functionalities recommended for thesaurus-based search user interfaces in the recently revised thesaurus construction standards in the U.K. and the U.S.

5.1 Rationale for the Integration of Thesauri Into Search User Interfaces

The selection of search terms for query formulation and expansion is a key phase in the information retrieval process. Saracevic (1997) describes search term selection as a dynamic process that involves interaction between a user and a computer at various levels. The dynamic nature of this process implies that search terms are selected from various sources and then adapted, changed, or abandoned at different stages during a search.

Thesauri have been recognized as a useful source for enhancing search term selection for query formulation and expansion (Fidel, 1991; Brajnik et al., 1996; Beaulieu, 1997). Research on searching behavior, information retrieval interface evaluation, search term selection, and query expansion has addressed the issue of providing users with terminological assistance to enhance information retrieval. Such assistance may be supplied through the inclusion of thesauri and classification schemes within information retrieval interfaces.

Researchers have investigated the searching behaviors of various types of users and in particular have looked at search term selection behavior. These studies suggest that the selection of terms can be improved if thesauri are incorporated into the search interface (Hsieh-Yee, 1993; Efthimiadis, 2000; Sutcliffe et al., 2000; Vakkari, 2000).

Another line of investigation that deals with interactive query expansion and interface evaluation also provides evidence of the benefits of incorporating thesauri into interfaces. In a series of experiments on designing interfaces to the Okapi search engine, both implicit and explicit use of a thesaurus during automatic and interactive query expansion were found to be beneficial (Jones et al., 1995; Beaulieu, 1997). It was also suggested that while the system can find useful thesaurus terms through the automatic query expansion process, terms explicitly selected by users were of particular value.

In addition to the studies already described, a significant number of search user interfaces enhanced with thesauri have been designed and developed during the past two decades. While some of these were experimental or prototypical, others have found their way into operational and active search systems and services. Thorough analysis and coverage of these interfaces are presented in Chapter 6.

Some of the key web-related developments that gave rise to the popularity of thesauri as a component of information retrieval systems in general and search user interfaces in particular are as follows:

- Web protocols, applications, and languages (e.g., HTML, XML, RDF)

- The rise of information architecture and its immediate attention to the importance of controlled vocabularies

- Development and growth of a large number of digital libraries, archives, and repositories on the web

- Innovative visualization technologies and techniques for the presentation of terminologies in general and thesauri in particular

- Semantic web standards, in particular the W3 Simple Knowledge Organization System standard, for encoding various controlled vocabularies

- Linked data as an environment for encouraging cross-searching and cross-browsing of open data repositories

These developments attracted and encouraged researchers, practitioners, and developers from domains and disciplines such as computer science, library and information science, information architecture, knowledge management, and software development to explore various ways in which thesauri can be incorporated into search systems and services to support users' information search behavior in web-based information environments. The advent of the web and its associated technologies has thus provided new opportunities for thesauri to be repackaged, repurposed, and reused in a broad range of web-based services, repositories, and digital information environments.

5.2 Networked Knowledge Organization Systems and Services

One of the noteworthy developments in the use of thesauri on the web is the Networked Knowledge Organization Systems/Services (NKOS) initiative. Lykke Nielsen (2010) provided the following description in the *Encyclopedia of Library and Information Sciences*:

> NKOS (nkos.slis.kent.edu) is an informal network of academics and practitioners who are interested in the use of knowledge organization systems (KOSs) in networked information environments. The general aim of the community is to enable KOSs to act as networked information services (both machine-to-machine and human-computer), and support the description and retrieval of information resources on the internet. The community is a forum for presentation and discussion of KOS applications and interchange of ideas, from technical issues to intellectual, semantic, and terminological problems related to the use of KOS. The participants come from a variety of disciplines, and from academia as well as practice, and interact and communicate by a diverse set of means: annual workshops in the U.S. and Europe, a website, a mailing list, and publication of special journal issues and working papers about contemporary issues.
>
> NKOS workshops were initiated in 1997 within the Association for Computing Machinery (ACM) Digital Library Conference to address the issues of creating interactive

knowledge organization systems on the web that would include thesauri. The first workshop focused on thesauri for searching and generating metadata. Among the main issues discussed were the use of thesauri in digital libraries, thesaurus-based metadata, subject vocabulary in distributed search environment, and automated classification of networked information. This workshop aimed to gather information on research and products relating to the use of thesauri as metadata content tools.

Since then, annual workshops have been held regularly to report and discuss the developments and trends associated with the use of various knowledge organization systems on the web. The 2010 European NKOS Workshop, held in conjunction with the European Conference on Research and Advanced Technology for Digital Libraries, had a particular focus on users and knowledge organization systems and addressed issues such as semantic mapping of knowledge organization systems for knowledge exploration, users and thesaurus-based query expansion, and search term recommendation based on thesauri. These topics indicate that the NKOS community is moving toward more user-centered issues and applications and placing particular emphasis on large-scale applications of knowledge organization systems in the web environment.

5.3 NISO Workshop on Electronic Thesauri

The growing number of web-based thesauri in the 1990s stimulated discussion on the need to review existing standards for thesauri. The National Information Standards Organization (NISO) workshop on Electronic Thesauri: Planning for a Standard, held November 4 and 5, 1999, under the sponsorship of NISO, the American Society of Indexers, and the Association for Library Collections and Technical Service, was an important attempt to address the issue of standards as they relate to thesauri.

The workshop specified that such standards should meet the following criteria:

- Speak to criteria and/or methods for generating thesauri by machine-aided or automatic means

- Show semantic relationships among terms as aids to text and information analysis and retrieval

- Support a variety of electronic thesaurus displays

- Support interoperability protocols, structures, and/or semantics applicable to thesauri

Among the issues highlighted in the workshop were vocabulary mapping, management, interoperability, and the need for flexible electronic thesaurus displays that would ease and augment indexing and retrieval. Standards such as XML and RDF were put forward as widely supported formats for different browsing tools.

Workshop participants noted that web browsers were not thesaurus-aware and that existing metadata formats made little use of thesauri. To address these issues, it was suggested that special emphasis should be placed on the use of thesauri within metadata. It was also suggested that the adoption of standards would allow developers to give full consideration to computer-displayed thesauri and their use by thesaurus browsers. Moreover, it was argued that the invisibility of thesaural use by search systems, in which a search engine expands the user's term without the user's knowledge of the route, is confusing, and should receive careful attention.

The following specific criteria related to user interfaces emerged during the breakout sessions in the workshop:

- Accommodate visual and graphical thesauri

- Accommodate a variety of flexible displays to meet the needs of many uses and users

- Collect examples of displays in current use

- Recognize the need for content displays that vary from minimal to literally everything in a record

- Make available for display both metrics (e.g., number of relationships) and metadata of the thesaurus

The NISO workshop concluded that a new standard was needed for thesauri. Of particular significance is the importance accorded to taking into account the variety and types of users of thesauri, ranging from end-user searchers, indexers, and library and information professionals to thesaurus software developers. The highlight of the workshop, in the context of the main theme of *Powering Search*, is that the new standard should allow for the design of more-accommodating user interfaces that would encourage the use of thesauri in more interactive and flexible ways.

5.4 BS 8723: Structured Vocabularies for Information Retrieval

The British standard (BS) 8723 *Structured Vocabularies for Information Retrieval* (British Standards Institution, 2005) was published in 2005 to supersede BS 5723, the 1987 British Standard Guide to Establishment and Development of Monolingual Thesauri. The BS 8723 standard was replaced by ISO 25964-1 in 2011. This standard was a major revision of BS8723 undertaken by an international committee. Further details about the standard can be found at www.bsi group.com.

The BS 8723 covers thesauri and other types of structured vocabularies, such as taxonomies, ontologies, and authority lists, together with structural models for interoperability across vocabularies. It gives specific attention to thesauri, including their use within computerized systems. The standard points out that most contemporary thesauri are electronic, created and maintained with the support of software and integrated into search engines and content management systems. In the past, thesauri were designed and used by information professionals for indexing and retrieval. However, with the rise and development of a wide range of new information environments on the web, there is a demand by a wide range of users for vocabularies as search aids.

The "Presentation and Layout" section of BS 8723 notes that, "when presented for human use on a screen or in a printed form, an indexing vocabulary can be displayed in multiple ways:

A. As a *single record*, showing the preferred term or non-preferred term itself and any or all other relationships

B. As an *alphabetical* arrangement, allowing access to concepts from the words in which they are initially expressed by the user, and in a computer display supplementing a direct search function

C. As a *hierarchical sequence*, based on broader term and narrower term relationships that expand or refine the concept being sought

D. As a *classified sequence*, allowing browsing in a subject area to draw attention to related concepts

E. As a *graphical display*, showing terms and their relationships laid out pictorially

F. As a permuted display, helping to find words embedded
in multi-word terms" (p. 33)

It should be noted that these displays are very general in nature,
and there are many variations in interface and display design within
the previously mentioned categories. Aitchison et al. (2000) provide a
detailed discussion of various thesaurus displays that are useful
mainly for thesaurus developers and indexers.

Below are examples of some of the popular web-based thesaurus
displays based on the types described in BS 8723. Unlike alphabetical
displays in print thesauri, in which each term is shown along with its
details and relationships, most web-based thesauri provide a brief
alphabetical list with clickable letters at the top of the page. Figure 5.1
shows a snapshot of the alphabetical listing of the Statistics Canada
Thesaurus. Users interested in exploring details of a term, for example, *economic accounts*, click on the term to view and/or to choose
the term for searching (Figure 5.2).

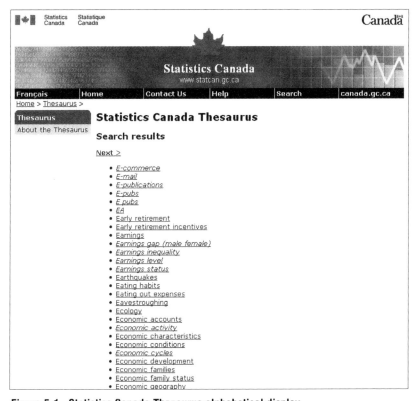

Figure 5.1   Statistics Canada Thesaurus alphabetical display

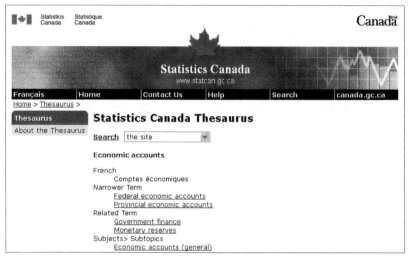

Figure 5.2   Statistics Canada Thesaurus term details

Some thesauri provide a rich set of entry terms to support users in finding the right term. A good example of alphabetical browsing with a large number of entry terms can be found in the Subject Index Term browsing feature in the Global Legal Information Network (Figure 5.3), where browsing entries under a letter will provide users with various terms and references to improve their search.

Hierarchical displays are very popular in thesauri design as they provide a rich hierarchical structure that can be used to graphically or visually present thesaurus terms to the user. A sophisticated example of a hierarchical display is illustrated by the AGROVOC Thesaurus from the Food and Agriculture Organization of the United Nations (Figure 5.4).

Classified displays have been used for thesauri with faceted structures and multiple subject areas. Many web-based applications and search systems use faceted displays and views generally, without any classification or numerical notations to facilitate users' understanding of the browsing feature. Figure 5.5 provides an example of a detailed classified display from the Alcohol and Other Drugs (AOD) Thesaurus used by the Alcohol and Alcohol Problems Science Database (from the National Institute on Alcohol Abuse and Alcoholism). The figure shows thesaurus terms in a classified display, along with related term (RT), narrower term (NT), synonymous term (ST), and scope note (SN) relationships, as well as with the classification notations in capital letters.

Look for	
☐ Search In Scope Notes	
	All # A B C D E F G H I J K L

- Click on a term to view additional terms or more information.
- To search GLIN using the Subject Term Index, select up to 20 terms and click "Search".

Results 21 - 40 of 304

Data security use Computer security	☐
Data warehouses use Databases	☐
Data warehousing use Warehouse management	☐
Database protection use Computer security	☐
Databases	☐
Date conversion problem of Year 2000 for computers use Year 2000 computer problem	☐
Date rape use Rape	☐
Dates and other dried fruits use Fruit	☐
Day care (for children) use Child care	☐
Daylight savings time use Time	☐

Figure 5.3   Global Legal Information Network subject index terms

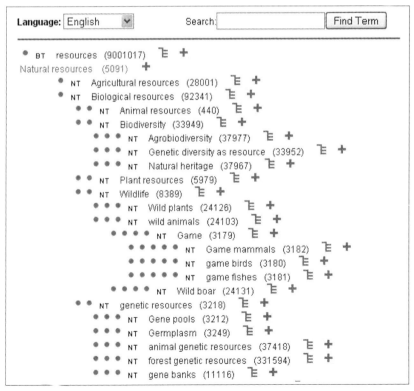

Figure 5.4   Hierarchical display in AGROVOC

GFₑ	**symptom** d-out gh		
	SN	In medicine as well as counseling and psychotherapy, a physical associated with a problem or a syndrome.	
	ST	general manifestation of disorders	
		symptoms, signs, and ill-defined conditions	
	NT	EA18.4.2.2e general adaptation syndrome gh sh	
		+GQ2 digestive system symptom gh sh	
		+GX4.2.2e headache gh sh	
		+GZ2 mental symptom gh sh	
	RT	FR14.2 decreased or increased activity gh sh	
		+HD2 physical examination gh sh	
GF2	**physical symptom** gh		
	ST	somatic manifestation	
	RT	+EA22.4.2e fatigue gh sh	
		GH8.6.2e hyperthermia gh sh	
		GH8.6.4e hypothermia gh sh	
GF2.2ₑ	. physical appearance gh		
GF2.2.2	. . unkempt physical appearance gh		
	ST	personal uncleanliness	
		untidy appearance	
GF2.2.4	. . facial expression gh		
	RT	NA12.6 nonverbal communication gh sh	

Figure 5.5   Alcohol and Other Drugs Thesaurus classified display

Permuted or rotated displays have been used in a number of thesauri; however, on the web they are not as popular as alphabetical and hierarchical displays. Figure 5.6 shows such a display for the term *fiber* in the NASA Thesaurus. The introduction to the thesaurus notes that the rotated display is a ready-reference tool providing thousands of additional "access points" to the thesaurus terminology.

BS 8723 also suggests that "alphabetical access is essential and should be provided by direct search or by alphabetical sequence. Either hierarchical or classified access should be provided to give an overview of the systematic arrangement. A useful overview of a field can sometimes be presented graphically, but graphical presentations are complicated to create, and they can be obscure if too much additional information is presented. A permuted display may prove useful for printed thesauri but not necessarily for electronic thesauri, in which searches for character strings are possible" (p. 33.)

Graphical displays help to show terms and their interrelationships in the form of a two-dimensional figure from which the user may select appropriate terms. Figures 5.7 and 5.8 capture two simple graphical displays that were created using the TheW32 software developed by Tim Craven at the University of Western Ontario. The

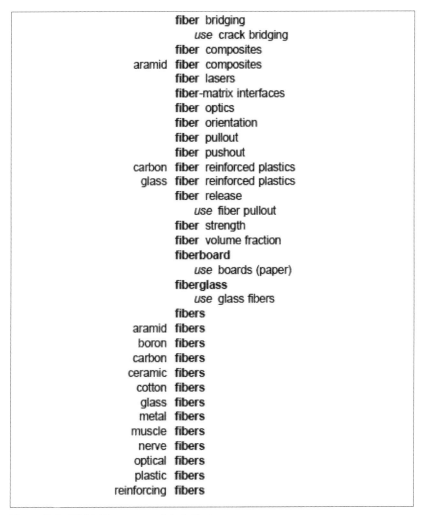

Figure 5.6 NASA Thesaurus rotated display

figures show the term *libraries*, along with its broader and narrower terms, in two different graphic displays.

Depending on the algorithm used for graphical representation, thesaurus terms can be organized in vertical or horizontal displays.

With recent developments in information visualization and human-computer interaction research, numerous visualization techniques have been proposed and developed to represent terms and their relationships in thesauri. In particular, user interfaces to information retrieval systems have adopted graphical and visual techniques to make the structure and content of thesauri more accessible to users.

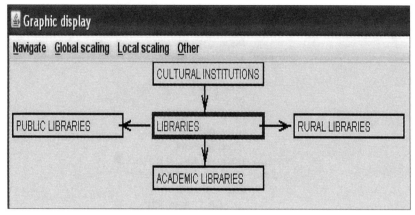

Figure 5.7   TheW32 graphic display 1

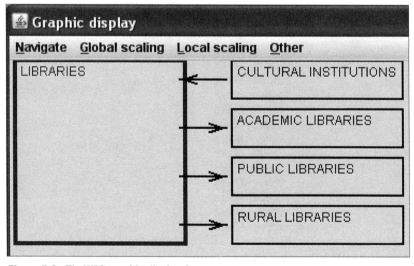

Figure 5.8   TheW32 graphic display 2

BS 8723 includes a section on thesaurus functions in electronic systems. It suggests the following "fundamental functionalities to support searching and browsing within thesauri:

A. The ability to search for terms

B. The ability to move from the record for one term to that of any of its BTs, NTs, and RTs

C. The ability to expand and contract levels when viewing a hierarchical or classified display (i.e., to gain an overview of the structure, it should be possible to start with a view of the top level and then expand progressively or selectively at one stroke.)

D. The ability to switch from one style of display to another" (p. 42)

User interfaces to many web-based thesauri accommodate most of the features highlighted before. However, the ways in which these features can be designed and implemented depend on the structure of the thesaurus and whether it is faceted. Chapter 6 provides examples of user interfaces that have implemented these features.

BS 8723 also suggests two additional functionalities: When the thesaurus is integrated into a document collection, the number of postings should be shown against each preferred term, and users browsing the thesaurus should be able to move directly to the searching phase. BS 8723 suggests the following features for these purposes:

- "The ability to select one or more search terms from a thesaurus display

- The ability to build a search statement by copying terms from the thesaurus without retyping (for example, double-click or drag-and-drop) and assistance in applying valid search syntax (for example, selecting Boolean operators)

- The ability to select subtrees from the thesaurus to be used in a search (i.e., to search for a given term and all of its narrower terms combined with Boolean OR, sometimes called the "explode" function)

- The ability to select a non-preferred term, leading to substitution for the corresponding preferred term in the search statement (and ensuring that the user is notified of what has been done), and in the event that the user enters a non-preferred term into a search statement without first browsing the thesaurus, offering the option of converting to the corresponding preferred term

- The ability, during the process of search refinement, to adjust the numbers of postings in any of the thesaurus displays to show the numbers that apply in the subset of the collection already selected" (pp. 42–43)

These recommendations are useful for designing thesaurus-enhanced search interfaces for digital collections. However, because of the general nature of these features, various approaches and techniques can be adopted in their design. For instance, the ability to select one or more terms from the thesaurus can be provided through check boxes or a search term pool so that several terms can be selected to form a query statement.

Another example of variety in design is a capability to redirect a user from a non-preferred to a preferred thesaurus term. To ensure that the user is aware of the process and the change, the interface can be created in such a way that the user is provided with a short note or instruction as to why the new term should be used for searching rather than the initial term(s) entered by the user. This feature can also offer a list of items retrieved from the collection.

5.5 ANSI/NISO Z39.19

The Guidelines for the Construction, Format, and Maintenance of Monolingual Controlled Vocabularies, also known as American National Standard Institute/NISO (ANSI/NISO) Z39.19, was published in 2005 and revised in 2010. This is the revised edition of the 1993 Standard titled Guidelines for the Construction, Format, and Management of Monolingual Thesauri.

The 2010 revised standard was based on the recommendations put forward by consensus at the NISO Workshop on Electronic Thesauri. The standard presents guidelines and conventions for the contents, display, construction, testing, maintenance, and management of monolingual controlled vocabularies. Similar to BS 8723, ANSI/NISO Z39.19 addresses various controlled vocabularies, such as lists, synonym rings, taxonomies, and thesauri.

It discusses effective display of controlled vocabularies and the effects of the display on the user's willingness and ability to make use of thesauri. One of the interesting aspects of this standard with regard to display format lies in its categorization of users. The standard outlines three categories of users who should be taken into account in the design of displays for controlled vocabularies:

- Controlled vocabulary maintenance personnel: Those users with indexing and controlled vocabulary construction experience, who must have access to all views of a controlled vocabulary and complete information about each term, with the ability to edit and manipulate term records, cross-references, classification notation, and hierarchies; they require "housekeeping" displays not needed by end users of a controlled vocabulary.

- Indexers and expert searchers: Those users with indexing experience and expertise in online searching and the use of controlled vocabularies, sophisticated users who require the ability to search and view cross-references, definitions, and notes for terms as well as various levels of the classification or hierarchies; higher-level controlled vocabulary displays and terminology are appropriate for these users.

- End users: Those users not likely to be experienced in the jargon and complexities of online information retrieval or the conventions of controlled vocabulary notation, but who nevertheless may have expertise in the subject field and understand its terminology; the types of displays available to expert searchers can be designed with the needs of end users in mind as well.

ANSI/NISO Z39.19 also recommends that "controlled vocabulary developers may want to produce two versions of the vocabulary:

- A basic list of terms, references, and relationships designed for the end user or occasional searcher

- A more complete version designed for the indexer and the expert searcher, which may include detailed scope notes, indexing instructions, information on term history, and postings data" (p. 58)

From a search and browsing perspective, it would be useful to take into account these user categories in designing displays or user interfaces for thesauri. Similar to basic and advanced search features in web search engines, search interfaces can be designed to provide basic as well as advanced thesaurus-enhanced search functionalities to accommodate different types of users.

Similar to BS 8723, ANSI/NISO Z39.19 discusses different types of displays, as well as some key design issues that will help developers of user interfaces to thesauri. The standard notes that "the decision to include a graphic display should take into account the domain, the search habits of users, and the overall design of the information system of which the controlled vocabulary is a component. Graphic displays can be more effective in an interactive computer environment where terms are hyperlinked to the term details or to a conventional flat format display" (ANSI/NISO Z39.19, 2010, p. 73).

The standard devotes a section to user interface design and suggests that "viewing information on a screen differs from viewing printed information in these ways:

- A screen display is harder to browse and remember one's context.

- Compared with print media, the screen is more difficult and tiring to view.

- The available screen window "page" size can make it difficult to grasp information that is perfectly comprehensible in printed form.

- The display format could be simplified and streamlined to assist users unfamiliar with the entire notion of a controlled vocabulary.

One of the key areas that the standard also stresses is the importance of applying usability and accessibility standards rigorously to all controlled vocabulary display designs" (p. 76).

5.5.1 Recommendations Related to Searching and Browsing

Electronic controlled vocabularies should provide keyword searching of all of the terms in the vocabulary. This search feature serves the same purpose as the permuted and/or rotated indexes that are commonly used in print formats. Keyword searches should retrieve all occurrences of the term, especially in compound terms. With regard to term details display, ANSI/NISO Z39.19 recommends that users should be able to view the details of each term, including scope notes, definition, history, and all term relationships. The standard does not, however, discuss which features might be more useful for each category of users (p. 79).

A useful design feature for hierarchical display is that it should be possible to display the first three levels of a controlled vocabulary. The following example (Figure 5.9) from the standard shows the facet *natural phenomena* from the Library of Congress Thesaurus for Graphic Materials (TGM I).

The inclusion of narrower terms for search expansion can be achieved through tree structures in controlled vocabularies (p. 78). Path hierarchical displays can also be used as an alternative method for viewing a vocabulary's hierarchies in context, as shown in Figure 5.10. (The terms in Figure 5.10 are selected from the Centre for Agricultural Bioscience [CAB] Thesaurus).

The standard includes considerations for displaying controlled vocabularies on web browsers and web-related technologies. It suggests that the use of hyperlinks makes it easy to move around a controlled vocabulary, particularly from one level to another and from one type of display to another, such as from an alphabetical listing to a hierarchical listing.

For browsing controlled vocabularies, an important recommendation in the standard is to provide an alphabetical browsing option.

Natural phenomena
. Weather
.. Fog
.. Hail
.. Rain
.. Snow
... Snowflakes
.. Storms
... Blizzards
... Cyclones
... Dust storms
... Hurricanes
... Tornadoes
... Typhoons
... Waterspouts
.. Winds

Figure 5.9   Thesaurus for Graphic Materials displaying three levels of hierarchy

Plants > Cereals > Rice > Deep water Rice
Plants > Cereals > Millets > Finger millet
Plants > Cereals > Wheat > Winter wheat

Figure 5.10 Example of a path hierarchical display

This feature can be facilitated by means of scroll bar, Up and Down navigation arrows, Page Up and Page Down keys, or plus and minus signs for expanding and collapsing a hierarchical list (p. 79).

Finally, the standard suggests that "a typical web-enabled controlled vocabulary might include links from a term to the following portions of the vocabulary:

- Narrower and broader terms
- Related terms
- Individual term records
- Scope notes
- History notes
- Facets
- Tree structures
- Classification code or structure" (p. 81)

5.6 Conclusion

This chapter discusses the rationale for incorporating thesauri into search user interfaces and introduces the NKOS initiative as a group of researchers and practitioners interested in the use of thesauri in web-based services. The revised versions of both the American and the British standards for the construction of controlled vocabularies are reviewed. Both include recommendations and best practices for the design of useful and usable thesaurus displays and user interface features that support various categories of users in their interaction with thesauri.

The two standards provide detailed information about different types of thesaurus displays as well as design recommendations for searching, browsing, and navigating thesaurus content, including terms, their relationships, scope notes, and the use of web-related technologies for making the content of thesauri more findable, flexible, and accessible. The American standard focuses especially on various categories of users, the challenges associated with the user interface design, and hyperlinks and web navigation techniques for thesauri, whereas the British standard gives attention to thesaurus search functions, such as term selection, query building, the use of Boolean operators, and the way in which cross-references between preferred and non-preferred terms should be handled.

The standards advocate similar measures for supporting users in making use of thesauri:

- Availability of alphabetical and hierarchical displays

- Flexible access to various levels of thesaurus hierarchies

- Keyword searching of thesaurus content

- Access to details of thesaurus terms

- Ability to navigate around the thesaurus via hyperlinks

- Ability to select terms from the thesaurus

The two standards complement each other and are very useful for designers of both thesauri and search user interfaces to thesauri and other types of controlled vocabularies. It should be noted, however, that these standards provide only general recommendations for thesaural display. They present little in the way of specific design guidelines for implementing searching and browsing functions in search user interfaces.

References

Aitchison, J., Gilchrist, A., and Bawden, D. (2000). *Thesaurus construction and use: A practical manual*, 4th ed. London: Routledge.

ANSI/NISO Z39.19: 2005. (Revised 2010). *Guidelines for the construction, format, and management of monolingual controlled vocabularies*, 4th ed. Bethesda, MD: National Information Standards Organization.

Beaulieu, M. (1997). Experiments of interfaces to support query expansion. *Journal of Documentation*, 53(1), 8–19.

Brajnik, G., Mizzaro, S., and Tasso, C. (1996). Evaluating user interfaces to information retrieval systems: A case study on user support. In: H. P. Frei, D. Harman, P. Schaübie, and R. Wilkinson (Eds.), *Proceedings of the 19th annual international ACM/SIGIR conference on research and development in information retrieval* (pp. 128–136). New York: ACM Press.

British Standards Institution. (2005). *BS 8723 Structured vocabularies for information retrieval: Guide. Part 2. Thesauri.* 2005. London: British Standards Institution.

Efthimiadis, E. N. (2000). Interactive query expansion: A user-based evaluation in a relevance feedback environment. *Journal of the American Society for Information Science,* 51(11), 989–1003.

Fidel, R. (1991). Searchers' selection of search keys: II. Controlled vocabulary or free-text searching. *Journal of the American Society for Information Science,* 42(7), 501–514.

Global Legal Information Network. Retrieved from www.glin.gov/search. action (accessed June 6, 2012).

Hsieh-Yee, I. (1993). Effects of search experience and subject knowledge on the search tactics of novice and experienced searchers. *Journal of the American Society for Information Science,* 44(3), 161–174.

ISO 25964-1: 2011. (2011). *Thesauri and interoperability with other vocabularies: Part 1: Thesauri for information retrieval.* International Organization for Standardization. Switzerland: ISO.

Jones, S., Gatford, M., Hancock-Beaulieu, M., Robertson, S. E., Walker, W., and Secker, J. (1995). Interactive thesaurus navigation: Intelligence rules OK? *Journal of the American Society for Information Science,* 46(1), 52–59.

Lykke Nielsen, M. (2010). Networked knowledge organization systems/services (NKOS). In: M. J. Bates and M. N. Maack (Eds.), *Encyclopedia of library and information sciences,* 3rd ed. Boca Raton, FL: CRC Press.

National Aeronautics and Space Administration. (2010). NASA thesaurus. Volume 1: Hierarchical listing with definitions. Retrieved from www.sti.nasa.gov/thesvol1.pdf (accessed June 14, 2012).

National Information Standards Organization. (1999). Report on the workshop on electronic thesauri, November 4–5, 1999. Retrieved from www.niso.org/news/events/niso/past/thesau99/thes99rprt.html (accessed March 17, 2011).

National Institute on Alcohol Abuse and Alcoholism (NIAAA). Alcohol and other drugs (AOD) thesaurus. Retrieved from etoh.niaaa.nih.gov/AOD Vol1/Aodthome.htm (accessed June 6, 2012).

Networked Knowledge Organization Systems/Services (NKOS). Retrieved from nkos.slis.kent.edu (accessed June 6, 2012).

Saracevic, T. (1997). The stratified model of information retrieval interaction: Extension and applications. In: Schwartz, C., and Rorvig, M. (Eds.), *ASIS'97: Proceedings of the American Society for Information Science* (Vol. 34, pp. 313–327). Silver Spring, MD: ASIS.

Statistics Canada. Statistics Canada Thesaurus. Retrieved from www47.stat can.gc.ca/th_r000-eng.htm (accessed June 6, 2012).

Sutcliffe, A. G., Ennis, M., and Watkinson, S. J. (2000). Empirical studies of end-user information searching. *Journal of the American Society for Information Science*, 51(13), 1211–1231.

Vakkari, P. (2000). Cognition and changes of search terms and tactics during task performance: A longitudinal case study. In: *Proceedings of RIAO 2000, content-based multimedia information access RIAO conference* (pp. 894–907). Paris: C.I.D.

CHAPTER 6

Design of Search User Interfaces for Thesauri

This chapter reviews and analyzes thesaurus-enhanced search user interfaces developed since the 1980s. Generally speaking, the design of search user interfaces enhanced with thesauri should take into account the information search process and its various stages, the design elements outlined in the standards for the construction of thesauri and other types of controlled vocabularies (Chapter 5), and guidelines for best practices in designing thesaurus-enhanced search user interfaces (Chapter 9).

Shiri et al. (2002) reviewed two categories of search interfaces enhanced with thesauri, namely, those associated with research-based programs and those developed as commercial web-based interfaces to bibliographic databases. Using Shiri's categorization, this chapter provides a comprehensive analysis of research proto-types and commercial web-based interfaces, with a particular focus on user interface features and functionalities and on the ways in which these interfaces support query formulation and reformulation.

6.1 Thesaurus Information Elements

Thesauri offer a rich set of information elements for use in the design and development of a broad range of search user interfaces to support various information-seeking strategies. Milstead (1990) provides a detailed discussion of the specifications for thesaurus software, with a focus on supporting the evaluation of existing packages for acquisition as well as the design of custom software. Will (2010) has been maintaining a website titled Software for Building and Editing Thesauri, which presents a detailed and annotated directory of thesaurus software with detailed descriptions of their functionalities.

Ganzman (1990) proposes a more specific set of thesaural elements for developing and evaluating thesaurus software, including a checklist. Some of the specific features included in Ganzman's checklist that are related to the focus in this chapter are as follows:

A. Terms, scope notes, notations, and information as to language of term

B. Relations, including equivalence, hierarchical, and associative

C. Displays: alphabetical, hierarchical, Keyword-in-Context (KWIC), systematic based on notations, and graphical

D. Interaction possible in thesaurus on screen: scrolling/browsing, navigation to semantically related terms, selection of terms for editing and deletion, direct modifications, and deletions in lists

E. Statistics on the use of thesaurus terms

This list identifies the key information elements found in thesauri that can inform the design and development of search user interfaces. As we will see in the following discussion, search user interfaces have taken various approaches to the use of thesaural information elements. Some approaches have relied on the use of thesaural relationships only, while others have made use of additional elements, such as scope notes and display options, and introduced ways to provide suggested term lists to users. Only some search user interfaces have made use of all of these elements and features.

6.2 The Information Search Process

Numerous information-seeking, searching, and interaction models have been proposed by researchers in library and information science, information retrieval, human-computer interaction, and computer science. Specific models that deal with the use of thesauri in the search and interaction process are reviewed in Chapter 2.

Hearst (1999) suggests that most accounts of the information access process assume an interaction cycle consisting of these phases:

- Query specification

- Receipt and examination of retrieval results

- Either reformulating the query and repeating the process until a perfect result set is found or stopping altogether

In his later work, adapted from Broder (2002), Hearst (2009) introduces the standard model of the search process (Figure 6.1).

It should be noted that this is a generalized view of the search process and does not include many specific information-seeking strategies that users may adopt throughout their search process. Not depicted in the general model, for example, are browsing a list of terms or choosing additional sources for search terms, as well as changing interaction with the system using either basic or advanced search mode. Hearst (1999) notes that the standard model downplays the interaction that takes place when a user scans thesaurus structures or views thematic overviews of document collections. Also, the model does not address specifically many browsing, navigation-

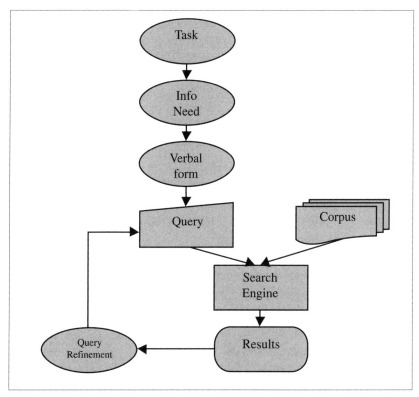

Figure 6.1   The standard model of the search process (Hearst, 2009), adapted from Broder (2002)

based, and exploratory search activities. At the same time, it is useful for explaining the broad general stages of the search process.

The importance of thesaurus support for effective searching has also been stressed by researchers in the field of human-computer interaction. Shneiderman (1998), for instance, in a discussion of user interface features for searching textual databases, proposes a four-phase framework: formulation; initiation of action; review of results; and, refinement. He suggests that in the search formulation phase, interfaces should provide broader, narrower, and synonymous terms from a thesaurus to help users clarify their search.

Bates (1990a) proposes a number of search term tactics and strategies that can be implemented in the interfaces to information retrieval systems. These specific term tactics include SUPER for broader search terms, SUB for narrower search terms, and RELATE for related terms comparable to the conceptual structure of thesauri and provide the user with alternative approaches to search term selection.

A significant number of user interfaces have made use of thesauri to support the search process. Some of these are prototype research-based interfaces, and some are stable operational user interfaces. Each is examined in the following sections, prefaced by a brief overview of early systems.

6.3 Thesaurus-Aided User Interfaces: Early Systems

The application of online versions of domain-specific thesauri for query formulation and expansion can be traced back to the late 1970s, when a number of information retrieval researchers began to advance prototype systems in order to explore ways of aiding user search within information retrieval systems.

The emergence of expert system and artificial intelligence technologies in the 1980s stimulated a growing parallel interest among developers of expert systems and intelligent front-ends in applying thesauri as the knowledge bases of their interfaces. Efthimiadis (1996) provides a detailed review of these thesaurus-enhanced systems, most of them using expert system techniques, which were designed and developed to assist users in formulating and expanding queries in one way or another.

Many of these expert and intermediary systems embedded thesauri as part of their search facilities in order to provide users with alternative search terms from which to choose. Some of these systems used mapping techniques for matching user-submitted terms with their thesaurus knowledge base and displayed hierarchical structures associated with the entered term. Most of these systems adopted standard thesauri such as Medical Subject Headings (MeSH) and Inspec to provide either thesaurus browsing or thesaurus mapping capabilities.

6.4 Research-Based, Thesaurus-Enhanced Prototype Search User Interfaces

One of the early thesaurus-enhanced search interfaces can be attributed to the High Resolution Interface for Database Specific Browsing and Searching (HIBROWSE) system developed by Steve Pollitt and his colleagues (1994) in the late 1980s and 1990s. The HIBROWSE system was implemented as a front end to a number of bibliographic databases, including MEDLINE, Inspec, EPOQUE (European Parliament Online Query System), and EMBASE. These interfaces used MeSH, Inspec, and EuroVoc thesauri.

The system presents a multiwindow search interface with the thesaurus at the center. The interface presents views of the database via navigable hierarchies of subject descriptors from thesauri and also provides simultaneous access to different bibliographic fields.

One of the notable features of the HIBROWSE interface is its ability to simultaneously show the thesaurus terms associated with two or more search facets in a single view. The interface caters to navigation up and down the hierarchy for further query refinement, and it provides a dynamic and multidimensional view of the database.

The key advantages of HIBROWSE are its faceted views of the underlying database, its effective use of thesauri for searching and browsing, and its ability to use Boolean operators to create sophisticated search statements. In addition, the user is able to view the titles of documents retrieved, along with other search features. Figure 6.2 shows the HIBROWSE interface and its provisions for conducting searches based on thesaurus terms, classification codes, author, document type, date, and language options.

In the design proposed by Bates (1990b) of a subject search interface and online thesaurus, the online thesaurus is made in such a way that synonyms and term variations are clustered. This proposal allows for a larger entry vocabulary and the inclusion of partial

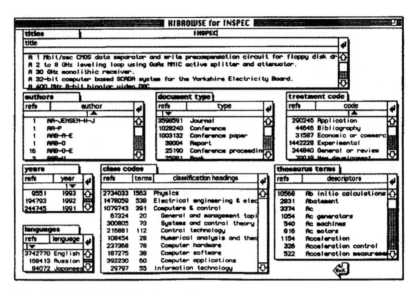

Figure 6.2   HIBROWSE for Inspec

matches between the user's term and those held in the thesaurus. The proposed design features allow the mapping of user-entered terms to those of the thesaurus and the use of the OR operator for combining all thesaurus terms selected by the user. The main feature of the interface is the display of alternative thesaurus terms without any hierarchical order or term type definition.

With this type of interface, it is assumed that users do not need an understanding of the thesaurus and its relationships; they are provided only with a number of terms close to their own search term. Figure 6.3 shows how the thesaurus terms matched with the user's term are displayed as additional terms.

Figure 6.3 illustrates a search for the term *wire*, which is matched with the subject term *wires*. Users are provided with a number of terms in which theirs occurs. This type of design allows users to disambiguate, modify, or expand their query and to examine an overview of what the collection may have on the subject. To deal with broad terms, such as shown in the above example, the thesaurus and interface make use of high-frequency clusters to display a limited number of terms on screen for user selection.

In the early 1990s, a number of thesaurus-enhanced search interfaces were developed that demonstrated the ways in which hypertext

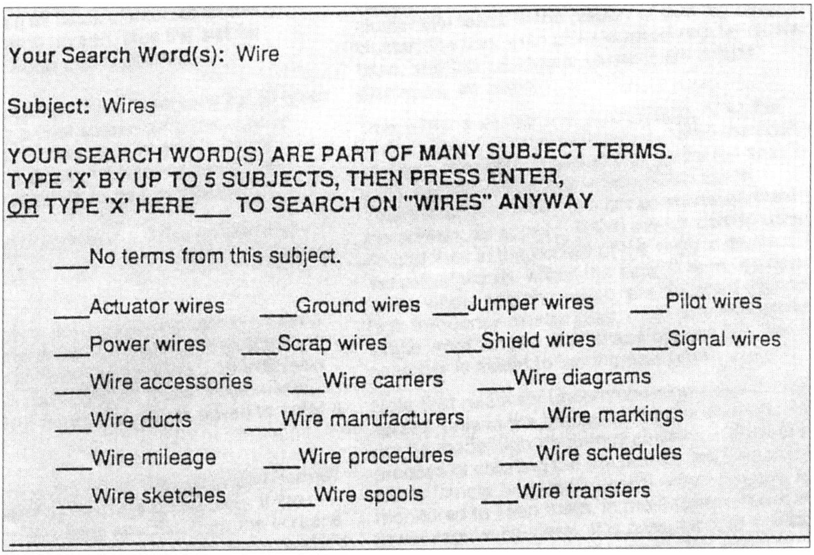

Your Search Word(s): Wire

Subject: Wires

YOUR SEARCH WORD(S) ARE PART OF MANY SUBJECT TERMS.
TYPE 'X' BY UP TO 5 SUBJECTS, THEN PRESS ENTER,
OR TYPE 'X' HERE___ TO SEARCH ON "WIRES" ANYWAY

___No terms from this subject.

___Actuator wires	___Ground wires	___Jumper wires	___Pilot wires
___Power wires	___Scrap wires	___Shield wires	___Signal wires
___Wire accessories	___Wire carriers	___Wire diagrams	
___Wire ducts	___Wire manufacturers	___Wire markings	
___Wire mileage	___Wire procedures	___Wire schedules	
___Wire sketches	___Wire spools	___Wire transfers	

Figure 6.3   Subject search interface (Bates, 1990b)

technology could be used to facilitate searching, browsing, and navigation of thesauri attached to bibliographic databases.

Hyperline (Agosti et al., 1992) is a conceptually enhanced interface that makes use of the Inspec Thesaurus and hypertext features to provide concept browse and navigation facilities. Developed for the Information Retrieval Service of the European Space Agency, it employs a mapping technique for matching words entered by users with thesaurus terms, after which the interface shows candidate concepts for browsing. Thesaurus browsing consists of two stages. In the first stage, the interface shows user input and related thesaurus terms from which the user can make a selection (Figure 6.4).

In the second stage, the searcher is provided with the details of the selected thesaurus term, including narrower, broader, related, top, and "used for" terms, together with the number of references indexed by that term (Figure 6.5). Offering access to the documents and the thesaurus at all stages of navigation is a major functionality of this interface, with the flexibility to move from thesaurus concepts to documents and vice versa.

One of the key features of this interface is its integration of the thesaurus with the Inspec database so that users can switch between the thesaurus and the bibliographic records. Another useful feature is that additional information is provided about the number of items

```
EsaQuest is looking for related candidate terms

Your Input:

   1 - INFORMATION RETRIEVAL USER INTERFACE
------------------------------------------------------------------------
Related thesaurus terms :

   2 - INFORMATION RETRIEVAL
   3 - USER INTERFACES
   4 - INFORMATION RETRIEVAL SYSTEMS
   5 - EXPERT SYSTEMS
   6 - DATABASE MANAGEMENT SYSTEMS

------------------------------------------------------------------------
Enter (C)ontinue, (N)avigate, (S)how item, (G)et term
(T)op list, h(I)story, (H)elp or (Q)uit : s1
```

Figure 6.4   Suggested terms based on the Inspec Thesaurus in Hyperline

```
----- thesaurus term DATABASE MANAGEMENT SYSTEMS -----------------------
Ref    Items term                                    Relationship
  1    15009 DATABASE MANAGEMENT SYSTEMS
  2     4755 FILE ORGANISATION                        Previous
  3     9503 MANAGEMENT INFORMATION SYSTEMS           Previous
  4      228 DEDUCTIVE DATABASES                      Narrower term
  5     1444 DISTRIBUTED DATABASES                    Narrower term
  6      153 OBJECT-ORIENTED DATABASES                Narrower term
  7     4208 RELATIONAL DATABASES                     Narrower term
  8      515 APPLICATION GENERATORS                   Related term
  9      677 CONCURRENCY CONTROL                      Related term
 10      706 DATA INTEGRITY                           Related term
 11     2055 DATABASE THEORY                          Related term
 12     4021 DECISION SUPPORT SYSTEMS                 Related term
 13      935 GEOGRAPHIC INFORMATION SYSTEMS           Related term
 14      789 HYPERMEDIA                               Related term
 15      782 INTEGRATED SOFTWARE                      Related term
 16      110 MULTIMEDIA SYSTEMS                       Related term
 17     1399 QUERY LANGUAGES                          Related term
 18      612 TRANSACTION PROCESSING                   Related term
                                                      -More  0.10-
------------------------------------------------------------------------
Enter (N)avigate, (B)ack navigate, (S)how item, (G)et term,
(T)op list, h(I)story, (H)elp or (Q)uit : s6
```

Figure 6.5   Thesaurus structure for the term *database management systems* in Hyperline

retrieved for each thesaurus term. The user interaction modeled in the interface takes advantage of the conceptual and semantic association of terms and documents, whereby searchers may change their information search strategies from viewing documents to browsing thesaurus terms.

Pollard (1993) reports the design of an experimental hypertext-based browsing interface for the ERIC thesaurus as a tool for subject access to the related bibliographic database. The user interface consists of two scrollable windows, and a typical search session starts with a keyword search. The user is then guided to the details of the terms, including display of different thesaurus terms, from which search terms can be selected. The interface uses hypertext features for navigating through various parts of the thesaurus. A search for the term *job* will display a list of partially or exactly matched terms. On clicking the keyword term, a list of terms and cross references to preferred thesaurus terms are presented. Users can choose to click on a preferred term to view the details of that term, as shown in Figure 6.6.

This experimental interface focuses on an alphabetical display of a thesaurus and on directing the user from a term found in the thesaurus to its specific details, thus allowing users to search for that term in the database. However, most of the emphasis in the interface is on the thesaurus, and little information is provided as to how search statements can be constructed.

In designing BRAQUE (BRowsing And QUEry formulation), an interface to support different information-seeking approaches, Belkin et al. (1993) employed the Hyperline system described earlier to provide a thesaurus-browsing functionality as one type of information-

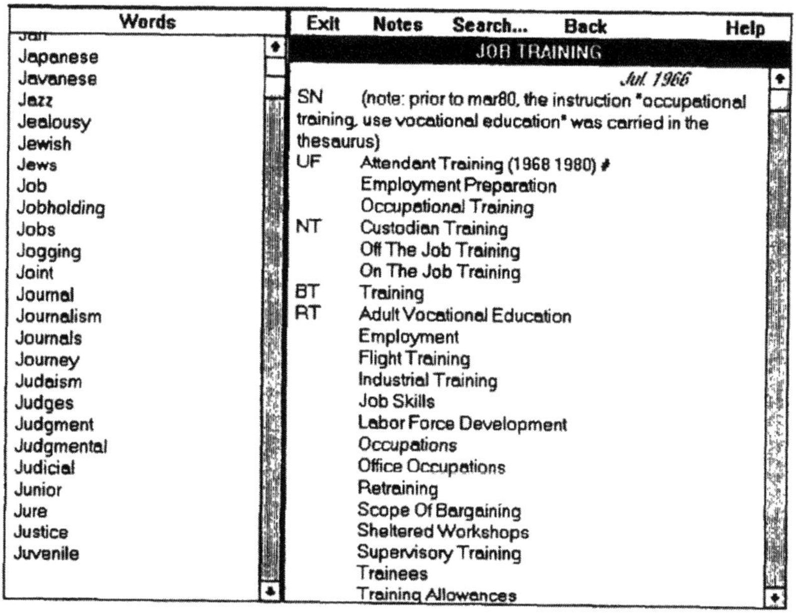

Figure 6.6   Hypertext-based thesaurus

seeking strategy. In their model, the use of thesauri, or what they termed *meta-information,* can be considered one such approach. BRAQUE supports various types of browsing and searching strategies that utilize thesaural knowledge. It incorporates a model for the transparent construction of Boolean queries to support search statement formulation. The user interface offers a number of thesaurus-enhanced features, namely, thesaurus browsing, access to the top of the term hierarchy in the thesaurus, and the ability to view related terms (Figure 6.7). The system also provides a Search Term Pool, allowing users to save their browsed and navigated thesaurus terms using the drag-and-drop function.

One of the useful features of this interface is its underlying matching function, which provides partial matching between the user terms and those in the thesaurus. This feature is particularly useful for thesauri as it enables searchers to view partially matched terms that may have the potential to meet their information need. It should be noted, however, that the interface shows only what it calls *related terms,* and rather than using various thesaural notions, it adopts a simple terminology to facilitate user interaction with this type of interface.

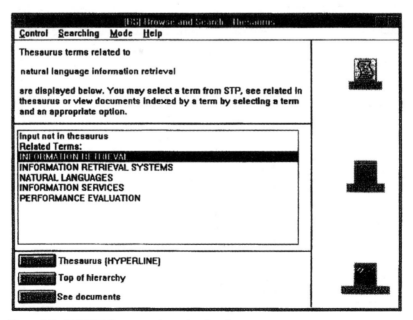

Figure 6.7   BRAQUE thesaurus browsing function

Once a term has been selected from the list of related terms, the searcher can choose either to see the documents containing that thesaurus term or to view the terms associated with the selected term.

If the user decides to view a particular document, the option is available to request that the concepts associated with the document be displayed. In fact, to take advantage of thesaurus terms within this interface, users can variously interact with the thesaurus, the retrieved documents, or the Search Term Pool. Users are able to engage in some or all of these steps, identified as multiple information-seeking strategies.

Johnson and Cochrane (1995) and Johnson (1997) developed a prototype of a hypertextual interface to the Inspec Thesaurus (Figure 6.8). The display represents an ordered, hypertextual concept space in which the user can move about at will, selecting search terms for immediate use or for use during subsequent searches, without leaving the thesaurus or going into a separate search mode. The interface displays both hierarchical and alphabetical lists of terms and shows the current term around which its related terms are displayed. It uses plus and minus icons to show broader or narrower terms, while taking advantage of visual features to display related terms for the selected term in an adjoining area of the unified interface.

The authors use the metaphor of *cloud* to describe the space in which related terms are shown. This is particularly interesting and innovative, given the recent appearance of tag cloud features on many social tagging websites. All terms shown on the interface are clickable and can be selected for searching the database. The interface also provides KWIC and keyword-out-of-context displays as alternative ways of accessing the thesaurus to support users in its navigation. The interface has a search history function called Hold File, which allows users to drag and drop thesaurus terms of interest for later searching.

Interesting and useful features of the interface are its display of multiple relationships among terms in a concept space, and its treatment of polyhierarchies. For instance, if a thesaurus term appears under two or three different hierarchies, displaying all the instances within a single screen would be challenging, so a dropdown menu is provided to allow users to switch to a different hierarchy if needed. Beaulieu (1997) reports on the design of a thesaurus-enhanced search interface using knowledge-based techniques. This design exploits thesaurus knowledge for query enhancement in a probabilistic information retrieval system. The interface provides a single

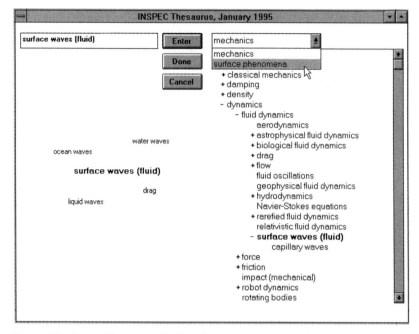

Figure 6.8 Inspec Thesaurus display with *surface waves* as the current term

window with multiple panes in which the retrieval task is treated as two related, equally important subtasks.

The interface provides a number of facilities to ease the term selection process. The query entered by the user is partially matched with the thesaurus terms, and the top document of the retrieved items is displayed, along with a list of suggested thesaurus terms. Users can choose thesaurus terms to add to their query terms, or they can navigate and browse the thesaurus further.

The simultaneous display of all original and selected terms, as well as the list of retrieved documents, is the key feature of the interface. As some matching terms are non-preferred terms, the interface also shows the preferred terms for possible substitution. This type of interface has been specifically designed to meet the requirement of query enhancement and expansion.

In addition to largely text-based thesaurus interfaces, a significant number of graphical and visual interfaces have been developed in order to demonstrate the power and utility of thesauri as tools for supporting the search process. McMath et al. (1989) developed thesaurus-enhanced graphical interfaces for two information retrieval systems.

One interface was TraverseNet (McMath et al., 1989), which made use of the Association for Computing Machinery (ACM) Computer Classification, a strictly hierarchical thesaurus in which each term has one parent. The conceptual model underpinning TraverseNet is that of an observer able to explore the thesaurus structure. This interface encourages exploration, both in investigating the thesaurus and in constructing queries.

The graphical representation of the thesaurus is designed to help novice searchers with a thesaurus. Queries can be formulated using thesaurus terms by selecting hierarchy terms and placing them in the query. As Figure 6.9 illustrates, the thesaurus is displayed as an inner circle surrounded by "children" (narrower term) nodes depicted as semantically related terms.

Figure 6.9 depicts the search term *computer science*, along with its children nodes. Users can move about in the hierarchy, traversing the links up and down the graph. This not only allows viewing of the thesaural terms but also helps convey the meaning of the terms by showing the relationships of one to another. Queries are formulated by moving about the network and by indicating that a term should be included in a query. When documents are retrieved, the resulting document list is also graphically displayed, with the relevance of each document to the query depicted visually. This process allows

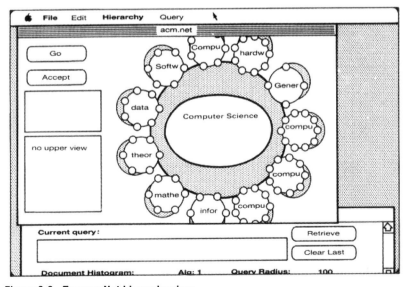

Figure 6.9 TraverseNet hierarchy view

for easy refinement of the query and for the display of multiple queries simultaneously.

The other user interface developed by McMath et al. (1989) makes use of the MeSH thesaurus and provides a different approach for browsing and navigation. Given the richness and term details in MeSH, this interface puts more emphasis on the display of various term hierarchies.

Figure 6.10 shows a search for the term *hyperlipemia* and its genetic etiology within the user interface. The user first has the choice of browsing the thesaurus or of entering a term directly. If the user enters the term *hyperlipemia*, the neighborhood around it

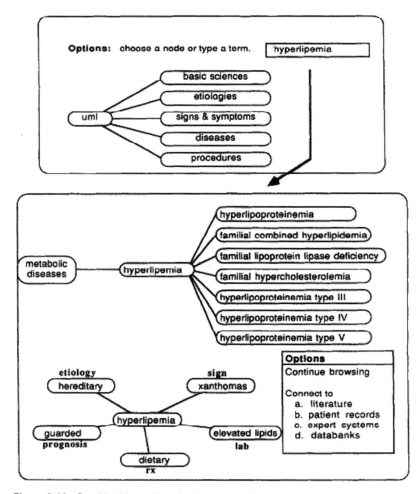

Figure 6.10 Graphical browsing of a thesaurus, showing multiple representations of the thesaurus

appears on the screen. That neighborhood includes both the broader-than and narrower-than terms, along with a constellation of terms connected by Etiology, Prognosis, Treatment, and other such links that are appropriate for the disease being searched. If the user now chooses to pursue the Etiology link, another screen appears that shows both a hierarchy of etiology-like relations and a hierarchy of the hereditary terms that are related to the original etiology presented for the disease.

The interface provides various control features to allow users to view documents on a particular thesaurus term or to use the term to search patient records, expert systems, and data banks.

MeSHBROWSE (Korn and Shneiderman, 1995) is a prototype interface for browsing the MeSH thesaurus. It uses a concept space approach and a node-link tree diagram of the concept space (Figure 6.11). Users can expand or contract each of the high-level categories and interactively explore hidden interrelationships. Clicking on each category will display its children or narrower terms. The user interface makes use of the colors green, yellow, and red to represent default, clicked, and interrelated terms. The graphical nature of the

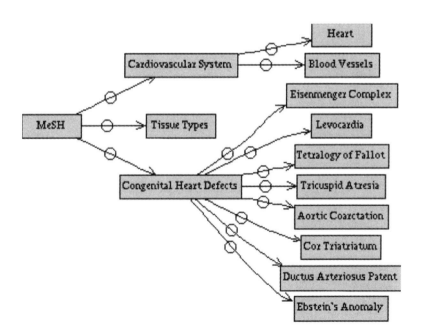

Figure 6.11   MeSHBROWSE

interface allows for related categories of terms to be displayed in a two-dimensional tree structure.

Because the clicked nodes or terms change color, users are able to form Boolean queries (AND and OR) using the already high-lighted terms.

Cat-a-Cone (Hearst and Karadi, 1997) has a three-dimensional visual interface designed to achieve two key goals: 1) to make large hierarchical category sets easier to view and understand and 2) to couple the viewing of categories with search and display of retrieved results. One of the novel aspects of the interface is the use of colors and paints for specifying Boolean queries. Users can select a combi-nation of colors to represent their chosen search terms.

The interface (Figure 6.12) initially shows all of the MeSH top-level categories and allows users to control the subsequent expansion. They can drill down the MeSH hierarchy to view specific terms under each facet or sub-facet.

The prototype implementation makes use of the ConeTree 3D+ animation visualization from the Xerox PARC Information Visualizer. An alternative mode of interaction is for the user to type in a category label and determine which parts of the hierarchy match or partially match that label. The interface also encourages a kind of relevance feedback by suggesting additional categories. Users can jump easily from one category to another and search on multiple categories simultaneously.

Two main advantages of this type of two-layered interaction model are that users can disambiguate the query terms appearing in several different places in a large thesaurus such as MeSH, and they can simultaneously interact with the thesaurus and the retrieved documents.

Visual MeSH is a graphical interface developed by Lin et al. (1998) and Lin (1999) to interact with the MeSH thesaurus and the MEDLINE database. It allows users to look up and interactively explore MeSH terms in a click-and-choose environment and assists them in browsing the MeSH terms through the display of several views of the concept. The user can double-click on a term to select it in any of the views.

The interface supports visual construction of Boolean queries. It provides instant feedback and uses the number of hits and document distributions on a map to help users modify their query. Within the interface, three views are provided, namely, Tree View, Neighbor View, and Map View.

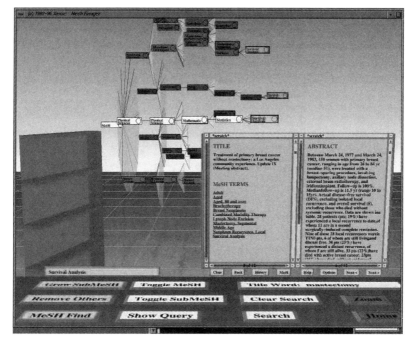

Figure 6.12   Cat-A-Cone user interface

The Tree View displays a MeSH term along with its synonymous, narrower, broader, and related terms. The Neighbor View allows a user to drag a term to the center of the interface to be able to view its broader, narrower, and related terms. These terms are then shown around the central concept.

The Map View consists of a term map and a document map. Figure 6.13 shows how a term map displays the hierarchical relationships of terms, as well as the semantic types of each term. The interface uses different colors to show the high-level categories of the thesaurus. For instance, Diseases & Pathologic Process is represented in red and the Procedures or Treatment category in green. Moving the mouse over the list of colored diamonds on the right reveals what each color represents.

Terms can be selected by dragging them to the four corners of the term map, where the user is then able to combine multiple terms using the AND operator to search and retrieve documents from MEDLINE. The bottom part of the interface affords control options for choosing different views of concepts. This thesaurus-enhanced search interface has the advantage of providing users with multiple

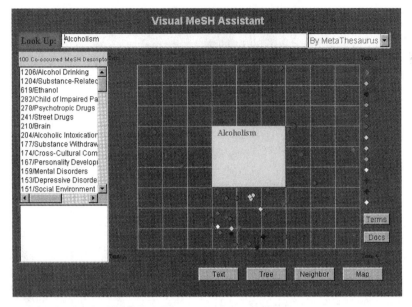

Figure 6.13   Visual MeSH Map View

views of the MeSH thesaurus terms, both for those who are interested in list-based presentation of search terms and for those who prefer visual representation of terms.

Sutcliffe et al. (2000) describe a visual interface enhanced with a thesaurus called the Integrated Thesaurus-Results Browser, which provides simultaneous access to a query bar, thesaurus terms, thesaural structure, and search results. The interface design was based on the idea that, in the early phases of articulating needs and forming queries, users should be supported by thesaurus and term suggestion features. The authors adopted a tiled window layout in order to increase the ease of a variety of functionalities, such as cross-referencing between queries, metadata representation in the thesaurus, visual summaries of the result sets, and document viewing.

The thesaurus is a major feature of the interface, allowing for search term selection and query specification or modification. The thesaurus terms are displayed in categorical boxes and lines connected to subcategories. Deeper levels of the thesaurus can be reached through single-clicking; double-clicking thesaurus terms puts them into the query bar at the top of the thesaurus area. Search results for *company news, merger* are displayed in Figure 6.14.

As Figure 6.14 shows, the results browser contains one or more "bull's eye" cluster displays for similar documents retrieved. The bull's-eye metaphor encodes two properties of the results: First, relevance is represented by rings, from higher relevance in the center of the bull's eye to marginal relevance in outer rings, and second, similarity between documents is expressed by clusters on the browser.

The key advantage of this interface lies in its integration of thesaurus browsing and results browsing to support users' information-seeking process. The dynamic interaction between the thesaurus and results panes allows users to easily switch between the thesaurus and the results display. It might be noted that, given the small space provided for the thesaurus component, this type of interface design may not easily lend itself to the presentation of large and polyhierarchical thesauri.

Dalmau et al. (2005) report the design of a user interface that provides faceted browsing of a photo collection based on the Thesaurus for Graphic Materials (TGM). Let's consider a query for *gardens and California*, with search term suggestions based on the thesaurus, in this instance, for the thesaural term *gardens*, offering broader and

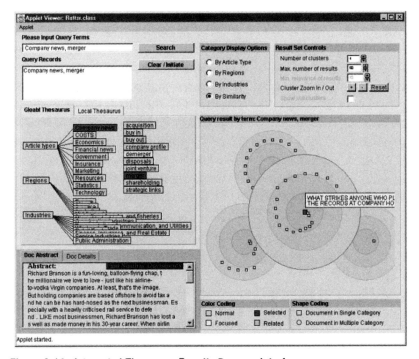

Figure 6.14   Integrated Thesaurus-Results Browser interface

narrower terms in TGM for further refinement and at the same time viewing of results. A useful feature of this interface is its Browse by Subject feature, which allows a user to see quickly which subjects are covered by the collection.

In some cases, if the list of narrower terms is too long, the interface shows a section of the list along with a More Terms feature for displaying the rest of the list in a pop-up window, as illustrated in Figure 6.15.

This interface provides a functional example of the use of thesaurus terms for query modification. It should be noted, however, that there is no specific feature designed to allow for the construction of sophisticated search statements using multiple thesaurus terms. In addition, the structure of the thesaurus is not explicitly available for browsing.

Using the Art and Architecture Thesaurus (AAT), Tudhope et al. (2006) designed a thesaurus-based search user interface with semantic query expansion, called FACET, for the U.K. National Museum of Science and Industry database. One of the objectives of the system and the FACET interface is to support thesaurus-based multiconcept

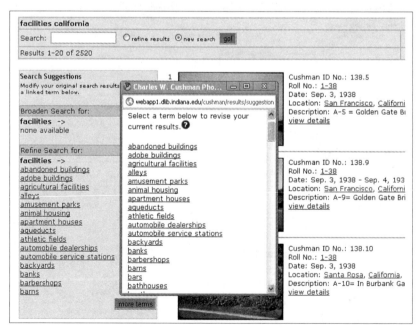

Figure 6.15   The More Terms feature and the pop-up window display in the Charles W. Cushman Photograph Collection user interface

query construction and expansion. The system and interface take advantage of a sophisticated partial matching of user terms and thesaurus terms. Users' terms can also be matched to those found in scope notes in order to create a larger entry vocabulary. The FACET interface provides a very good example of making effective use of faceted thesauri such as the AAT to support searching and browsing of digital collections.

Figure 6.16 depicts the Query Builder screen of the user interface. The left pane combines a number of navigable views of the thesaurus, namely, a mapping facility to controlled terms, a hierarchical browser, and a "semantic browser." Once controlled thesaurus terms are selected (by any of the methods), they can be dragged, or added via the Context menu, to the query on the right, where they are automatically associated with the appropriate facet.

Figure 6.16 also shows the Query Expansion view in the right pane, representing a color-coded visualization of terms affected by the current expansion setting. Functionality includes term navigation history, bookmarking, display of scope notes, and display of related terms. Color-coded icons indicate facet membership, and also the presence of related terms. At any point, users may double-click a term to browse the thesaurus and explore local context in order to discover whether a term corresponds to their information need (there may be homonyms).

The FACET interface has a number of thesaurus browsing options. There are three different thesaurus views, as shown in Figure 6.16. The Ancestry view shows all ancestry terms back to the root, or facet, term, while the Hierarchy view additionally shows siblings of the selected term (and in the web demonstrator shows immediate narrower terms).

An Expansion view of the concept *mahogany* in the left pane allows the user to do further interactive browsing by selecting any displayed concept. The hierarchical display is replaced by a linear ranked list, with relative semantic closeness symbolized by longer and shorter bars. This may be a useful browsing option when a simpler view of thesaurus content is desired.

De Vorsey et al. (2006) created for the American Museum of Natural History a simple user interface to a local thesaurus based on the AAT. The thesaurus was designed with TheW32 open source application, specifically for the archaeological and ethnographic collections of the museum.

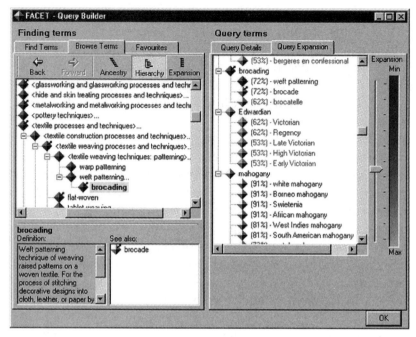

Figure 6.16   FACET Query Builder screen

Figure 6.17 shows a faceted view of a search for *carrying basket*. The left pane of the interface shows the faceted structure of the thesaurus. The right pane shows both the results and brief metadata records for the results set. Also, a scope note for the selected term *carrying basket*, along with the user's search term, are displayed at the top.

The advantage of this type of user interface lies in its integration of thesaurus browsing and results display. Users are able to modify a search term and examine the immediate effect on the results. The brief display of metadata records on the right side of the interface allows users to form a better context for reviewing their thesaurus-based search results.

Shiri et al. (2006) report on the design and implementation of a prototype thesaurus-enhanced search interface for the Government of Canada Core Subject Thesaurus (Figure 6.18). The interface design is based on a theoretical framework grounded in two key components. The first involves the concept of the "rich prospect" interface, in which individual representations of every item in a collection can be combined with emergent tools to allow access to a digital collection (Ruecker, 2003).

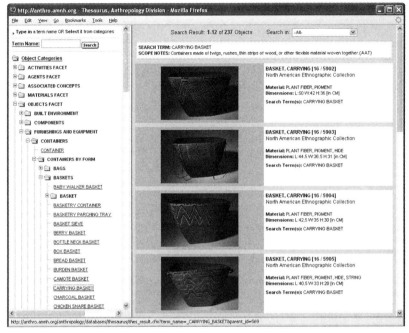

Figure 6.17   American Museum of Natural History thesaurus interface

The second component is the use of several design ideas for thesaurus-based search interfaces that were suggested earlier by Shiri et al. (2002). Key design features are summarized as follows:

- Hierarchical and alphabetical lists to support different browsing and searching strategies

- Flexible ways of choosing terms for posting to the search system, such as drag and drop, check boxes, hypertext features, and double clicking

- Clearer representation of moving from a descriptor to its hierarchical structure using hypertext navigation

- Alternative Boolean operators for combining different thesaurus terms

- A Term Pool option for saving for later use the descriptors chosen during thesaurus browsing

- Integrated thesaurus and retrieved documents displays for more-effective search and retrieval

- Availability of thesaurus options in all stages of the search process, whether query formulation, query modification, or query expansion

The aim of the proposed interface is to provide the user with the following types of spaces within it:

- Query space, for formulating search statements

- Thesaurus space, for browsing and navigating the thesaurus

- Document space, for viewing document representations

As Figure 6.18 shows for the search term *animals*, the side panel on the left presents a list of the highest-level categories in the thesaurus. The middle table allows users to browse terms associated with each high-level facet and to view the standard types of thesaurus relationships by using microtext and visual elements. The right side of the interface offers a query formulation facility whereby users are able to gather terms in the search term pool area and construct Boolean query statements. A language switch provides a means of checking for corresponding terms in another language; such terms are in any case always visible as microtext satellites of the query terms.

Shiri et al. (2010) designed and developed a visual thesaurus-enhanced search interface for the UNESCO multilingual digital library. The interface, called T-Saurus, makes use of the UNESCO multilingual thesaurus, and its functional prototype is available at thesaurus-index.markbieber.ca/Main.html. The user interface makes use of visual objects, size, color, location, and zoom in and zoom out features in order to distinguish between various types of thesaurus terms and their relationships.

Figures 6.19 and 6.20 show the T-Saurus search and the retrieved document spaces. Figure 6.19 depicts a core of visual elements, consisting of a set of "buckets" organized in the center of the screen. The size of each bucket represents the number of matches for a particular term, while proximity and opacity, or degree of shading, represent scope and accuracy of the term in relation to pre-established hierarchies for the query as follows: Main Term, Related Term, More Specific, More General, and Synonyms.

The Query space is located across the top and on the right side of the screen, while the Thesaurus space is located on the left and in the center. Users can search for a single term in the thesaurus by entering

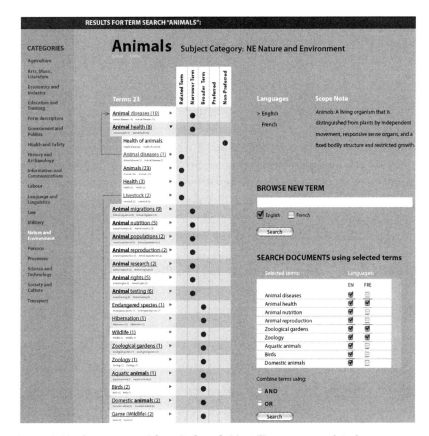

Figure 6.18   Government of Canada Core Subject Thesaurus user interface

it in the query box at the top of the page and clicking the Find button. The query box is equipped with an auto-completion feature that allows users to view up to five terms as they type in their search query. The list of auto-completion terms is also browsable, allowing users to view a longer list of thesaurus terms available for search. If the term exists in the thesaurus, it appears in the center of the screen with a number in parentheses beside it, indicating the number of documents in the collection that include the selected term.

Users can also browse all the thesaural terms using the panel on the left, which can then be sorted either alphabetically or hierarchically by category. Again, each term has a number beside it in parentheses indicating how many documents in the collection contain the term. When a term in the list is clicked, it will appear in the center of the screen.

When a term is selected by either method, it is represented by a square in the central thesaurus space. With the check boxes in the bottom right panel, users can compare their selected term with thesaurus terms that are related, narrower (more specific), broader (more general), and preferred or non-preferred (synonyms). These associated terms are also represented in the thesaurus space by squares or diamonds, and their relationships to the user's selected term are represented by their relative proximity and opacity.

Users can also use the check boxes in the right-hand panel to show thesaural terms in multiple languages and to view scope notes for selected terms. When users decide to add a term to their query, they do so by clicking on its square in the center of the screen, at which point it is added to the Summary of Terms list, or term pool, at the top of the right-hand panel. Users can add as many terms as they wish, delete terms at any time, choose to keep them in only one language rather than multiple languages, or combine them using the Boolean operators below the list.

When searchers have finished formulating their query, they click Retrieve Documents to view the results, as shown in Figure 6.20 for the search term *thesauri*. The darker green box in the middle shows

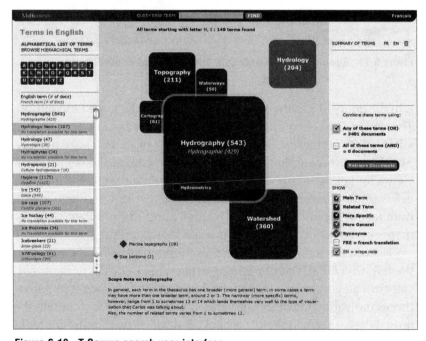

Figure 6.19   T-Saurus search user interface

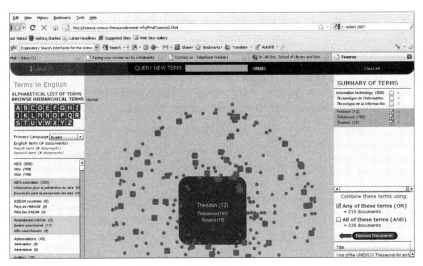

Figure 6.20   T-Saurus results presentation interface

the thesaurus term *thesauri* and its French and Spanish equivalents, as well as the number of documents indexed using that term. The red dots around the darker green box represent the results retrieved for the chosen term.

A chronological review of those research-based prototype user interfaces previously discussed shows that various techniques and approaches have been adopted to make thesauri more accessible to support the browsing and searching of electronic collections. The user interfaces developed in the late 1980s and 1990s focused on the ways in which hypertext technology could be used to create more-flexible thesaurus-enhanced user interfaces, while the web-based technological developments in the late 1990s and early 2000s allowed researchers to explore, examine, and apply graphical and visualization techniques to thesaurus-enhanced designs. The later developments are, to some extent, attributable to growing collaboration among researchers in the various disciplines of information science, information retrieval, and human-computer interaction. The recent introduction of information visualization techniques provides new opportunities to design more-interactive and more-engaging user interfaces for thesaurus-based search systems.

These interfaces share a number of common capabilities, available in most of the research-based interfaces reviewed here:

- Linking users' search terms with those of thesauri using different mapping techniques

- Informing users of the number of documents indexed by a given thesaurus term

- Finding thesaurus terms by means of look-up and browse options

- Saving thesaurus terms for later use by means of search term pool options

- Integrating thesaurus and document displays to allow for easy query modification

- Using hypertext techniques for navigating and selecting thesaurus terms

- Showing all types of thesaurus term relationships

- Implementing search term suggestions based on thesauri

- Supporting high-level view of the collection by means of faceted browsing options

- Visualizing of thesaurus and retrieved results displays

6.5 Commercial Thesaurus-Enhanced Search User Interfaces

Chan and Pollard (1988) compiled an analytic guide to commercial databases that made use of thesauri at the time they were writing. The guide identified the indexing vocabularies used in specific online databases, the syndetic structures employed in specific thesauri, and the arrangement of descriptor displays.

Since then, there have been major developments associated with the migration of commercial bibliographic databases onto the web. Major search user interface designs have found their way into these commercial databases. This section introduces several examples of search user interfaces that have made effective use of thesauri in searching, browsing, and navigation.

Because a number of database vendors and providers publish a wide range of databases in various areas, and because their products use the same interface, the examples that follow have been selected to show the variety of approaches to thesaurus-aided search interface design.

One well-designed search user interface that incorporates thesauri into various databases was developed by Ovid Technologies. The interface provides a mapping feature that maps a user's term to the terms in a thesaurus. When a user searches in MEDLINE for a term such as *leukemia*, the term is mapped to one or several of the thesaurus terms, and the terms are displayed. The user is able to select the exact match, as shown in Figure 6.21, or to see the tree or hierarchical view of the term, including broader and narrower terms.

The interface allows a searcher to use the Explode option to include narrower terms of a selected term in the search, to limit a search to those documents in which the user's subject heading is considered the major point of the article, to review the scope note for the term, and to create Boolean queries using the AND and OR operators. The plus and minus features facilitate expansion or contraction of the tree structure. The detailed view of the term *leukemia* illustrated in Figure 6.22 also shows the number of documents indexed using the term entered.

The interface also provides search functions for its permuted index, scope notes, and sub-headings. One of the useful features of

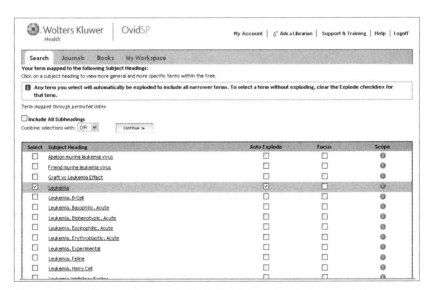

Figure 6.21   Ovid user interface for MEDLINE [*Reproduced with permissions granted from Ovid Technologies, Inc./ Copyright © 2008 Wolters Kluwer Health/Ovid*]

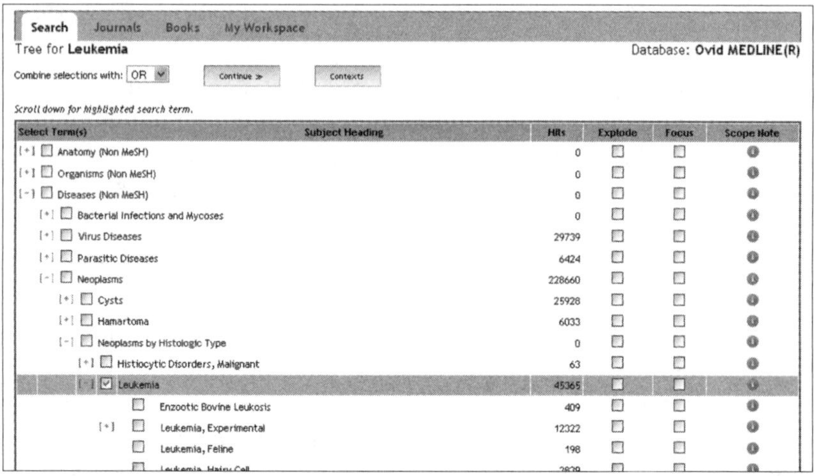

Figure 6.22   The Tree View of Ovid MEDLINE thesaurus-based search [*Reproduced with permissions granted from Ovid Technologies, Inc./ Copyright © 2008 Wolters Kluwer Health/Ovid*]

this interface is Search as Keyword, which allows users to carry out free-text searching of a term in addition to controlled-vocabulary searching. Another useful feature is the ability to find partial matches for the term entered, thereby allowing searchers to gain a better overview of terms they might not be aware of at the beginning of their search.

In general, because of the availability of the mapping feature in the advanced search functionality, Ovid provides seamless access to subject-based searching. It offers a Filter by Subject option in order to support users in refining and reformulating their search while viewing the results. It also supplies thesaurus-based search features for other databases, including ERIC and PsycINFO.

The ERIC database, provided by EBSCOhost, offers a different approach to the availability of thesaurus-based searching. Users choose the Thesaurus option on the homepage in order to get access to the thesaurus. The interface provides a more traditional view of the ERIC thesaurus terms, consisting of broader terms, narrower terms, and scope notes.

Figure 6.23 illustrates that, for the search term *leaves of absence*, two search options are available for users, Term Begins With and Term Contains. The latter provides a KWIC search functionality. The labeling of the permuted index as Term Contains provides an easy-to-understand search function.

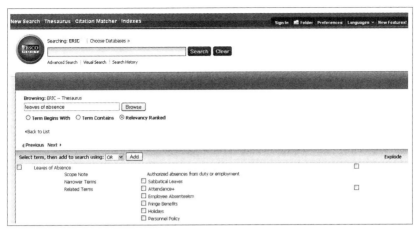

Figure 6.23   ERIC database thesaurus-based search provided by EBSCOhost
[*Reproduced with permission of EBSCO*]

Similar to Ovid, the Explode option in the EBSCOhost interface allows users to include narrower terms of a search term for simultaneous searching. Boolean searching of thesaurus terms is incorporated, and further exploration of them is facilitated by means of a plus sign in front of some terms, indicating that those terms have narrower or broader terms. Searchers can also move to other thesaurus terms through Previous and Next buttons. The Add option allows searchers to insert the thesaurus term into their query.

However, one of the limitations of the interface is that if users want to select their initial term for searching, along with a term chosen from the thesaurus, there is no easy way to add both of them to the query. The Add feature incorporates only the selected thesaurus term. To add the initial query term as well, the user has to copy it and paste it in manually. Another limitation is that the juxtaposition of the thesaurus browsing search bar and the database search bar may pose challenges for users, who may not appreciate the implications of each search strategy for the search results.

Once the thesaurus-based search is completed, the user interface provides an option to refine results via suggested subject terms, as shown in Figure 6.24 for a search on displayed terms. This feature is particularly useful because it provides an opportunity, at the results display stage, for users to narrow down or broaden their queries using thesaurus terms. The EBSCOhost help file does not indicate how these suggested terms are extracted from the thesaurus.

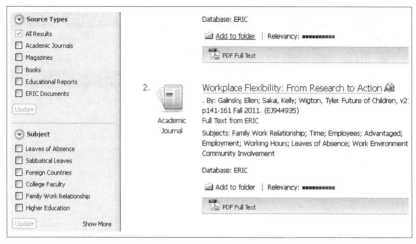

Figure 6.24   Suggested subject terms in the EBSCOhost interface [*Reproduced with permission of EBSCO*]

It should be noted that the CINAHL Plus EBSCOhost interface for with full-text database provides an additional feature called Major Concept. When the Major Concept box is ticked, the system creates a search query that finds only records for which the subject heading is a major point of each indexed document.

The database vendor WilsonWeb, recently acquired by EBSCO, publishes Library Literature and Information Science Full-Text and provides a thesaurus-based search interface. Figure 6.25 shows a search for the term *online searching* in the thesaurus. An exact match for the term is found, and broader and narrower terms are shown through a Tree View indentation. At the top right of the interface are icons for users to expand, collapse, or view broader terms. One of the useful features of the interface is the View Records link next to each thesaurus term, which allows searchers to gain quick access to the documents indexed by that term.

Users can select a number of terms for searching with the Search Marked Subjects button. However, this feature carries out a Boolean OR search only, leaving users unable to use other Boolean operators to create more-sophisticated search statements. Similar to EBSCOhost, WilsonWeb provides a list of suggested subject terms along with the result set so that users can narrow down their initial search by using new terms from the thesaurus.

Cambridge Scientific Abstracts (CSA) Illumina provides access to thesauri for searching in its databases under a feature called Search

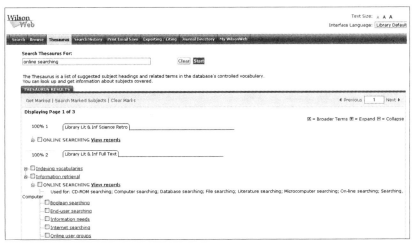

Figure 6.25 WilsonWeb Library Literature and Information Science Full-Text database [*Reproduced with permission of EBSCO*]

Tools. The thesaurus option provides three different views of thesaurus terms, alphabetical, hierarchical, and rotated. Figure 6.26 shows a search for the term *syntax* in the Linguistics and Language Behavior Abstracts database.

The interface provides Boolean AND and OR search operators for combining terms as well as an Explode option for including narrower terms. Clicking on any term allows the searcher to view the details of that term, including narrower and related terms; the plus sign indicates that a term has narrower terms. The interface provides a feature for viewing Previous Term and Next Term. The rotated view of the thesaurus shows all the terms that contain the searched term.

CSA Illumina takes a different approach to the provision of subject terms at the query reformulation stage. When users retrieve results from a search for thesaurus terms, the thesaurus descriptors assigned to each document are displayed on the right side of the interface, as shown in Figure 6.27 with a search for the term *syntax*. This feature can help users view a wider range of thesaurus terms and form a broader context for their search.

A suggested improvement to this type of interface is to use terminology that is familiar to searchers. For instance, instead of the term *descriptors*, terms such as *additional terms*, *subject terms*, or *suggested terms* would facilitate better user understanding.

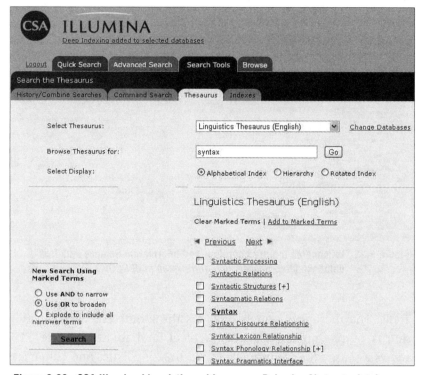

Figure 6.26　CSA Illumina Linguistic and Language Behavior Abstracts database thesaurus search user interface [*Screenshots and their contents published with permission of ProQuest LLC. Further reproduction is prohibited without permission.*]

Thomson Reuters Web of Knowledge provides a uniform interface for a wide range of databases. One example is how the Centre for Agricultural Bioscience (CAB) Abstracts Database Thesaurus is used for searching within Thomson Reuters Web of Knowledge. In this interface, gaining access to the thesaurus is a multistep process, and users can enter the CAB Thesaurus by choosing the Descriptor field. However, even if a term in the Descriptor field is selected for searching, the user will still be instructed to carry out a search in the thesaurus. Once in the thesaurus area, users have to search for a term to see the details. Figure 6.28 shows a search for the term *aciduria*, with the option for users to view the hierarchy for that term or to see its thesaurus details.

In the Thomson Reuters Web of Knowledge CAB Thesaurus hierarchical view, users are able to browse the structure of the thesaurus and choose to add their term or select more terms for their search

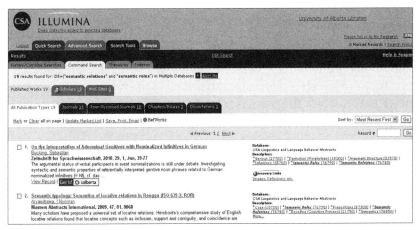

Figure 6.27   CSA Illumina Linguistic and Language Behavior Abstracts database
result display [*Screenshots published with permission of ProQuest
LLC. Further reproduction is prohibited without permission.*]

WEB OF KNOWLEDGE℠ | DISCOVERY STARTS HERE

CABI: CAB Abstracts® and Global Health®

CAB Thesaurus -- Descriptors field

Use the Find feature to locate terms to add to your query.

Enter text to find terms containing or related to the text .
Example: acid*

    aciduria   Find

Browse Descriptors Hierarchy

JUMP TO ITEM

KEY: (Add) = add to query   T = view thesaurus details

⊞ GENERAL

⊞ PHYSICAL SCIENCES

⊞ EARTH SCIENCES

⊞ LIFE SCIENCES

⊟ APPLIED SCIENCE AND TECHNOLOGY

    ⊞ (health and pathology)

    ⊞ (applied human and animal nutrition)

Figure 6.28   Thomson Reuters Web of Knowledge CAB Abstracts Database
thesaurus search [*Reproduced with permission of Thomson Reuters
©2011 Thomson Reuters*]

statements (see Figure 6.29). Once the Add button is clicked, the term appears at the bottom of the page in a search bar. Choosing two or more terms will trigger the OR operator to combine the selected terms. Users are not able to make changes to Boolean operators.

Once the selected terms are transferred to the main search box, the user has to click the search button to carry out a search on the

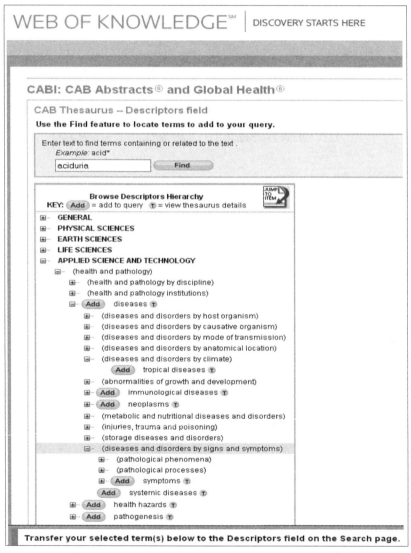

Figure 6.29   Thomson Reuters Web of Knowledge CAB Thesaurus hierarchical view [*Reproduced with permission of Thomson Reuters ©2011 Thomson Reuters*]

selected terms. Along with the list of retrieved results, the Refine by Descriptor feature allows users to narrow down their search by using one of the suggested descriptors.

It should be noted that, in general, this type of design is challenging for users who are not familiar with a given thesaurus. Such interfaces are more useful for indexers, information professionals, and search specialists. The multistep nature of the interface design does not provide an accommodating and easy-to-use approach for thesaurus-based search.

Engineering Village provides a wide range of engineering databases, including the well-known Inspec and Compendex databases. The user interface for the Inspec database allows users to choose multiple databases or select a particular thesaurus. Users can choose the Thesaurus option from the navigation bar at the top. The thesaurus search function provides Exact Match as well as Partial Match features.

Figure 6.30 shows a screenshot of the Inspec Thesaurus search for the term *nanofabrication*. If any of the check boxes for search terms are ticked, they will automatically appear in the search box at

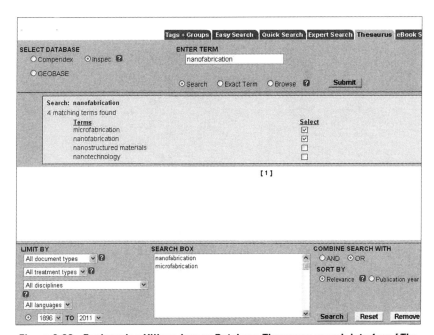

Figure 6.30   Engineering Village Inspec Database Thesaurus search interface [*The Inspec database is published by The Institution of Engineering and Technology © The Institution of Engineering and Technology*]

the bottom of the page. Users will then be able to use Boolean operators and/or other delimiters to refine their search. Also, the terms are clickable if details of a term are needed, such as broader or narrower terms.

The Browse option allows users to see the searched term in its alphabetical order. Users are able to view the Search box and the terms selected throughout their thesaurus searching and browsing. For instance, as Figure 6.31 illustrates, if a user decides to view narrower terms for a new term such as *electromagnetism*, the user can access the Search box and previously selected terms. If users decide to remove previously selected terms and add new terms, they can do so with the features provided next to the Search box.

For query reformulation, the Results Display interface allows users to choose from a list of terms labeled Controlled Vocabulary. An interesting and novel feature of the interface is its visual representation of the controlled vocabulary terms. One of the main advantages of Inspec thesaurus-based search interface is that it allows users to quickly select terms to formulate sophisticated queries and to maintain their search context as they proceed in their search process.

Figure 6.32 shows the number of documents indexed for each of the selected thesaurus terms, as well as the number of documents

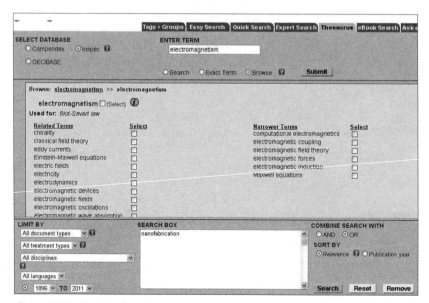

Figure 6.31   Engineering Village Inspec Database Thesaurus term details [*The Inspec database is published by The Institution of Engineering and Technology © The Institution of Engineering and Technology*]

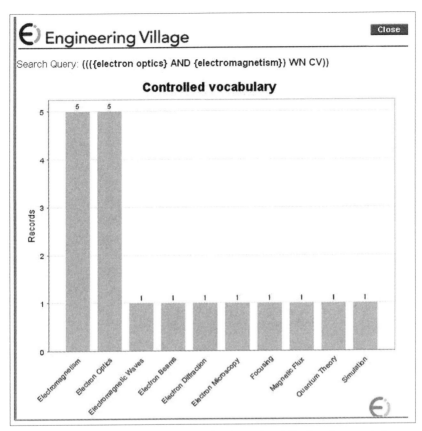

Figure 6.32   Engineering Village Inspec database visual display of suggested
controlled vocabulary terms [*The Inspec database is published by
The Institution of Engineering and Technology © The Institution of
Engineering and Technology*]

available for the Controlled Vocabulary terms that the interface displays along with the retrieved results.

ProQuest provides a thesaurus-based search option on the homepage interface. It is initiated by clicking on the Thesaurus button on the homepage, which opens a new window with a thesaurus search bar. As shown in Figure 6.33, a search for the exact match term *cognitive therapy* produces the entry for the term along with its details. There is a tab labeled Add to Search that allows searchers to put this term in their search statement.

The interface provides a simple alphabetical navigation bar at the top to allow users to choose a specific letter to browse. The thesaurus

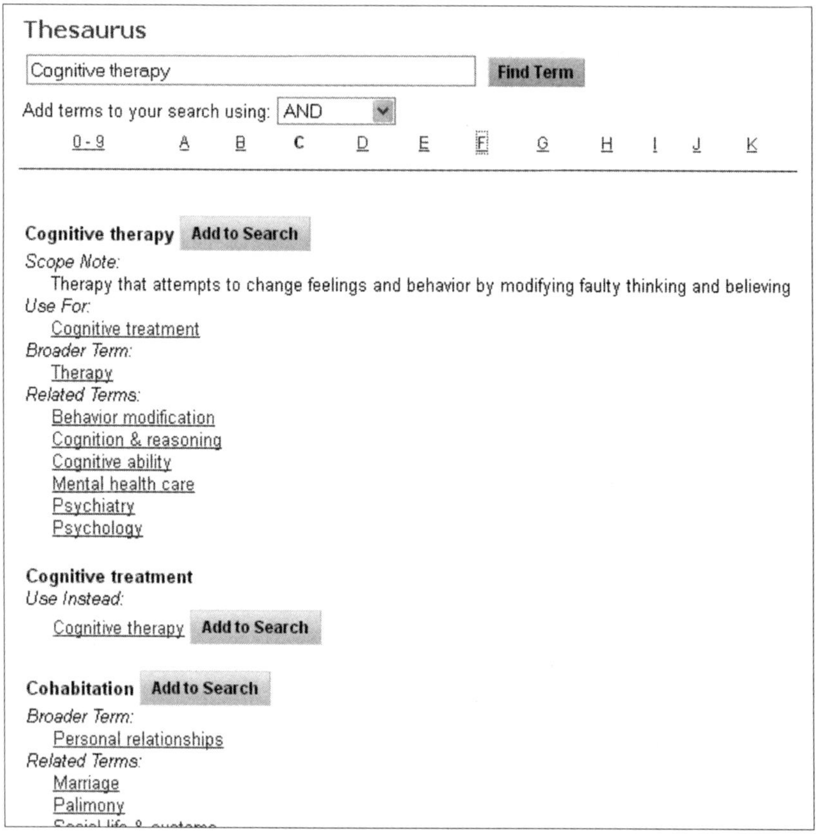

Figure 6.33   ProQuest Education Journals thesaurus search interface [*Screenshots and their contents published with permission of ProQuest LLC. Further reproduction is prohibited without permission.*]

search interface also has three Boolean operators, namely, AND, OR, and AND NOT. The interface also provides cross-references from non-preferred to preferred terms. There are no hierarchical or permuted displays available in the thesaurus interface.

It should be noted that, because the thesaurus search page opens up as a different window, no activity can be observed on the interface when the user clicks on the Add to Search tab; instead, the user has to go back to the basic search page window to determine whether the term has been added, as Figure 6.34 demonstrates. Therefore, if the user decides to include several thesaurus terms, the back-and-forth between the two search page windows can be quite distracting and difficult to work with. Figure 6.34 shows the subject *cognitive style*

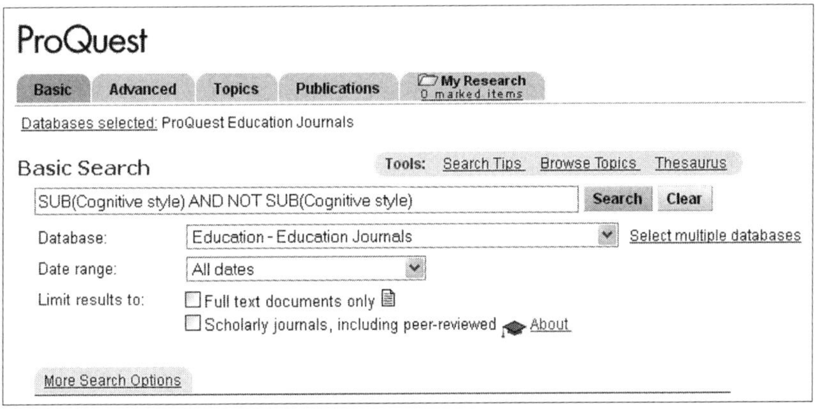

Figure 6.34   ProQuest Education Journals basic search page showing the terms
added from the thesaurus [*Screenshots and their contents published
with permission of ProQuest LLC. Further reproduction is prohibited
without permission.*]

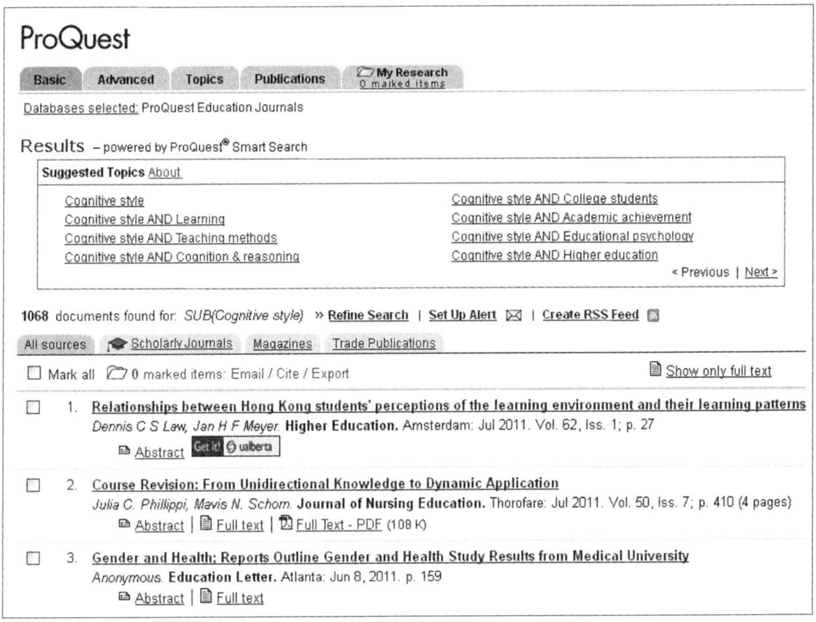

Figure 6.35   ProQuest Education Journal Suggested Topics feature [*Screenshots
and their contents published with permission of ProQuest LLC.
Further reproduction is prohibited without permission.*]

selected in the basic search bar. The interface makes use of the notation SUB as the abbreviated form of the term subject.

An effective and useful feature of the interface is the ProQuest Smart Search function. When search results are displayed, a box appears at the top of the Results set to show Suggested Topics (Figure 6.35). Suggested Topics are additional terms extracted from the thesaurus to allow users to reformulate or narrow down their searches. A novel feature of this list of thesaural term suggestions is the offer of the Boolean operator AND to save users time combining multiple terms for query reformulation. In addition to Suggested Topics, the interface provides a Topics search function that appears in the navigation bar at the top of the homepage. This is the source list of the suggested topics. It supplies a number of suggestions and ways in which multiple terms can be selected for searching the database.

In general, ProQuest makes effective use of the thesaurus to provide search support. However, thesaurus browsing is not the focus of the search user interface.

Almost all of the web-based interfaces to bibliographic databases made available by commercial vendors exploit a number of functionalities in common for thesaurus-based searching and browsing that support users in query formulation and expansion. To provide an easy-to-follow overview of thesaurus-based searching and browsing features in commercial database interfaces, Table 6.1 summarizes and compares the key thesaurus-based search functionalities made available by seven commercial providers.

A comparison of this table with an earlier examination by Shiri et al. (2002) shows that commercial database vendors have made a number of improvements in their thesaurus-based search functionalities. These changes are associated with the increased visibility of thesaurus search options, the greater use of thesaurus terms at various stages of the search process, more-effective provision of diverse thesaurus displays, and an increased flexibility in using thesauri for searching.

Important trends emerging in commercial database interfaces are the growing use of partial matching of users' terms to thesauri and of the prompting of thesaural term suggestions both at the term selection and at the results display stages. These developments stem from the emergence of exploratory search interfaces that allow users to view and explore facets before, throughout, and following a search.

In addition to the search user interfaces reviewed in this chapter, a number of commercial software providers have developed visual

Table 6.1   Comparative summary of thesaurus-based search features in commercial database interfaces

Interface features	WilsonWeb	Cambridge Scientific Abstracts	Engineering Village	Ovid	Thomson Reuters Web of Knowledge	EBSCOhost	ProQuest
Thesaurus button on main search page	X	--	X	X	--	X	X
Thesaurus search bar	X	X	X	--	X	X	X
Hypertext navigation	X	X	X	X	X	X	X
Hierarchical display	X	X	--	X	X	--	--
Alphabetical display	--	X	X	--	--	X	X
Permuted list	--	X	--	X	X	X	--
Scope notes	--	X	X	X	X	X	X
Explode option (including narrower terms)	--	--	--	X	--	X	--
Browsing previous and next thesaurus terms	X	X	X	--	--	X	X
Non-descriptor to descriptor redirection	X	--	--	X	--	X	X
Feedback on the term not found in thesaurus	X	--	X	X	--	X	--
Explicit Boolean operators	--	X	X	X	--	X	X
Display number of hits for each descriptor	--	--	--	X	--	--	--
Subject term suggestion option (term selection stage)	X	--	X	X	--	X	--
Subject term suggestion (results display stage)	X	X	X	X	X	X	X

interfaces for language thesauri rather than for information retrieval thesauri, in order to show animated visual displays of the meanings of words. Some well-known examples of visual thesaurus software developments on the web are by Thinkmap, Lexipedia (Vantage Linguistics), and Visuword (LogicalOctopus).

6.6 Conclusion

The design of thesaurus-enhanced search user interfaces is a challenging task, mainly because of the complexity of thesaural structures and the variety of thesaural elements that can be incorporated into a search user interface. This chapter discusses briefly the information search process and then provides a review of features and functionalities implemented in both research-based prototypes and commercial thesaurus-based search user interfaces.

The review of research prototypes is presented in chronological order to demonstrate the gradual evolution of user interface design functionalities and to show the scope of research and development in this area. In addition, seven well-known commercial database user interfaces are examined to provide an overview of the variety of user interface designs and features. In contrast to research prototypes, commercial database providers tend to have a relatively uniform set of thesaurus features in their interfaces.

Some of the functionalities suggested by information retrieval researchers have also been incorporated into commercial design for web-based interfaces; web technologies afford flexible ways of designing these types of interfaces. In general, many and various approaches, of both a textual and a graphical nature, have been adopted in the design and development of prototype and research-based interfaces enhanced with thesauri. Recent thesaurus-enhanced search user interfaces, both commercial and prototype, have adopted advanced visualization techniques and implemented auto-completion and term suggestion features in order to provide highly interactive and exploratory user interface experiences.

References

Agosti, M., Gradenigo, G., and Marchetti, P. G. (1992). A hypertext environment for interacting with large textual databases. *Information Processing and Management*, 28(3), 371–387.

Bates, M. J. (1990a). Where should the person stop and the information search interface start? *Information Processing and Management*, 26(5), 575–591.

Bates, M. J. (1990b). Design for a subject search interface and online thesaurus for a very large record management database. In: D. Henderson (Ed.), *Proceedings of the 53rd annual meeting of the American Society for Information Science* (pp. 20–28). Medford, NJ: Learned Information.

Beaulieu, M. (1997). Experiments of interfaces to support query expansion. *Journal of Documentation*, 53(1), 8–19.

Belkin, N. J., Marchetti, P. G., and Cool, C. (1993). BRAQUE: Design of an interface to support user interaction in information retrieval. *Information Processing and Management*, 29(3), 325–344.

Broder, A. (2002). A taxonomy of web search. *SIGIR Forum*, 36(2), 3–10.

Chan, L. M., and Pollard, R. (1988). *Thesauri used in online databases: An analytical guide*. Westport, CT: Greenwood Press.

Dalmau, M., Floyd, R., Jiao, D., and Riley, J. (2005). Integrating thesaurus relationships into search and browse in an online photograph collection. *Library Hi Tech*, 23(3), 425–452.

De Vorsey, K. L., Elson, C., Gregorev, N. P., and Hansen, J. (2006). The development of a local thesaurus to improve access to the anthropological collections of the American Museum of Natural History. *D-Lib Magazine*, 12(4). Retrieved from www.dlib.org/dlib/april06/devorsey/04devorsey. html (accessed April 15, 2011).

Efthimiadis, E. N. (1996). Query expansion. In: M. E. Williams (Ed.), *Annual review of information science and technology* (pp. 121–187). Medford, NJ: Information Today.

Ganzman, J. (1990). Criteria for the evaluation of thesaurus software. *International Classification* 17(3/4), 148–157.

Hearst, M. A. (1999). User interfaces and visualization. In: R. Baeza-Yates and B. Ribeiro-Neto (Eds.), *Modern information retrieval* (pp. 257–323). New York: ACM Press.

Hearst, M. A. (2009) *Search user interfaces*. Cambridge, UK: Cambridge University Press.

Hearst, M. A., and Karadi, C. (1997). Cat-a-Cone: An interactive interface for specifying searches and viewing retrieval results using a large category hierarchy. In: *Proceedings of the 20th annual international ACM/SIGIR conference on research and development in information retrieval of the Association for Computing Machinery Special Interest Group on Information Retrieval* (pp. 246–255). New York: ACM.

Institution of Engineering and Technology. Inspec database. www.theiet.org/ resources/inspec (accessed June 7, 2012).

Johnson, E. H. (1997). Using IODyne: Illustrations and examples. In: P. A. Cochrane and E. Johnson (Eds.), *Visualizing subject access for 21st century information resources: Proceedings of the 34th annual clinic on library applications of data processing* (pp. 80–93). Champaign, IL: University of Illinois at Champaign-Urbana, School of Library and Information Science.

Johnson, E. H., and Cochrane, P. A. (1995). A hypertextual interface for a searcher's thesaurus. In: *Digital Libraries '95: Proceedings of the second annual conference on the theory and practice of digital libraries*. June 11–13, 1995, Austin, Texas, USA. Hypermedia Research Lab, Computer Science Department, Texas A&M University.

Korn, F., and Shneiderman, B. (1995). *Navigating terminology hierarchies to access a digital library of medical images*. University of Maryland Technical Report HCIL-TR-94-03. College Park, MD: University of Maryland.

Lin, X. (1999). Visual MeSH. In: F. Gey, M. Hearst, and R. Tong (eds.) *Proceedings of the 22nd annual international ACM SIGIR conference on research and development in information retrieval (SIGIR'99)* (pp. 317–318). New York: ACM Press.

Lin, X., Hassell, L., Song, I., and Doszkocs, L. (1998). Visual interactions with web database content. In: *Workshop on new paradigms in information processing and visualization* (pp. 100–104). New York: ACM Press.

LogicalOctopus. Visuword online graphical dictionary. Retrieved from www.mpcollab.org/MPbeta1/node/1720 (accessed June 7, 2012).

McMath, C. F., Tamaru, R. S., and Rada, R. (1989). A graphical thesaurus-based information retrieval system. *International Journal of Man-Machine Studies*, 31(2), 121–147.

Milstead, J. (1990). Specifications for thesaurus software. *Information Processing and Management*, 27(2/3), 165–175.

Pollard, R. (1993). A hypertext-based thesaurus as subject browsing aid for bibliographic database. *Information Processing and Management*, 29(3), 345–357.

Pollitt, A. S., Ellis, G. P., and Smith, M. P. (1994). HIBROWSE for bibliographic databases. *Journal of Information Science*, 20(6), 413–426.

Ruecker, S. (2003). *Affordances of prospect for academic users of interpretively-tagged text collections.* PhD dissertation, University of Alberta, Edmonton, Canada.

Shiri, A. A., Revie, C., and Chowdhury, G. (2002). Thesaurus-enhanced search interfaces. *Journal of Information Science*, 28(2), 111–122.

Shiri, A., Ruecker, S., Anvik, K., and Rossello, X. (2006). Thesaurus-enhanced visual interfaces for multilingual information retrieval. *Proceedings of the American Society for Information Science and Technology (ASIS&T) annual conference*, Austin, Texas, U.S., November 3–9.

Shiri, A., Ruecker, S., Fiorentino, C., Stafford, A., Bouchard, M., and Bieber, M. (2010). Designing a semantically rich visual interface for cultural digital libraries using the UNESCO multilingual thesaurus. In: F. Sudweeks, H. Hrachovec, and C. Ess (Eds.), *Proceedings of cultural attitudes towards technology and communication 2010 conference: Cultural diversity in e-learning and/or m-learning.* University of British Columbia, Vancouver, Canada.

Shneiderman, B. (1998) *Designing the user interface: Strategies for effective human–computer interaction.* Menlo Park, CA: Addison-Wesley Longman.

Sutcliffe, A. G., Ennis, M., and Hu, J. (2000). Evaluating the effectiveness of visual user interfaces for information retrieval. *International Journal of Human-Computer Studies*, 53(5), 741–763.

Thinkmap, Inc. Visual thesaurus. Retrieved from www.thinkmap.com/visual thesaurus.jsp (accessed June 7, 2012).

Tudhope, D., Binding, C., Blocks, D., and Cunliffe, D. (2006). Query expansion via conceptual distance in thesaurus indexed collections. *Journal of Documentation*, 62(4), 509–533.

Vantage Linguistics. Lexipedia. Retrieved from www.lexipedia.com/english (accessed June 7, 2012).

Will, L. (2010). Software for building and editing thesauri. Retrieved from www.willpowerinfo.co.uk/thessoft.htm (accessed July 13, 2011).

CHAPTER 7

Design of User Interfaces for Multilingual and Meta-Thesauri

A thesaurus that exists in more than one language is generally called a *multilingual thesaurus* (Soergel, 1997). This chapter examines search user interfaces that have been enhanced with the features and functionalities of multilingual thesauri. It also reviews a number of projects that have developed meta-thesauri, with a particular focus on their user interface features and functionalities. Examples of meta-thesauri and multiple thesauri systems that have made use of the Simple Knowledge Organization System (SKOS) are presented.

7.1 Multilingual Thesauri

Aitchison et al. (2000) note that bilingual and multilingual thesauri are needed if queries are searched in more than one language. Jorna and Davies (2001) point out the importance of tools to support multilingual information retrieval, suggesting that multilingual thesauri can play a significant role in facilitating cross-cultural communication in an increasingly globalized information society. They observe the growing popularity of multilingual tools as different user groups with a variety of cultural and linguistic backgrounds search for a diverse range of information objects.

Hudon (1997) argues that the true multilingual thesaurus offers complete conceptual and terminological inventories for each of its languages and that in a multilingual thesaurus, all languages are equal. She further stresses the importance of taking into account the sociocultural and political implications of semantic solutions and display options in multilingual thesauri.

Several multilingual thesauri have been developed in Europe, Canada, and the U.S., and some of them are integrated into search user interfaces and function as searching and browsing tools across different languages. Thesaurus construction standards discuss the challenges and issues in constructing multilingual thesauri and briefly address displays and user interface issues. For instance, the new British standard (BS) ISO 25964-1:2011 *Thesauri and interoperability with other vocabularies*, which is a major revision of BS 8723 undertaken by an international committee, focuses on the use of multilingual thesauri to support searching and retrieval. This new standard is published in two parts: Part 1 is titled *Thesauri for information retrieval* and Part 2, which is published for discussion, is titled *Interoperability with other Vocabularies*. The standard states that the display of multilingual thesauri can be alphabetical, systematic, or in a correspondence table. The *Guidelines for Multilingual Thesauri*, developed by the Working Group on Guidelines for Multilingual Thesauri under the International Federation of Library Associations Classification and Indexing section, focus mainly on construction techniques and issues.

7.2 Multilingual Thesauri Search User Interfaces

A number of researchers have commented on the ways in which multilingual thesauri should be presented to the user. Soergel (1997) notes that, whether searching free-text or with controlled vocabularies, it is always useful to allow users to browse a well-displayed hierarchy of concepts and that hierarchical display and guidance through facets and their concepts must be available in the language of the user. Hudon (2003) comments that matters relating to display have consistently received little attention, either in the scientific and professional literature or in the standards and textbooks relating to thesaurus construction.

Jorna and Davies (2001) argue that multilingual thesauri should be structured semantically, rather than alphabetically, to allow for an equal representation of languages involved, as well as to ensure that the conceptual context of each term and its translations are presented in a more explicit manner. Using the facet analysis technique, they developed a multilingual thesaurus for English, French, and German called InfoDEFT, which uses faceted classification. The thesaurus has five facets, namely, *things*, *people*, *activities*, *places*, and *environment*. The languages are treated equally, and users are able to switch among languages and facets to browse a particular term or its related terms. Figure 7.1 shows the key facets and an English language entry along with options for switching to German or French.

This type of interface allows searchers to see the whole context of the term, as well as to navigate easily without losing that context. There are links to the nearest equivalent pages in the other two languages, so that users can immediately compare translations of their search terms and respective contexts.

Numerous long-established multilingual thesauri that are integrated into searching and browsing user interfaces are now available on the web. One of these is EuroVoc, a multilingual, multidisciplinary thesaurus covering the activities of the European Union, particularly the European Parliament; it contains terms in 22 European Union languages. The interface requires that the searcher select a specific language and allows for browsing by high-level subject categories and alphabetical permuted terms. When a particular term is searched in the thesaurus, users are able to see the details for that term and a list of equivalent terms in the 22 languages supported by the thesaurus. Equivalent terms are also hyperlinked, and if the user clicks on any of them, the term and its details in the chosen language appear on the screen. The content language also changes automatically. There is an option for users to change the language of the interface as well. However, it should be noted that, because of the large number of languages supported by this thesaurus, the interface is not

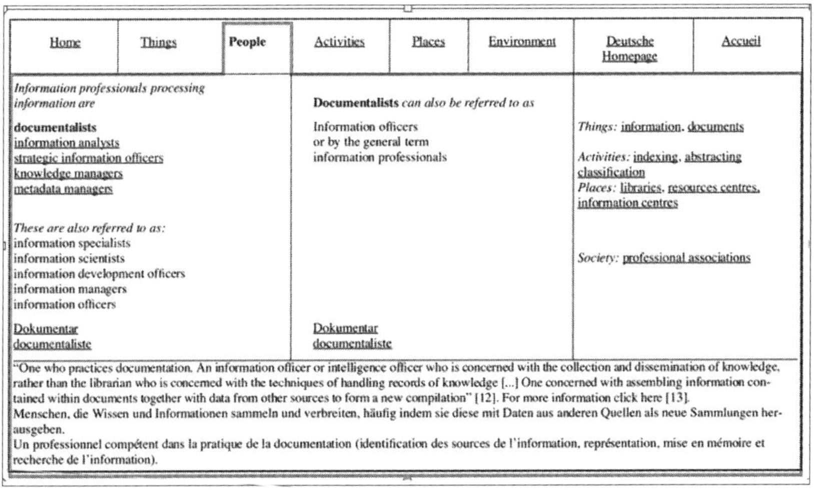

Home	Things	People	Activities	Places	Environment	Deutsche Homepage	Accueil

Information professionals processing information are

documentalists
information analysts
strategic information officers
knowledge managers
metadata managers

These are also referred to as:
information specialists
information scientists
information development officers
information managers
information officers

Dokumentar
documentaliste

Documentalists *can also be referred to as*
Information officers
or by the general term
information professionals

Dokumentar
documentaliste

Things: information, documents

Activities: indexing, abstracting classification
Places: libraries, resources centres, information centres

Society: professional associations

"One who practices documentation. An information officer or intelligence officer who is concerned with the collection and dissemination of knowledge, rather than the librarian who is concerned with the techniques of handling records of knowledge [...] One concerned with assembling information contained within documents together with data from other sources to form a new compilation" [12]. For more information click here [13].
Menschen, die Wissen und Informationen sammeln und verbreiten, häufig indem sie diese mit Daten aus anderen Quellen als neue Sammlungen herausgeben.
Un professionnel compétent dans la pratique de la documentation (identification des sources de l'information, représentation, mise en mémoire et recherche de l'information).

Figure 7.1   InfoDEFT multilingual thesaurus interface

designed for users to view details of a search term in multiple languages simultaneously.

Figure 7.2 shows a search for the term *diritto commerciale*, the Italian equivalent for *commercial law*. On the left side of the interface, the Italian term is presented, along with its narrower terms, related terms, and the micro-thesaurus terms. "A micro-thesaurus is a specialized thesaurus that is mapped onto and is entirely integrated within the hierarchical structure of some broader thesaurus, that is called a macro-thesaurus" (Aitchison et al., 2000, p. 177). On the right are the equivalents to the Italian term in all 22 languages, with the Italian term highlighted.

The Advanced Search feature allows users to choose from a flexible range of search options, including Exact Match Search, Starting With, Ending With, and Containing. In addition, Advanced Search allows searchers to narrow a search to preferred terms, non-preferred terms, acronyms, or scope notes.

EuroVoc offers an alternative visual display of a term and its details called Map. Figure 7.3 shows a map for *diritto commerciale*. The colors red, yellow, and blue represent narrower terms, related terms, and micro-thesaurus terms, respectively. It should be noted, however, that the visual display presents a term in one language only, that chosen by the searcher.

AGROVOC (from the Food and Agriculture Organization of the United Nations) is a multilingual agricultural thesaurus of 40,000

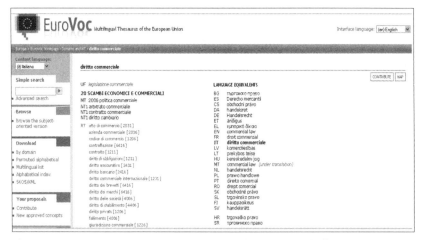

Figure 7.2   A search for *diritto commerciale (commercial law)* in the EuroVoc multilingual thesaurus [© *European Union, 2010, eurovoc.europa.eu*]

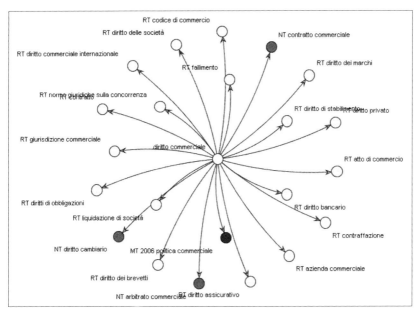

Figure 7.3   A search for *diritto commerciale* in the EuroVoc Thesaurus Map feature [© *European Union, 2010, eurovoc.europa.eu*]

terms in 20 languages. Used in the indexing of the AGRIS (International System for the Agricultural Sciences and Technology) database, AGROVOC is a global public domain database with 2.6 million structured bibliographical records on agricultural science and technology. The AGROVOC database thesaurus interface allows both browsing and searching. Users are able to search for terms to add to their search statements.

While AGROVOC supports 20 languages, the AGRIS database interface provides for searching in only the five United Nations official languages. Figure 7.4 shows the AGRIS database interface, with the AGROVOC search function on the right side of the interface.

Users must choose one of the languages at the top of the page if they want to search in a language other than English. The AGROVOC search function is very limited in that it does not allow effective browsing of the thesaurus.

The search function depicted in Figure 7.4 shows a general search for *natural*, which displays a brief list of terms that start with the word *natural*. Two query formulation features are available: The double arrow sign (<<) allows a user to search for the particular thesaurus term, and the plus sign allows a user to refine the search using that

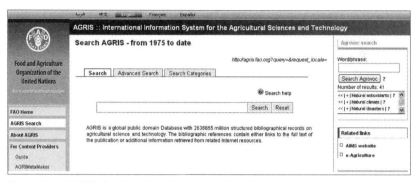

Figure 7.4   AGRIS database interface with AGROVOC search function

term. The latter is used when the user has already put a term in the AGRIS search bar. The Boolean operators are very challenging to work with and would be difficult for a user who is not familiar with advanced searching.

It should be noted that there is no cross-language information retrieval function within the AGRIS database, even though both AGROVOC and AGRIS provide multilingual functionalities. For example, searching for a Spanish thesaurus term in the AGRIS interface does not retrieve any documents. When users search in Spanish in AGROVOC, they can add terms to the query. However, the retrieved results will be in English, and users have to look at the details of each retrieved document to be able to see the AGROVOC Spanish term that was searched for.

In general, it could be noted that the AGROVOC is not used effectively within the AGRIS interface. For instance, a larger browsing and searching space for exploring AGROVOC and its very useful language features would provide a more interactive and engaging experience for users. The AGROVOC thesaurus has a number of especially useful capabilities and display options that could be incorporated into AGRIS to provide more effective search experiences.

The European Thesaurus on International Relations and Area Studies is a multilingual thesaurus containing around 8,000 terms arranged in a hierarchical manner. The thesaurus is available within the International Relations and Area Studies Gateway (IREON) from the German Information Network. The thesaurus supports nine languages: English, French, German, Spanish, Italian, Polish, Czech, Croatian, and Russian. The thesaurus is available and advertised on the IREON Gateway homepage.

Figure 7.5 shows a search for *civil defence facilities* in the IREON thesaurus. A link on the left navigation column provides access to the thesaurus. Users must choose a particular language to start their search. Once the term is searched, the magnifying glass icon in front of the thesaurus terms allows users to carry out a database search using any of the terms. Following the initial thesaurus term search, the translation option becomes available just below the main search bar, allowing users to choose a different language to see the equivalent term and its broader, narrower, and related terms.

The example depicted in Figure 7.5 shows the searcher has clicked the Translation box for German, which prompts the display of German thesaurus terms at the bottom of the page. However, users have to click on an arrow, not easily accessible, to see the equivalent terms. While the interface allows users to view equivalent terms in as many languages as they wish, equivalent terms are neither navigable nor clickable and do not have the magnifying class icon for searching in the IREON databases. At the same time, a search for the term *civil defence facilities* in British English, for example, will retrieve results in German, French, and other languages, depending on the availability of documents in those languages. This example indicates that the thesaurus can be used effectively for cross-lingual search and retrieval.

The interface also provides thesaurus browsing features, namely, alphabetic and systematic lists of thesaurus terms, both available on the right side of the interface. Figure 7.6 shows a search for *power*

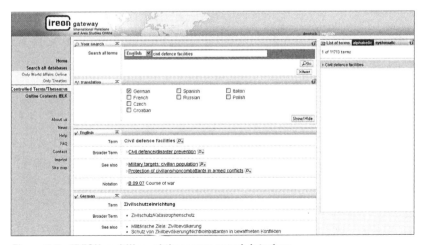

Figure 7.5   IREON multilingual thesaurus search interface

politics and the two browsing options. If a user browses either list and selects a term of interest, that term and its associated terms will appear at the bottom left side of the browsing option, with the magnifying glass icon available for searching the database. The browsing options are useful for providing a context for the thesaural term and for reformulating the query.

Although the IREON interface makes effective use of the thesaurus to provide searching, browsing, and navigation facilities, the language options are not sufficiently flexible to, for instance, allow users to choose an equivalent term for searching without having to copy and paste it into the main search box.

The European Language Social Science Thesaurus (ELSST) is a broad-based multilingual thesaurus for the social sciences that was produced by the U.K. Data Archive and funded by the European Union as part of the Language Independent Metadata Browsing of European Resources (LIMBER) project. ELSST is used by the Council of European Social Sciences Data Archives (CESSDA) portal. It was derived from an in-house English monolingual Humanities and Social Science Electronic Thesaurus (Balkan et al., 2002).

ELSST is currently available in four languages—English, French, German, and Spanish—and in various formats. Effectively incorporated into the CESSDA portal and browsable from it, the thesaurus supports both searching and browsing tasks.

Users can choose the Browse by Keyword option on the left side navigation bar, as shown in Figure 7.7 for the search term *industrial*

Figure 7.6   **Alphabetical and systematic browsing options on the IREON multilingual thesaurus interface**

tribunals, and then drill down the hierarchy. The concepts from the ELSST multilingual thesaurus are displayed in multilevel hierarchies, and the initial top-level terms can be expanded to show the narrower terms in the hierarchy. Note that not all the thesaurus concepts are presented in this hierarchical tree. Only those concepts are listed that will lead, either directly or through a narrower term, to resources being discovered.

A free-text search can be performed on all areas of the metadata by entering a search term or phrase in the search box at the top left side of the interface. When the search terms match a concept in the thesaurus, the search is performed in all the languages ELLST supports, reflected in the drop-down list; a complete list of resources containing the search term and its language equivalents is displayed in the panel on the right side. Related terms are also offered as suggestions for refining or broadening the search. Furthermore, the bottom of the results display section offers the option to narrow the search to one language. In addition to cross-language retrieval of records, the interface has a language option that allows users to change the language of the thesaurus. This means that the left-side navigation feature can be used to browse the thesaurus in all of the languages supported.

As shown in Figure 7.7 at the bottom right side of the page, users can view related terms, the top term, or narrower terms. One of the advantages of this interface design lies in its integration of thesaurus browsing, searching, and results display; users can navigate around the thesaurus, select a term, and view the results immediately, without

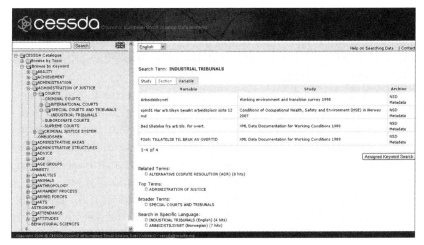

Figure 7.7   ELSST Multilingual thesaurus search in CESSDA

losing the context. Another advantage of the interface is that the multilingual thesaurus is used effectively for multilingual information retrieval; whichever language users choose for searching the collection, the results in different languages will be presented to them. However, it should be noted that one of the limitations of the language features is that the interface operates on the basis of the selection of individual languages and that viewing the thesaurus term equivalents simultaneously in multiple languages within the same interface is not supported.

The Centre for Agricultural Bioscience (CAB) Thesaurus (2011) is a large multilingual agricultural thesaurus used by the CAB Abstract database for indexing and retrieval in three languages—English, Spanish, and Portuguese—with a drop-down list of all three for searching and browsing. There are alphabetical and hierarchical browsing options for each language. Users can view a list of terms, terms and relationships, or terms and hierarchies. Another useful feature of the interface is the choice between Terms begin with and Terms contain, options that provide access to alphabetical and permuted indexes.

Figure 7.8 shows a search for the Portuguese term *florestas*, or *forests*. The English and Spanish equivalents are displayed at the top of the term list, along with broader and narrower terms. Users can click the equivalent terms to view a term and its relationships in that particular selected language.

This type of hyperlinking allows easy multilingual navigation within the thesaurus. Users can then select and include thesaurus terms for searching by using the Add icon that appears after each term. Clicking on the Add icon prompts the selected term to appear in the top right box. Once a query has been formulated, the user can send it to CAB Direct, the CAB database available to subscribers, or to search engines such as Google or Yahoo!

The default interface feature for combining terms is the Boolean OR operator. If users want to create more-sophisticated search statements, however, they have to enter the AND and NOT operators manually. An improved functionality would be to make these two operators available for selection in the vicinity of the search box, because users might not realize the interface supports them, too.

A disadvantage of the interface is that the Add icon for choosing terms to be searched is not available for selecting term equivalents in other languages unless the user clicks on an equivalent term and switches to its language. This indicates that, even though the interface

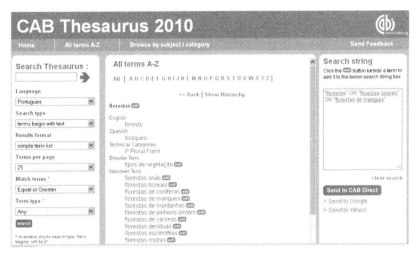

Figure 7.8   A Portuguese search for *florestas* in the CAB Thesaurus interface

provides flexible features for browsing and searching for terms in the three languages supported, cross-language searches are not easy and straightforward, particularly if the user wants to make use of Boolean operators. While the interface provides useful thesaurus-based searching and browsing in the three languages, query reformulation functionalities are not available that would provide users with seamless access either to the Results display screen or to the thesaurus throughout the search process.

A recent project funded by the Social Sciences and Humanities Research Council (SSHRC) investigated the design and development of a number of visual user interfaces for the UNESCO Multilingual Thesaurus for searching the UNESCO digital library in three languages, English, French, and Spanish (Shiri et al., 2010). Two prototype functional interfaces were developed for the thesaurus, Searchling and T-Saurus, both available on the web (www.thesaurus browser.info). The main ideas behind them are to make effective use of the multilingual features of the thesaurus and to make language options available for browsing, searching, and retrieval.

An initial version of the Searchling interface was designed and developed for the Government of Canada Core Subject Thesaurus, which is a bilingual thesaurus to support the searching of the Government of Canada site as well as Canada Portal (Stafford et al., 2008). This interface provides hierarchical, alphabetical, and high-level facet browsing of the UNESCO thesaurus and provides relationship details for the thesaural terms. The thesaurus terms in all three languages are available for viewing and choosing; clicking on a Spanish term, for instance, positions it as the main term at the top of the interface. The number of documents for each thesaurus term in each language is also shown following each term.

The interface provides explicit Boolean operators to support the creation of sophisticated search statements. A search term pool allows users to keep all of the terms they have selected visible and available for later use in the search process. The query formulation option also allows users to quickly switch between languages to view equivalent terms in a language of interest. The interface is designed in such a way that it supports cross-language information retrieval. Users can choose one, two, or all three languages to view results in those languages.

The example depicted in Figure 7.9 illustrates results displayed in French and English for the English language term *academies of science*. The results display pane is shown at the bottom of the search interface. Searchers enjoy seamless access to the thesaurus for query reformulation or expansion.

Figure 7.10 shows the result display pane in Searchling, which appears at the bottom of the search interface. The interface is

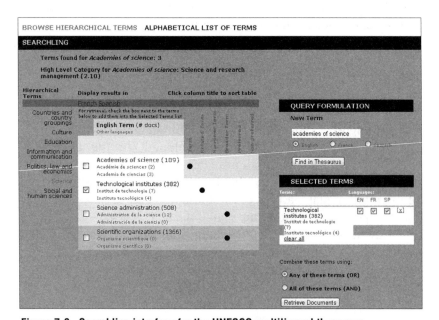

Figure 7.9 Searchling interface for the UNESCO multilingual thesaurus

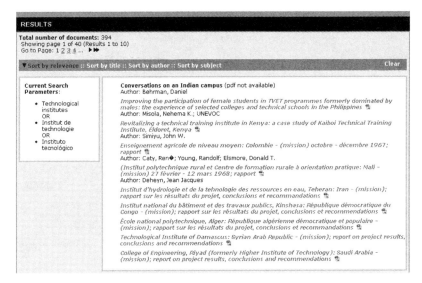

Figure 7.10 Searchling results display interface

designed to support cross-language information retrieval. The results display section shows the user's current search terms and the Boolean operators used. The retrieved results can be sorted by such metadata elements as relevance, title, author, and subject.

The second interface, T-Saurus, was designed to provide a more interactive and more visual user interface for the UNESCO multilingual thesaurus (Shiri et al., 2010). It uses the power of multilingual thesauri to support searching, browsing, and information retrieval.

Like Searchling, T-Saurus provides searching and thesaural browsing in both alphabetical and hierarchical modes. The multilingual options support, in all three languages, functionalities for browsing, query formulation, and results presentation.

Figure 7.11 shows a search for the Spanish term *biblioteca escolar*, or *school libraries*. The language option at the top left allows users to choose one primary language. The alphabetical browsing feature above it on the left shows thesaurus terms in all three languages. The main selected term, *biblioteca escolar* in this example, appears in the central box in the middle of the screen. Using the control option on the bottom right, users can view broader, narrower, and related terms for the selected term, as well as scope notes. These thesaural terms then appear surrounding the main selected term in the screen center.

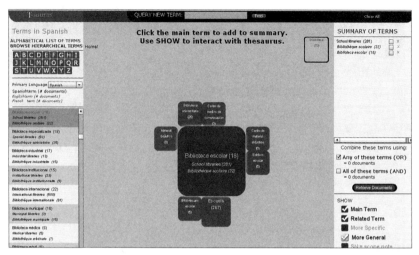

Figure 7.11   T-Saurus user interface

The interface also shows how many documents are available for retrieval in each language.

When users decide to add a term to their query, they do so by clicking on its square in the center of the screen, which adds it to the Summary of Terms list, or term pool, at the top right of the interface. Users can have the functional flexibilities to add as many terms as they wish, delete them at any time, choose to keep them in only one language rather than in multiple languages, or combine them using the Boolean operators displayed underneath the list of selected terms.

When they have finished formulating their query, they click Retrieve Documents to view the results, as shown in Figure 6.20 earlier in this book. The green box in the middle of the interface shows the thesaurus term and its French and English equivalents, as well as the number of documents indexed in each language. The red dots represent the results retrieved for the chosen term(s) in the language(s) selected.

Hovering the mouse over the red dots shows the title for each retrieved document. Users can click on a single red dot to retrieve a particular document. In addition, a textual list of results appears in the bottom right corner of the screen. Searchers can also change their context if they switch to searching or thesaural browsing for further query reformulation.

Several other multilingual thesauri are available online, but they are not integrated as essential parts of web-based searching and browsing systems.

A number of bilingual thesauri have been created in Canada; again, however, the majority function as stand-alone thesauri available on the web and are not integrated into search systems for browsing and searching. Here are some examples of these online bilingual thesauri:

- The Canadian Literacy Thesaurus

- Canadian thesaurus of Construction Science and Technology

- HIV/AIDS Treatment Thesaurus

- eHealth Thesaurus (Health Canada)

One Canadian bilingual thesaurus that does serve as an integral part of a search system is the Statistics Canada thesaurus in English and French (Figure 7.12). The interface provides searching and alphabetical browsing, as well as thesaural browsing by high-level facets. To start browsing or searching, users choose one of the two supported languages. If, for example, a user chooses to view details of an English thesaurus term, the French equivalent will be shown.

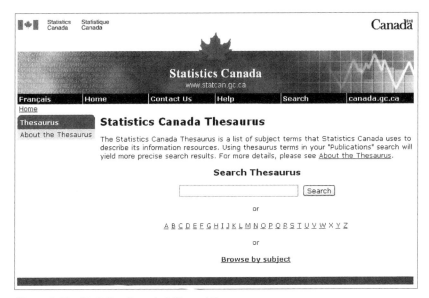

Figure 7.12 Statistics Canada bilingual thesaurus

However, the thesaurus can be searched only in the first language selected; users would not be able to choose the French term to submit to the search system. The French and English thesaurus terms are maintained in separate lists.

Figure 5.2, earlier in this book, shows a snapshot of the Statistics Canada thesaurus search for the term *economic accounts*. Users can search either the site or the library catalog of Statistics Canada.

However, even though the thesaurus is a well-constructed controlled vocabulary, one of the disadvantages of the interface is that it does not allow simultaneous bilingual searching and browsing. Because the interface is not designed for cross-language retrieval, users who choose, for example, the English version of the thesaurus will be able to search or browse only the English thesaurus and retrieve only English documents; the same holds true for French language searchers.

One of the useful features of the interface is that, when a set of documents is retrieved, searchers can reformulate their queries by taking advantage of a refining feature called Subject, which is displayed in Figure 7.13 on the left side of the interface for the previously searched term *tax rebates*. However, the interface does not indicate the number of documents available for each term at the query formulation stage. Users are provided with an indication of the number of documents after they have received results from their initial thesaurus-based search.

Users can narrow their search by using the subject terms displayed. It should be noted, however, that the thesaurus is not available at this stage for further searching and browsing unless searchers go back to the initial thesaurus page.

7.3 Meta-Thesauri and Subject Interoperability

A meta-thesaurus is a synthesis of existing controlled vocabularies; it is achieved by linking, merging, and integrating them. The constituent thesauri are mapped onto one another, creating pointers from every concept in one thesaurus to the most equivalent concept in the others. The vocabularies are also merged, creating a more enriched and comprehensive knowledge base (Aitchison et al., 2000).

The history of meta-thesauri—or, more precisely, of the history of discussions about the issues relating to the integration, merger,

Figure 7.13   Statistics Canada thesaurus-based search: Query reformulation using the subject feature

reconciliation, and mapping of thesauri, classification schemes, and other types of controlled vocabularies—dates back to the 1970s.

Following the development of the web, the term *interoperability* became pervasive in the literature (Saumure and Shiri, 2008), in large part because of the rapid increase in the number, volume, and availability of digital collections; the proliferation of metadata formats and standards; and the need to connect and integrate tools, resources, and knowledge organization systems. The terms *semantic interoperability* and *subject interoperability* have been used in the literature to refer to the various methods for creating connections among knowledge organization tools such as thesauri and classification schemes in order to support cross-browsing and cross-searching of various digital collections. For instance, Hunter (2001) uses the term *semantic interoperability* to refer to the process of creating inter-thesaurus semantic relationships.

Since then, numerous projects have investigated subject interoperability using such terms as *reconciliation of thesauri* (Neville, 1970), *integration* (Niehoff, 1976; Dahlberg, 1982), *compatibility* (Lancaster and Smith, 1983; Chamis, 1991), *merging* (Milli and Rada, 1988), *switching* (Silvester, 1993), and *mapping* (Whitehead, 1990; Chaplan, 1995). A detailed account of these terms and their definitions is provided by Zeng and Chan (2004).

Recently, a number of European projects have addressed the issue of subject interoperability across languages. For instance, Content Analysis, Retrieval and Metadata: Effective Networking, known as CARMEN, is a German project that focused on the creation of "cross concordances of classifications and thesauri." Its aim was to allow an integrated search for subject aspects of distributed data repositories, assisted by cross-concordances to address the conceptual differences among applied thesauri and classifications.

Another European project that addressed subject interoperability in the context of multilingual content was Multilingual Access to Subjects (MACS). This project aimed to provide multilingual subject access to library catalogs through the creation of links among three subject heading lists in English, French, and German (Landry, 2000).

McCulloch and Macgregor (2008) studied equivalence mapping of four controlled vocabularies for terminology services and provided a list of validated match types that should be used for the development of terminology-mapping initiatives. These match types include exact match, exact match with intervening characters, plural form, species-genus subordination, genus-species superordination, part-of-speech difference, further specification, spelling variation, and concept match.

The American National Standards Institute–National Information Standards Organization (ANSI/NISO) Z39.19 *Guidelines for the Construction, Format, and Management of Monolingual Controlled Vocabularies* provides a specific section on the notion of thesaural interoperability to support different types of users. The standard refers to using the searcher's preferred query vocabulary to metasearch multiple content resources as one of the interoperability needs that controlled vocabulary designers should take into account.

There is substantial literature on the concept of interoperability for knowledge organization systems. Zeng and Chan (2004) provide a very useful account of the trends and issues in establishing interoperability among knowledge organization systems, as well as of the methodological issues involved in creating, sharing, and maintaining links among several different knowledge organization systems.

McCulloch (2004) notes that the vast variety of knowledge organization schemes has resulted in disparate terminologies being implemented throughout various sections of web-based search systems and services. This development, in turn, has given rise to marked differences across sectors and subject areas, rendering cross-sectoral or multidisciplinary searching an arduous undertaking for users.

These incongruities and obstacles point to the importance of subject and semantic interoperability across multiple collections and knowledge organization schemes. The High Level Thesaurus (HILT) project at the Centre for Digital Library Research at the University of Strathclyde has been experimenting with the development of various terminology services since 2000 (Nicholson, 2002). Its website provides detailed information about the projects and demonstrator services.

Focusing on cross-searching and cross-browsing of distributed digital libraries and collections, Nicholson and Shiri (2003) suggest that interoperability in subject searching and browsing is a key issue and will likely become more important as we strive to take advantage of the potential inherent in the semantic web. The next section focuses on the discussion and evaluation of examples of those user interfaces to meta-thesauri that support cross-browsing and cross-searching of various digital collections and materials.

7.4 Search User Interfaces for Meta-Thesauri

The Unified Medical Language System (UMLS), developed by the U S. National Library of Medicine, is a long-standing, and the largest, biomedical meta-thesaurus. It has more than 2 million names for some 900,000 concepts from more than 60 families of biomedical vocabularies, including the Medical Subject Headings (MeSH) and Systematized Nomenclature of Medicine—Clinical Terms (SNOMED), as well as 12 million relations among these concepts (Bodenreider, 2004). The website of the UMLS describes its role:

> The Unified Medical Language System (UMLS) integrates and distributes key terminology, classification and coding standards, and associated resources to promote creation of more effective and interoperable biomedical information systems and services, including electronic health records. All UMLS Knowledge Sources and associated software tools are free of charge to U.S. and international users.

The UMLS meta-thesaurus has been used in several information retrieval studies and has many applications, including enhancement of medical search engines, use in text and web mining of medical information, and terminology searching in the medical domain. Figure 7.14 shows a snapshot of the UMLS meta-thesaurus tree display, in which various controlled vocabularies are available for browsing and searching. The search function allows a user to search across all the controlled vocabularies held in UMLS. In the left pane, searchers can choose a controlled vocabulary to browse, and if they select a particular term, terminological details of the selected term will appear in the right pane.

The UMLS has a particularly useful term suggestion feature that shows a number of useful terms for users to choose from and to narrow down their search. One of the key advantages of the interface is that it is easy to use and provides users with immediate feedback for both browsing and searching the meta-thesaurus. In addition, the integrated interface design view allows users to choose a vocabulary category or search for the term and view the results within the same interface. This type of interface design ensures that users do not lose the context of the search and at the same time can view details as they wish. Figure 7.15 shows a search for the term *restraining*.

The UMLS meta-thesaurus is a sophisticated and rich vocabulary that can be incorporated in various ways into biomedical search and

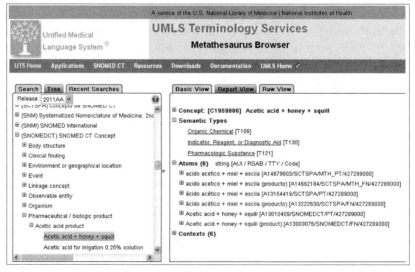

Figure 7.14 UMLS meta-thesaurus tree display

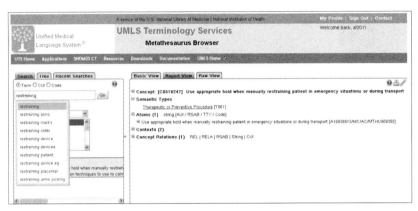

Figure 7.15   Suggestion feature in the UMLS search for *restraining*

retrieval services such as medical portals, digital libraries, subject gateways, and institutional repositories. The meta-thesaurus has a web browser that can be installed locally and an application programming interface for querying the UMLS data within specific applications. Users need to request a license and a UMLS Terminology Services account.

The HILT project, mentioned earlier, investigated subject interoperability and the cross-searching and browsing of distributed services among the archives, libraries, museums, and electronic services sectors in the U.K. The project was funded by the U.K. Joint Information Systems Committee (JISC), which provides leadership and support to U.K. educational organizations at a local, national, and international level. To develop a switching mechanism that would support subject searching across numerous higher education digital collections, the project made use of several knowledge organization systems, including the MeSH, the UNESCO thesaurus, the Library of Congress Subject Headings, and the Dewey Decimal Classification (DDC) system (Nicholson and Shiri, 2003). The HILT project made use of the DDC classification system as a switching language or scheme for the translation of equivalent terms in the other controlled vocabularies. The project also developed a terminologies server with a user interface for cross-searching and cross-browsing (Shiri et al., 2004).

Figure 7.16 shows the homepage of the HILT pilot interface, highlighting a search for the term *teeth*. The homepage consists of a search bar, a brief description of the service, a link to search tips, and DDC-specific subject categories for browsing.

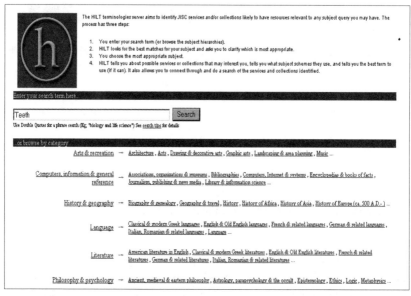

Figure 7.16   Homepage of the HILT pilot terminologies service

Figure 7.17 shows the disambiguation stage of the HILT pilot service, with possible options retrieved from DDC. At this stage, the user contextualizes a search term and decides which option to choose. A number of possible options and their contexts in terms of the DDC hierarchy are presented, and a button labeled More Results enables users to search for additional similar results.

When searchers select one of the options, they will be taken to the next stage, called the "collection selection stage," which is illustrated in Figure 7.18. This page includes a variety of features: a search bar; the DDC hierarchy for the selected term; a browsable list of JISC collections retrieved; information on the subject scheme used, with mapping from the unprocessed DDC number to the appropriate term in the subject scheme used by the highlighted collection; the DDC number for the collection; and a link to the host service search screen option.

Renardus (Heery et al., 2001) is a project funded by the European Union and established to create a collaborative framework for European subject gateways that would benefit both users, in terms of enhanced services, and the gateways themselves, in terms of shared solutions. An important part of the Renardus service is its attempt to

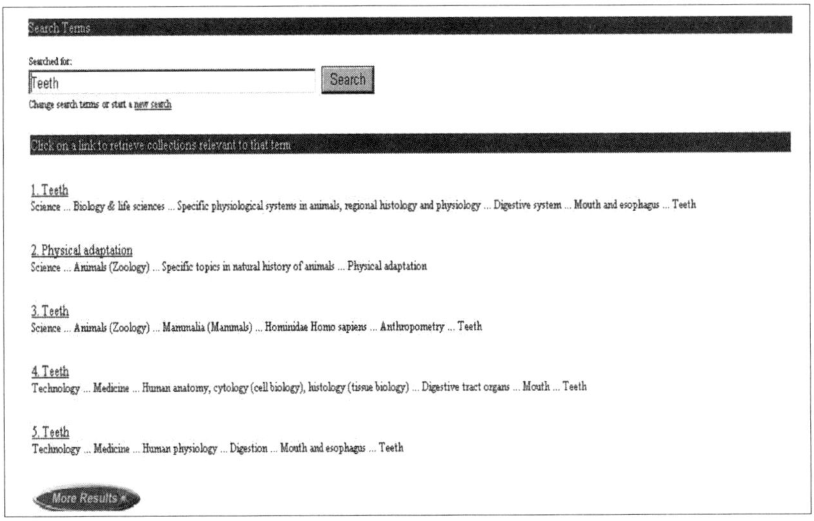

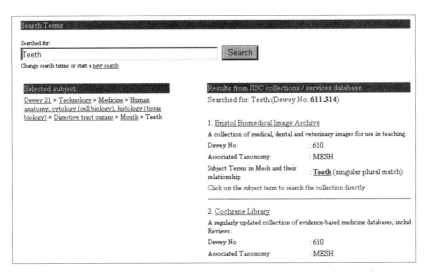

Figure 7.17 Disambiguation page of the HILT pilot terminologies service

Figure 7.18 Collection selection page of the HILT pilot terminologies service

provide some kind of subject directory browsing service across the participating gateways.

The classification scheme chosen by the project to create a central browse structure was the DDC system. The mapping was made from the DDC to the subject browse hierarchies used by participating gateways. However, a number of classification schemes and thesauri are used by individual subject gateways, so they have been asked to map their classification systems to DDC.

The DDC mapping information is used in two different ways by the Renardus prototype: first, to create the cross-browse service and second, to provide information for the advanced search feature. The cross-browse feature is designed to allow users to navigate through the subject hierarchies of the DDC classification and to "jump" from a chosen class to related (i.e., mapped) classes and directories in the local subject gateways. This type of navigation can be called *browse and jump*.

The Renardus system specifies the different equivalencies and degrees of overlap in the user interface. This approach allows users to visualize the resources in the context of their local browsing structures and to continue browsing there, as shown in Figure 7.19 for the search term *mining and related operations*. The upper part of every page displays the available categories in the relevant section of the hierarchy, with links for searchers to proceed to all levels above and one level below. The lower half of the browsing pages shows one or more links to related resource collections. Also displayed are the local classification caption, the local classification code, and the icon of the gateway to which the user would "jump" when clicking on the link. The related collections are presented in a ranked order according to the recorded mapping relationship: Fully equivalent classes are displayed first, and minor overlapping classes last, thus encouraging the user to explore initially the collections that are closest in coverage to the chosen DDC class (Koch et al., 2001).

The Renardus project also developed a graphical navigation interface (Figure 7.20) to support visual overview of all the available categories that surround a chosen subject term, normally at one level above and two levels below within the hierarchy. Colors are used to help display the selected class within its context, as well as all other classes that contain mappings. This feature is intended to increase the speed of navigation by searchers of the browse structure and to provide an immediate subject overview. Clicking on categories within the graphical display shows the relevant Renardus browsing page for the subject of interest.

The Biocomplexity Thesaurus, maintained by the U.S. Geological Survey's National Biological Information Infrastructure (NBII) program, was the product of the merging of multiple thesauri in the areas of biology, ecology, environmental sciences, and sustainability. It is used to facilitate and improve access to information. The NBII

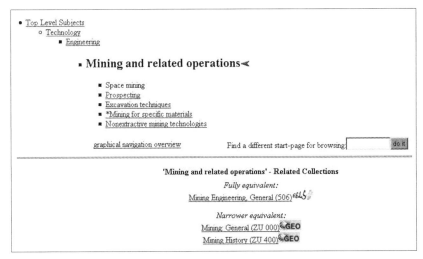

- Top Level Subjects
  - Technology
    - Engineering

    ▪ Mining and related operations◄

      ▪ Space mining
      ▪ Prospecting
      ▪ Excavation techniques
      ▪ *Mining for specific materials
      ▪ Nonextractive mining technologies

      graphical navigation overview   Find a different start-page for browsing: [   ] do it

      'Mining and related operations' - Related Collections

      Fully equivalent:
      Mining Engineering, General (506)ᵉᵉᴸˢ

      Narrower equivalent:
      Mining: General (ZU 000)GEO
      Mining History (ZU 400)GEO

Figure 7.19   Renardus DDC browsing page for *mining and related operations*

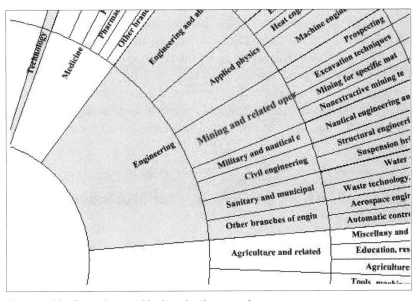

Figure 7.20   Renardus graphical navigation overview

makes use of the thesaurus behind the scenes, mainly as a search term suggestion facility. The large size of the thesaurus makes it a suitable entry vocabulary for searching the NBII collections. Although the NBII program was terminated in January 2012, the fully functional Biocomplexity Thesaurus is available on the U.S. Geological Survey website.

Figure 7.21 illustrates a search for the term *microbial contamination*. The retrieved results are shown, along with a list of expandable Related Topics terms at the upper right side of the screen. These terms are all thesaurus terms. Depending on the availability of Broader, Narrower, and Related Terms, the interface provides the user with additional terms. The See More option at the lower right corner of the Related Topics list allows users to explore additional terms associated with the searched term.

It should be noted that the NBII project was working closely with partners in the European Environment Agency (EEA) on a prototype to provide multilingual searching capabilities to both the NBII and EEA, as well as other global resources, through semantic interoperability between the Biocomplexity Thesaurus and the GEneral Multilingual Environmental Thesaurus (GEMET; Access Innovations, 2011). The demonstration versions of the NBII/GEMET thesaurus web service are available on the Biocomplexity Thesaurus website, and both are encoded in SKOS format. The web services developed for meta-searching and browsing of the two thesauri make use of the SKOS format to create semantic interoperability.

Gray et al. (2010) report the design of Vocabulary Explorer, a user interface for multiple astronomical vocabularies that is also encoded in SKOS format. The authors used the International Astronomical

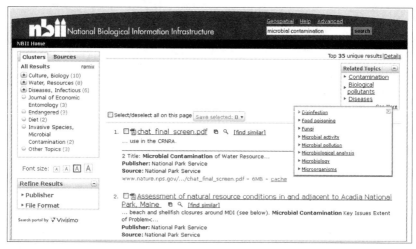

Figure 7.21   Search for *microbial contamination* on the National Biological Information Infrastructure website

Union Thesaurus, the International Virtual Observatory Alliance Thesaurus, and Astronomy Visualization Metadata, as well as journal article descriptors. The Vocabulary Explorer interface allows these controlled vocabularies to be searched and browsed by users, and query terms may find matches in some of them.

The Vocabulary Explorer uses the Terrier Information Retrieval Platform with the Porter Stemmer to index and search the vocabulary concepts. The system weights all controlled vocabulary terms for their exact or partial match with the terms submitted by users. This eliminates the problems of singular or plural search terms and case sensitivity. The interface has the ability to match concepts across vocabularies.

Figure 7.22 shows a search for the term *star*, with the result "Stars" from the journal article keywords expanded. Under the Equivalent Concepts heading in the screenshot, there is a link to the concept "3. Star" from the Astronomy Visualization Metadata vocabulary. The mapped vocabularies are shown on the right-hand side of the screen below the heading Configuration. Under the heading Narrower Terms are links to the vocabulary concepts in the journal keywords vocabulary that represent a narrower relationship with the *stars* concept.

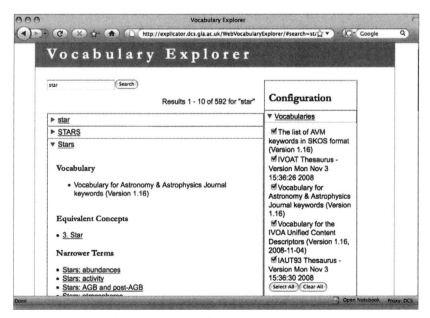

Figure 7.22   A search for *star* in Vocabulary Explorer

Also found here are links to concepts with a narrow match mapping. There are similar headings for Broader Terms and Related Terms.

Helping Interdisciplinary Vocabulary Engineering (HIVE) is a project headed by the Metadata Research Center at the University of North Carolina's School of Information and Library Science, working with several institutional partners. HIVE is both a model and a system that supports automatic metadata generation by drawing descriptors from multiple controlled vocabularies encoded according to the SKOS standard (Greenberg et al., 2011). Among the controlled vocabularies to which the HIVE vocabulary server provides access are AGROVOC, the Library of Congress Subject Headings, MeSH, NBII's Biocomplexity Thesaurus, and the Getty Thesaurus of Geographic Names. The Concept Browser allows users to choose any of these controlled vocabularies for searching.

The user interface provides search and browsing functionalities for all of the controlled vocabularies. Figure 7.23 shows a search for the term *water pollution* in MeSH, with mapped terms displayed from other controlled vocabularies. The complete record for the search term appears at the bottom of the screen. The interface provides quick and easy access to all the controlled vocabularies, and users can search or browse the terms from a selected controlled vocabulary either alphabetically or hierarchically. Another useful and interesting browsing feature is that users can quickly select or click on a mapped term from a different controlled vocabulary. Because all these controlled vocabularies are encoded in SKOS format, the interface also allows users to view the SKOS version of every term from these vocabularies.

A particularly effective current example of vocabulary integration in the context of government information management practices is the Integrated Public Sector Vocabulary (IPSV). It is a controlled vocabulary that was developed in the U.K. through the merger of three taxonomies, the Government Category List, owned by the Cabinet Office; the Local Government Category List, owned by the Effective Service Delivery toolkit; and the seamless UK taxonomy, owned by Essex County Council (Dextre Clarke, 2005). The vocabulary is compliant with ISO 2788 and BS 8723, the international and British standards for monolingual thesauri, and is recommended for use in assigning subject metadata to public sector resources.

The web interface for the IPSV vocabulary provides a two-pane interface, allowing users to browse or search within the vocabulary. Figure 7.24 shows the browsing interface with the search term

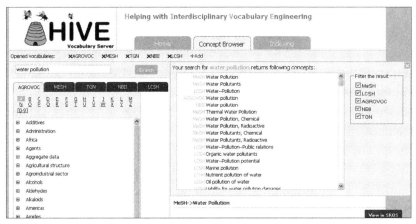

Figure 7.23 HIVE concept browser search for *water pollution*

environmentally sensitive areas. The details of the selected term appear in the right-hand pane. Hierarchical browsing permits up to four levels of categories to be drilled down and viewed.

The search function allows a free-text search of the whole vocabulary and provides term suggestions for modifying or narrowing search statements. Figure 7.25 shows the search interface with a highlighted search for the term *benefit.* The search bar on the left of the interface displays a list of Narrower and Related terms. Selection of any of the suggested terms shown in the drop-down list presents details of the term in the right pane. This type of interface provides a semantically rich environment for user interaction with the vocabulary.

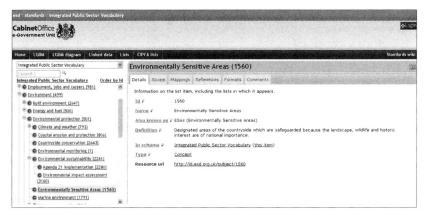

Figure 7.24 Integrated Public Sector Vocabulary (IPSV) browsing interface [*IPSV copyright of UK © Crown copyright*]

In addition to search and browsing functionalities, the interface allows users to view the mapping of each term within the integrated vocabularies. The IPSV is encoded in the SKOS Resource Description Framework (RDF) permitting it to be used and repurposed across various collections and linked data sources.

Other thesauri have been encoded in the SKOS format to facilitate semantic interoperability among various thesauri and digital collections. For instance, using SKOS, the AGROVOC thesaurus has been mapped to a large number of controlled vocabularies, including EuroVoc, the multilingual thesaurus for the European Union; the National Agricultural Library Thesaurus; GEMET; Library of Congress Subject Headings; and the Thesaurus for Economics.

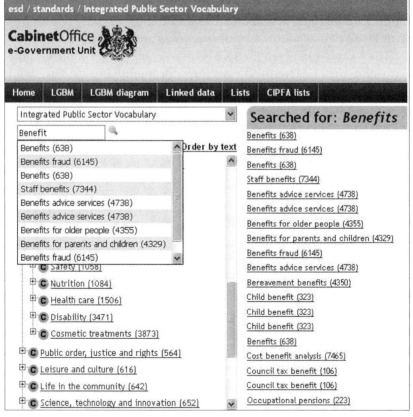

Figure 7.25   Integrated Public Sector Vocabulary search interface [*IPSV copyright of UK © Crown copyright*]

In a discussion of thesaurus web services and the use of multiple thesauri to improve subject access on the web, Johnson (2004) identifies the following functionalities that can be designed for the interlinked use of multiple thesauri:

- Provision of each thesaurus with a unique identifier and the means to locate a thesaurus, given its name, anywhere on the internet

- Reference to any thesaurus by name within another thesaurus, and to any given term within that thesaurus

- Discovery of thesauri using either keyword searching or references from related thesauri, yielding identifiers of previously unknown thesauri

- Reference to any substructure of a thesaurus, typically a sub-tree rooted in a particular term, but also, for example, a neighborhood of related terms surrounding a given term

- Meta-thesaurus links among individual terms, hierarchies, and other substructures within different thesauri

- Integrated and simultaneous access, based on Keyword in Context, to multiple thesauri

- Meta-thesaurus structures that express equivalence between terms in different thesauri

- Conventional hypertext links from scope notes or other textual elements of term description records to webpages

- Links between thesauri and other types of term suggestion services, such as concept spaces

- History of a term across multiple thesauri and other term suggestion services, including a chronology of the use of the term, any prior terms, and subsequent terms

- Multiple external meta-thesaural views, allowing different communities of practice to build their own topical maps of the world from pieces of other thesauri and vocabularies

- User-defined general rules for meta-linking of newly discovered thesauri based, for example, on regular expressions describing terms

- A thesaurus query language, allowing for retrieval of terms, as well as for identification of other terms related in particular ways to the term or terms specified in the query

These functionalities offer ways in which the semantic and structural features of thesauri can be integrated to produce a web-based meta-thesaurus that not only supports domain-specific searches but also represents a new service that many search engines and other web-based search services can use to provide semantically rich search environments for various communities and subject domains.

7.5 Conclusion

The increasing growth of multilingual and multicultural digital collections on the web necessitates the development of meta-thesauri supporting multiple languages to facilitate various information-seeking tasks such as searching, browsing, and navigation. This chapter discusses and reviews the user interface features and functionalities of a number of multilingual thesauri and meta-thesauri that support cross-browsing and cross-searching of various digital collections.

The review of these multilingual thesaurus-based user interfaces reveals both the wide variety of search user interface designs and the diversity of ways in which thesaural elements and information can be presented. Some user interfaces dedicate a major portion of the interface to thesaurus browsing, for instance, while giving little attention to result display features. Some interfaces offer quick access to the various languages supported, while others provide limited information about the ways in which languages or language features can be consulted.

This chapter also examines a number of projects that have developed user interfaces for meta-thesauri and multiple thesauri search systems in the context of both subject interoperability and the mapping of various controlled vocabularies. Finally, efforts are briefly discussed that make use of the SKOS to support semantic interoperability and to facilitate information seeking through multiple thesauri search systems.

References

Access Innovations, Inc. Taxobank terminology registry. Retrieved from www.taxobank.org (accessed June 7, 2012).

AGRIS (International Information System for the Agricultural Sciences and Technology). Retrieved from agris.fao.org (accessed May 27, 2011).

Aitchison, J., Gilchrist, A., and Bawden, D. (2000). *Thesaurus construction and use: A practical manual*, 4th ed. London: Routledge.

ANSI/NISO Z39.19: 2005 (2005). *Guidelines for the construction, format, and management of monolingual controlled vocabularies*, 4th ed. Bethesda, MD: National Information Standards Press.

Balkan, L., Miller, K., Austin, B., Etheridge, A., Bernabé, M. G., and Miller, P. (2002). ELSST: a broad-based multilingual thesaurus for the social sciences. In: *Third international conference on language resources and evaluation* (pp. 1873–1877). Retrieved from gandalf.aksis.uib.no/lrec2002/pdf/3.pdf (accessed May 21, 2011).

Bodenreider, O. (2004). The Unified Medical Language System (UMLS): Integrating biomedical terminology. *Nucleic Acids Research*, 32(1), 267–270.

British Standards Institution. (2005). *BS 8723 Structured vocabularies for information retrieval: Guide. Part 2. Thesauri*. 2005. London: British Standards Institution.

CAB International. CAB thesaurus 2011. Retrieved from www.cabi.org/cab thesaurus/mtwdk.exe?yi=home (accessed June 7, 2012).

CARMEN. WP12: Cross concordances of classifications and thesauri. Retrieved from www.bibliothek.uni-regensburg.de/projects/carmen12/index.html.en (accessed May 17, 2011).

Centre for Digital Library Research, University of Strathclyde. Retrieved from hilt.cdlr.strath.ac.uk/index.html (accessed June 7, 2012).

Chamis, A. Y. (1991). *Vocabulary control and search strategies in online searching*. Westport, CT: Greenwood Press.

Chaplan, M. A. (1995). Mapping Laborline thesaurus terms to Library of Congress Subject Headings: Implications for vocabulary switching. *Library Quarterly*, 65(1), 39–61.

Council of European Social Science Data Archives (CESSDA). CESSDA catalog. Retrieved from www.cessda.org/accessing/catalogue (accessed June 8, 2012).

Dahlberg, I. (1982). The Broad System of Ordering (BSO) as a basis for an integrated social science thesaurus? *International Classification*, 7(2), 66–72.

Dextre Clarke, S. G. (2005). Integrated public sector vocabulary: Editorial policy version 1.2. Retrieved from www.esd.org.uk/documents/IPSVEditorial Policy.pdf (accessed July 19, 2011).

European Union. EuroVoc thesaurus. Retrieved fromeurovoc.europa.eu/drupal (accessed June 8, 2012).

Food and Agriculture Organization of the United Nations. Agricultural information management standards: AGROVOC. Retrieved from aims.fao.org/website/AGRO VOC-Thesaurus/sub (accessed June 8, 2012).

German Information Network International Relations and Area Studies (FIV). International relations and area studies gateway (IREON). Retrieved from www.ireon-portal.de (accessed June 8, 2012).

Gray, A. J. G., Gray, N., Hall, C. W., and Ounis, I. (2010). Finding the right term: Retrieving and exploring semantic concepts in astronomical vocabularies. *Information Processing and Management*, 46(4), 470–478.

Greenberg, J., Losee, R., Pérez Agüera, J. R., Scherle, R., White, H., and Willis, C. (2011). HIVE: Helping interdisciplinary vocabulary engineering. *Bulletin of the American Society for Information Science and Technology*, 37(4), 12–14.

Heery, R., Carpenter, L., and Day, M. (2001). Renardus project developments and the wider digital library context. *D-Lib Magazine*, 7(4). Retrieved from www.dlib.org/dlib/april01/heery/04heery.html (July 6, 2011).

Hudon, M. (1997). Multilingual thesaurus construction: Integrating the views of different cultures in one gateway to knowledge and concepts. *Knowledge Organization*, 24(2), 84–91.

Hudon, M. (2003). True and tested products: Thesauri on the web. *Indexer*, 23(3), 115–119.

Hunter, J. (2001). MetaNet: A metadata term thesaurus to enable semantic interoperability between metadata domains. *Journal of Digital Information*, 1(8), 234–253.

ISO 25964-1: 2011. (2011). *Information and documentation: Thesauri and interoperability with other vocabularies: Part 1: Thesauri for information retrieval*. International Organization for Standardization. Switzerland: ISO.

Johnson, E. H. (2004). Distributed thesaurus web services. *Cataloging & Classification Quarterly*, 37 (3/4), 121–153.

Jorna, K., and Davies, S. (2001). Multilingual thesauri for the modern world—no ideal solution? *Journal of Documentation*, 57(2), 284–295.

Koch, T., Neuroth, H., and Day, M. (2001). *Renardus: Cross-browsing European subject gateways via a common classification system (DDC)*. Paper presented at the International Federation of Library Associations satellite meeting: Subject retrieval in a networked environment, OCLC, Dublin, OH, August 2001.

Lancaster, F. W., and Smith, L. C. (1983). *Compatibility issues affecting information systems and services*. Paris: UNESCO General Information Programme.

Landry, P. (2000). The MACS Project: Multilingual access to subjects (LCSH, RAMEAU, SWD). In: *Proceedings of Sixty Sixth International Federation of*

Library Associations Council and General Conference. Jerusalem (Israel) 13–18 August 2000. Retrieved from archive.ifla.org/IV/ifla66/papers/165-181e.pdf (accessed June 15, 2012).

McCulloch, E. (2004). Multiple terminologies: An obstacle to information retrieval. *Library Review*, 53(6), 297–300.

McCulloch, E., and Macgregor, G. (2008). Analysis of equivalence mapping for terminology services. *Journal of Information Science*, 34(1), 70–92.

Metadata Research Center (MRC), School of Information and Library Science, University of North Carolina at Chapel Hill. HIVE (Helping Interdisciplinary Vocabulary Engineering). www.nescent.org/sites/hive/Main_Page (accessed June 8, 2012).

Milli, H., and Rada, R. (1988). Merging thesauri: Principles and evaluation. *IEEE Transactions on Pattern Analysis and Machine Intelligence*, 10(2), 204–220.

Neville, H. H. (1970). Feasibility study of a scheme for reconciling thesauri covering a common subject. *Journal of Documentation*, 26(4), 313–336.

Nicholson, D. (2002). Subject-based interoperability: Issues from the High Level Thesaurus (HILT) project. Paper presented at 68th International Federation of Library Associations council and general conference, August 2002, Glasgow, UK. Retrieved from archive.ifla.org/IV/ifla68/papers/006-122e.pdf (accessed April 17, 2011).

Nicholson, D., and Shiri, A. (2003). Interoperability in subject searching and browsing. *OCLC Systems & Services*, 19(2), 58–61.

Niehoff, R. T. (1976). Development of an integrated energy vocabulary and the possibilities for on-line subject switching. *Journal of the American Society for Information Science*, 27(1), 3–17.

Saumure, K., and Shiri, A. (2008). Knowledge organization trends: A comparison of the pre- and post-web eras. *Journal of Information Science*, 34(5), 651–666.

Shiri, A., Nicholson, D., and McCulloch, E. (2004). User evaluation of a pilot terminologies server for a distributed multi-scheme environment. *Online Information Review*, 28(4), 273–283.

Shiri, A., Ruecker, S., Fiorentino, C., Stafford, A., Bouchard, M., and Bieber, M. (2010). Designing a semantically rich visual interface for cultural digital libraries using the UNESCO multilingual thesaurus. In: F. Sudweeks, H. Hrachovec, and C. Ess (Eds.), *Proceedings of cultural attitudes towards technology and communication 2010 conference: Cultural diversity in e-learning and/or m-learning*, June 2010, University of British Columbia, Vancouver, British Columbia, Canada.

Silvester, J. P. (1993). An operational system for subject switching between controlled vocabularies. *Information Processing and Management*, 29(1), 47–59.

Soergel, D. (1997). Multilingual thesauri in cross language text and speech retrieval. In: *American Association for Artificial Intelligence* (*AAAI*)

Symposium on Cross-Language Text and Speech Retrieval. Stanford University, March 24–26, 1997.

Stafford, A., Shiri, A., Ruecker, S. et al. (2008). Searchling: User-centered evaluation of a visual thesaurus-enhanced interface for bilingual digital libraries. In: *Proceedings of the European conference on research and advanced technology for digital libraries: ECDL 2008* (pp. 117–121). Heidelberg, Germany: Springer.

Statistics Canada. Statistics Canada Thesaurus. Retrieved from www47.stat can.gc.ca/th_r000-eng.htm (accessed June 8, 2012).

U.S. Geological Survey. National Biological Information Infrastructure (NBII). Biocomplexity thesaurus. Retrieved from www.usgs.gov/core_science_systems/csas/biocomplexity_thesaurus (accessed June 19, 2012).

U.S. National Library of Medicine. Unified Medical Language System (UMLS). www.nlm.nih.gov/research/umls (accessed June 19, 2012).

Whitehead, C. (1990). Mapping LCSH into thesauri: The AAT model. In: T. Petersen and P. Molholt (Eds.), *Beyond the book: Extending MARC for subject access* (pp. 81–96). Boston, MA: G. K. Hall.

Zeng, M. L., and Chan, L. M. (2004). Trends and issues in establishing interoperability among knowledge organization systems. *Journal of the American Society for Information Science and Technology*, 55(5), 377–395.

CHAPTER 8

User-Centered Evaluation of Thesaurus-Enhanced Search User Interfaces

This chapter reviews the literature on free-text versus controlled vocabulary searching. It also addresses selected user studies focused on interactions of users and thesaurus-enhanced search interfaces. Examination and analysis are reported for selected user studies that have a particular focus on considering the interactions of users with thesaurus-enhanced search interfaces, in order to highlight the various evaluative approaches and strategies adopted to assess their impressions and understandings of thesaurus interface features and functionalities. The advantages of thesaurus-based applications for the semantic web and linked data environments are also discussed.

8.1 Free-Text Versus Controlled Vocabulary Searching

Studies about searching behavior, information retrieval interface evaluation, search term selection, and query expansion have addressed the challenges of terminological assistance to enhance user search effectiveness. Such assistance may be arranged through the inclusion of thesauri and classification schemes within information retrieval interfaces. Researchers have investigated the searching behavior of various types of users and looked in particular at their search term selection behavior. Findings suggest that term selection can be improved if thesauri are incorporated into search interfaces (Hsieh-Yee, 1993; Efthimiadis, 2000; Sutcliffe et al., 2000; Vakkari, 2000). (Chapter 3 contains a detailed account of these studies.)

Numerous studies have evaluated the performance and effectiveness of controlled vocabularies versus free-text terms in information retrieval (Markey et al., 1980; Perez, 1982; Svenonius, 1986; Dubois, 1987; Fidel, 1991; Cousins, 1992; Rowley, 1994; Muddamalle, 1998).

Rowley (1994), for instance, has reviewed the literature on the debate over controlled vocabularies and indexing languages. She suggests that, with the development of end-user searching and the prevalence of online public access catalogs (OPACs) and biblio-graphic databases, we are witnessing a rebirth of the value of con-trolled vocabularies in the context of user-friendly interfaces. We are also witnessing the unprecedented development of sophisticated, cross-disciplinary knowledge bases. She concludes there is general agreement on the effectiveness of using controlled language and nat-ural language in conjunction, and on the relative merits of each of these systems.

Muddamalle (1998) studied the effectiveness of natural language and controlled vocabularies in information retrieval and concludes that both show very effective retrieval results, with only marginal limitations. He suggests that optimum retrieval can be achieved through a combination of natural language and thesaurus retrieval techniques.

Savoy (2005) compared free-text and controlled vocabulary searching in a bibliographic database and finds that combined index-ing strategies always produce the best retrieval performance. He also concludes that, when users wish to conduct exhaustive searches with minimal effort, manually assigned terms are essential and useful.

Golub et al. (2009) investigated the effects on indexing and retrieval of social tagging alone compared with social tagging in com-bination with suggestions from a controlled vocabulary. The results show the importance of controlled vocabulary suggestions for both indexing and retrieval for several purposes: helping to produce ideas of tags to use, making it easier to find focus for the tagging, ensuring consistency, and increasing the number of access points in retrieval.

The evidence from these and other studies suggests that con-trolled vocabularies complement natural language searching and that terminological support can be provided through thesaural accessibility as part of information access user interfaces.

8.2 User Evaluation Methodologies

The information retrieval interaction models reviewed in Chapter 2 take into account a range of cognitive, physical, and affective aspects of the search process that should be considered in conducting evaluation studies of information retrieval systems and services.

Robertson and Beaulieu (1997) emphasize the importance in such evaluations of taking into account users' interactions with, cognitive views of, and satisfaction with the search process. These researchers suggest that information retrieval evaluations should not merely consider the issue of how good or how bad a particular system is but should also contribute to improvements in our understanding of the search processes involved and their relationships in an interactive searching environment. Accordingly, evaluation should also provide the basis for the design of better systems.

Saracevic (1995) points out a number of user-centered evaluation criteria, including utility, success, completeness, satisfaction, worth, value, time, and cost. He comments that such criteria seem to be well-suited to the evaluation of information retrieval interactions.

Harter and Hert (1998) studied user-oriented research and identified two classes of evaluation measures: those associated with users' perceptions and attitudes, such as utility, usefulness, impact, satisfaction, and other affective dimensions, and measures whose major focus is attempting to capture user-system interaction. The second class of measures is derived from the human-computer interaction usability literature and includes such measures as accuracy and completeness, error rate, process variables (e.g., number of commands, descriptors, screens accessed, and search cycles), training time, retrieval (e.g., number of entries retrieved, and unit cost), perceptions of ease of use, satisfaction, and ability to articulate system models.

In a review of user-centered perspectives of information retrieval research, Sugar (1995) divides this research into two main categories, cognitive and holistic. The cognitive approach focuses on the discovery of the mental models and cognitive characteristics of users' information-seeking behavior. The holistic approach concentrates not only on the cognitive aspects of an information search, but also on the affective and physical aspects, such as user satisfaction and perception and the actual use of system features.

From a human-computer interaction perspective, Shneiderman and Plaisant (2004) identify five key components of interface usability:

- Learnability: How easy is it for users to accomplish basic tasks the first time they encounter the interface?

- Efficiency: How quickly can users accomplish their tasks after they learn how to use the interface?

- Memorability: After a period of nonuse, how long does it take users to reestablish proficiency?

- Errors: How many errors do users make, how severe are these errors, and how easy is it for users to recover from these errors?

- Satisfaction: How pleasant or satisfying is it to use the interface?

These are general usability criteria for the evaluation and improvement of user interfaces. This section discusses and analyzes the methodologies and frameworks adopted in 10 studies selected on the basis of the following criteria:

- Availability of a thesaurus-enhanced search user interface

- Use of the thesaurus in tandem with a document collection

- Users' direct interaction with thesauri and their user interfaces

- Examination of both thesaurus and interface variables in the study

- Use of combined methodologies from information retrieval and human-computer interaction

These studies use a wide range of evaluation techniques and data-gathering methodologies to determine users' interactions with, impressions of, and satisfaction with thesaurus-enhanced search interfaces. A representative variety of usability and search behavior evaluation approaches are described. Table 8.1 summarizes these data-gathering and methodological considerations in the 10 studies selected according to seven descriptive categories: collection; subject domain; thesaurus; population; data collection; evaluation method; and variables, measures, and criteria.

Table 8.1 shows that a variety of collections and thesauri have been used for evaluation purposes. Equally diverse are the subject domains of the thesauri, ranging from medicine and the arts to life sciences, audiovisual materials, and engineering. An interesting observation is that all these studies have made combined use of usability and search behavior evaluation methodologies, an area that has recently been called human-computer information retrieval.

Table 8.1   Evaluation settings for thesaurus-enhanced search user interfaces

Author	Collection	Domain	Thesaurus	Population	Data collection	Evaluation method	Variables, measures, criteria
McMath et al. (1989)	MEDLINE	Medical	MeSH	Students (12)	Questionnaire	Experimental	Satisfaction, preference, understandings
Jones et al. (1995)	Inspec	Electronics, info science	Inspec	Students and faculty (39)	Transaction logging, survey	Controlled experimental	Success and failure, query effectiveness, behavior patterns
Sutcliffe et al. (2000)	Articles database	Business and industry	Locally developed	Researchers (12)	Pre- and post-test questionnaire, interviews, video recording	Usability evaluation	Relevance, comprehension, behavior patterns
Blocks et al. (2002)	Science museums collections	Museums	Art and Architecture Thesaurus	Museum professionals (8)	Think-aloud, screen capture videos, audio recording, log files	Usability evaluation	Success, user reasoning
McKay et al. (2004)	FAO collections	Agriculture	AGROVOC	Students (8)	Think-aloud, audio and video recording, screen capture, retrospective verbal protocol	Usability evaluation, expert evaluation	Preference, response time, satisfaction
Shiri & Revie (2005)	CAB abstracts	Life sciences and veterinary	CAB Thesaurus	Students and faculty (30)	Pre- and post-search questionnaire, screen capture, think-aloud, interviews	Controlled experiment	Subject knowledge, satisfaction, behavior patterns
Malaise et al. (2006)	Sound and vision archives	Various subjects	Common Thesaurus for Audiovisual Archives	Catalogers (9)	Video recording, questionnaire	Formative, usability evaluation	Efficiency, satisfaction, success
Tudhope et al. (2006)	Science museums collections	Museums	Art and Architecture Thesaurus	Cataloguers, collections managers, curator (23)	Think-aloud, screen capture videos, log files	Formative, qualitative user evaluation	Relevance, behavior patterns, user understanding
Tang (2007)	MeSH	Medical	PubMed	Students (19)	Pre- and post-search questionnaire, exit interview	Naturalistic, longitudinal	Subject knowledge, satisfaction, behavior patterns
Shiri et al. (2011)	Government of Canada site	General	Government of Canada Core Subject Thesaurus	Students and faculty (15)	Pre- and post-search questionnaire, think-aloud, screen capture, interviews	Usability evaluation	Satisfaction, behavior patterns, language

The most common evaluation measures adopted in these studies include search and browsing behavior patterns, search success, satisfaction, efficiency, relevance, user preference, and subject knowledge. Among the most popular data-gathering methods reported in the studies are think-aloud, screen capturing, pre- and post-search questionnaires, and post-session interviews.

Academic users, namely, students, faculty members, and cata-logers, constitute the main participants in these studies, with samples ranging from eight to 39 participants. It should be noted that engaging larger populations would provide more coherent and generalizable findings. With new technological developments such as software for simultaneous capturing of screen, audio, and video, the tasks attract-ing and involving more participants and exploiting more web-based data gathering techniques for user evaluations have become easier. However, the task of analyzing large audio, video, and screen capture files remains both time-consuming and labor intensive.

8.3 Key Findings From User Evaluation Studies

A more detailed examination of these evaluation studies is provided in Table 8.2, with succinct accounts of the key findings relating to thesaurus-enhanced search interfaces, the problems and challenges experienced by searchers, and the suggestions for improvement and implications put forward by researchers. These three categories pro-vide interesting insights into the variables and factors affecting users' interactions with thesaurus-enhanced search interfaces.

A close examination of these findings, problems, challenges, sug-gestions, and implications reveals several predominant themes:

- Thesaurus navigation was found useful and informative and provided a context for a given search term.

- Users prefer interactive query formulation using thesaurus-enhanced search interfaces as opposed to automatic, behind-the-scenes query expansion.

- The nature and characteristics of search tasks impact users' interactions.

- Full or partial presentation of the structure of the thesaurus may have different advantages and implications for users.

- Individual differences may impact users' interactions; for example, beginning and sophisticated searchers may benefit differently.

- Topic familiarity and prior search experience may influence users' understanding and impressions of thesaurus terms and thesaural relationships.

Table 8.2 Key findings, problems, and implications of usability studies

Study	Key findings	Problems and challenges	Suggestions for improvement and implications
McMath et al. (1989)	• Significant agreement that graphics added to the understanding of the thesaurus. • Many would trade sophisticated query construction facilities for graphical depictions of the query and retrieved documents. • The background of the user played a critical role in determining the user's view of the system.	• Users are unable to directly type a term into the computer and see its neighborhood. • The user may know exactly what terms are desired for the retrieval, and at those times, the thesaurus traversal would be an unnecessary restriction. • Users could get disoriented while searching the deep trees in MeSH.	• The user should be allowed parallel modes of presentation of data and not one deep menu. • To increase thesauri's explanatory power, it might be useful to show, for the text to which the keywords point, the context in the text where the key concepts occurred.
Jones et al. (1995)	• The successful users had twice as many terms to choose from, tended to navigate less far through the network, and picked a high proportion of their terms. • Success seems to be correlated with finding good matches for one's query in the thesaurus to start with. • Preliminary thesaurus navigation should be useful and informative. • Some users were prepared to navigate and select terms up to five moves away from their starting point. • Users get good results when they have plenty of terms to choose from (so they need well-designed thesauri giving good coverage of their particular field), and they are discriminating in their choice. • Thesaurus-based query expansion does indeed increase recall success and seems to be correlated with finding good matches for one's query in the thesaurus to start with.	• Users failed to find good matches for their original query in the thesaurus.	• A thesaurus can be viewed as a bridge between queries phrased in natural language and an abstract classification structure constitutes a "map" of a particular domain. • The accuracy, depth, and coverage of thesaurus information are the most important issues here, as well as the quality of the user interface for exploring it. • The initial match between queries and terms has already been identified as crucial to the success of a thesaurus. • Navigation needs to be improved.
Sutcliffe et al. (2000)	• Better-performing subjects actively explored and navigated both the thesaurus and results browser visualizations. • There were considerable individual differences in people's elective use of thesaurus and results visualization. • Longer task completion times and exploration of both thesaurus and results browser displays were associated with better-performing subjects. • Query facilities and thesaurus were rated above average.	• Several users commented that the terms in the thesaurus did not match their expectations and typed in their own queries. • Selecting thesaurus terms is a challenge, as is confusing representation of thesaurus hierarchy. • Thesaurus categories and views are not clear. • Thesaurus links between hierarchy levels are not clear.	• A larger thesaurus would be better. • Display with customization facilities would be preferable. • Visual structure is no substitute for either. • A well-designed thesaurus or user-customizable thesaurus is important.
Blocks et al. (2002)	• Interaction techniques used by the interface were successful in allowing a person with little knowledge of the interface to use the functionality. • Prototype interface does not provide nonexpert searchers with sufficient guidance as to query structure and when to use the thesaurus in the search process. • Thesaurus browsing to find a	• Profusion of separate windows is viewed as problematic. • The use of overlapping windows is problematic. • Breaking down the query into concepts that match thesaurus terms will improve results through repeated reformulation. • Browsing the thesaurus from the root level to find a term on a relatively low level or including a	• Query histories would allow comparisons of query versions and give an opportunity to easily return to the best result set. • Use of the thesaurus should be channeled so that users employ techniques at search stages at which the benefit is optimal. • Better design should be used to reflect the search process and the thesaurus as a source of terms for

Table 8.2   (cont.)

	particular term is useful as long as the entry point is low enough that users navigate within the term's local context. • Browsing the local context of a term can be useful to fine-tune the query and reassure users that they are on the right track.	number of closely related terms in a query could be problematic.	the query.
McKay et al. (2004)	• Participants preferred that the thesaurus act semi-automatically (that it suggested search terms) rather than automatically inserting thesaurus terms into the search. • Participants used the thesaurus less frequently when it was in a separate window. • Users appreciated that they could take in the relationship among a series of terms at a glance. • There were positive reactions from both experts and users regarding its learnability and predictability.	• Experts thought that the thesaurus returned a substantial number of terms, possibly causing information overload. • Users wonder if searching in the thesaurus should help users find documents (by showing document lists, for example) or concentrate on showing relationships among terms. • Slow response time frustrated, distracted, and sometimes distressed the participants. • Independent window interfaces were awkward to use.	• Participants wished to see thesaurus term relationship indications (broader, narrower, and related terms) when browsing the thesaurus. • Elimination of duplicate terms and terms that are not present in any documents in the collection would be helpful.
Shiri and Revie (2005)	• Interface usability is a factor affecting thesaurus browsing and navigation as well as other information-searching behaviors. • Those who evaluated the use of the interface as very easy required significantly less time to carry out searches. • Users who evaluated the learning or use of the interface as very easy also rated thesaurus browsing and navigation very easy. • Students focused on the broadening effect of the thesaurus and the provision of new terms. Faculty members stressed the narrowing-down effect of the thesaurus, the provision of alternative terms, and an appreciation of the fact that topic familiarity plays a role in thesaurus browsing and navigation. • The results indicated that thesauri are capable of assisting end users in the selection of search terms for query formulation and expansion, in particular by providing new terms and ideas. This resulted in the majority of users' expanding their queries and being successful in retrieving relevant information.	• Use of Boolean operators was an issue. • The size, position, and labeling of buttons was problematic. • Excessive scrolling up and down was needed in thesaurus browsing. • Switching between thesaurus browsing and results display was difficult. • Students experienced more difficulties than did faculty members.	• Explicit availability of Boolean operators can be particularly useful within a thesaurus-enhanced search interface. • Physical efforts, such as scrolling, should be reduced, particularly for browsing thesaurus terms. • Basic and advanced thesaurus-based search features can provide users with varying degrees of domain and subject knowledge.
Malaise et al. (2006)	• Users were more satisfied with the alphabetical search than with the hierarchical search. • Participants used mainly alphabetical search as they already knew the term they were looking for; therefore, hierarchical search is not appropriate. • In the hierarchal search, they mainly used the user-for and related-term relationships.	• Case sensitivity is an issue. • Search and lack of auto-completion proved problematic. • The screen layout was inefficient. • There was insufficient feedback on the action performed. • It takes too long to find the appropriate main category in the hierarchy.	• There should be disambiguating terms, showing the respective places in the hierarchy. • There should be a quick means for selecting the right concept. • Thesaurus browsing facility could be helpful to the general public for searching the public website.

Table 8.2   (cont.)

	• Browsing was not preferred as a first step to search for a term because the categories are too broad. • Screen layout and insufficient feedback on actions performed caused users to make a large number of steps.		
Tudhope et al. (2006)	• Given training and a user guide, users were able to interact with the thesaurus and complete tasks with the final system. • The interface required training and was seen as complex by these users. • Users vary in the time they are willing to spend in browsing a thesaurus. • A list simply showing expanded terms is appropriate in many contexts.	• There was confusion in using the slider with the scroll bar for the query expansion visualization. • The similarity between the browser's display of hierarchical relationships caused occasional confusion. • The amount of choice proved excessive and the control more complicated than generally required. • Some users expressed a wish for more interactive control of the expansion, including individual expansion control of query terms.	• For more casual users, a "simple search" interface, with the thesaurus in the background, should be considered. • There is a need for more-active system support for the search process itself (particularly for reformulation). • Hierarchical display of query expansion terms would help. • The application of semantic expansion to hypertext browsing of the thesaurus may be useful in interfaces where thesaurus content is made available but details of thesaurus structure are hidden.
Tang (2007)	• Most of the participants considered the browsable thesaurus most useful when they were unfamiliar with the topics. • Participants avoided the querying methods that involve thesaurus browsing, which demands more time and effort.	• The two most frequent complaints about the browsable thesaurus were the lack of specificity of the thesaurus descriptors and the difficulty in finding a term in the hierarchies. • Several of the participants mentioned that the terms in the thesaurus were not specific enough for their purpose	• The interaction of the nature of search tasks and different interface features should be considered.
Shiri et al. (2011)	• Users find the interface most useful at the beginning of a research project on an unfamiliar topic because they could start by browsing through general categories for relevant terms and the thesaurus could help them narrow or broaden their search. • Query formulation features, including Boolean control and search term pool, were evaluated as being very useful. • Users found the combination of search and browse functions useful and easy to use. • Searchling's ability to facilitate searches simultaneously in multiple languages is very useful, although it is most useful if it allows them to collect a larger quantity of information, not just the same information repeated in two languages. • Researchers are not interested in using the interface as a translation tool.	• Some users were unable to distinguish between searching the documents and the thesaurus terms. • Document records do not display enough information about the documents.	• The possibility of hiding parts of the thesaurus under a more user-friendly interface where users will not have to struggle to interact with the interface should be considered. • Explicit and implicit thesaurus features for novice and advanced searchers should be added respectively. • Use of thesaurus as a source for term suggestion should be a feature.

- Searchers may have particular preferences for various thesaural presentations, such as hierarchical or alphabetical.

- Visualization of thesauri may appeal to some users and may assist them in their understanding of the links and relationships.

- Integrating thesauri as part of the search or browsing system may pose design and user comprehension challenges.

- Interface usability affects users' experiences and interactions.

- Query formulation and reformulation features are important interface functionalities in supporting users to achieve success and satisfaction.

- The stage at which the user interface allows users to access and interact with thesauri may have an effect on users' success and satisfaction.

- Individual differences may have a bearing on users' preferences for searching or browsing.

- The coverage, specificity, and comprehensiveness of the thesaurus on the interface may affect the way users view it and its advantages.

- User-centered variables such as success, efficiency, and satisfaction are complex and may be examined at various levels, namely, interface usability, thesaurus interaction, term selection, and result analysis and judgment; as a consequence, evaluation of thesaurus-enhanced search interfaces should take into account these interrelated factors that may impact users' experiences.

In a nutshell, the findings suggest that the target audience of searchers is a key determinant in the design and development of an effective thesaurus-enhanced search interface. Even within one target audience, there are individuals with varying levels of search and subject knowledge who may benefit from the availability of two versions of the interface, one for novice searchers and the other for advanced user groups.

8.4 Thesaurus-Based Searching in the Semantic Web Environment

Berners-Lee et al. (2001) note that "traditional knowledge-representation systems typically have been centralized, requiring everyone to share exactly the same definition of common concepts such as *parent* or *vehicle*" (pp. 37–38). In contrast, the new information environment is distributed and decentralized and encompasses a broad variety of information and meta-information sources and services. This new environment provides ample opportunity for reusing and repurposing knowledge organization systems, such as thesauri and classification systems, to support search systems and services. The authors emphasize the importance of ontologies for enhancing the functioning of the web and the accuracy of web searches, through the creation of ways in which users and search systems and agents can reach a shared understanding by exchanging ontologies.

The introduction of flexible and semantically aware data formats such as Resource Description Framework (RDF) and XML as semantic web languages has given rise to a wide variety of semantically enhanced web services and applications that support the exchange of information between search systems and users.

The Simple Knowledge Organization System (SKOS), for example, is a World Wide Web Consortium standard and a common data model that aims to connect knowledge organization systems, such as thesauri, classification schemes, subject heading lists, and so forth, to linked data sources within the semantic web environment. Using the RDF, thesauri can be encoded in such a way as to be shareable, interoperable, and usable across various computer applications. The SKOS standard provides a framework for mapping and connecting multiple thesauri in order to create cross-browsing and cross-searching applications for linked data repositories, open archives, digital libraries, and various search systems and services. SKOS also provides a framework for ensuring semantic interoperability among different collections and services and facilitates the creation of more flexible thesaurus-based search services and applications.

Currently, a number of thesauri have been encoded in the SKOS format and are made available on the web. Examples include the AGROVOC thesaurus; EuroVoc, the multilingual thesaurus for the European Union; the National Agricultural Library (NAL) Thesaurus; the GEneral Multilingual Environmental Thesaurus (GEMET), and the Thesaurus for Economics (STW). Examples of thesauri used in the context of linked data were introduced in Chapter 4.

The developments associated with semantic web and linked data provide new opportunities for thesauri to be reused and repurposed in a wider variety of web-based collections and services. Thesauri encoded in SKOS can be used by computers and people to bridge the semantic gap that exists between what the searcher wants and what the search systems and services contain. These developments provide numerous opportunities for individuals and organizations interested in exploiting thesauri for information representation and retrieval purposes.

Some of the potential applications of thesauri in the semantic web and linked data environment can be summarized as follows:

- Facilitate the merger, reconciliation, and integration of SKOS-encoded thesauri

- Create terminology and thesaural web services

- Promote semantic interoperability across systems that use different thesauri

- Link thesauri to other web applications such as OPACs, search engines, digital libraries, and institutional repositories

- Support searching and browsing across various information collections

- Offer flexible information organization and representation techniques and strategies

- Enhance machine readability of thesauri and their semantic structures

- Expand the search functionalities of various search systems, through the provision of various semantic and thesaural links

- Facilitate precision-focused searching and browsing within large digital repositories and collections

- Allow for novel visualization techniques and interface design to show linked data sources and subject repositories

- Provide features and functionalities for disambiguation of terms in linked data sources

In addition to these applications, the new thesaurus-based services will provide interesting and exciting opportunities for the conduct of user-centered interface design and evaluation studies.

8.5 Conclusion

This chapter provides a brief summary of the literature on the comparison of controlled vocabulary searching versus free-text searching, concluding that a combination of both techniques achieves the best results. As with many web-based applications, successful design and development of usable thesaurus-enhanced search user interfaces depends, to a large extent, on the active and ongoing involvement of searchers throughout the process.

This chapter also summarizes user evaluation methodologies employed in the studies that have investigated searchers' interactions with thesaurus-enhanced search user interfaces. It reviews and synthesizes the key findings from these studies, the problems and challenges faced by users, and the suggestions and implications for future research and development. The role and importance of thesauri are emphasized in the context of the semantic web and linked data environment, and potential applications of thesauri in the new information environments on the web are suggested.

References

Berners-Lee, T., Hendler, J., and Lassila, O. (2001). The semantic web. *Scientific American*, 284(5), 34–43.

Blocks, D., Binding, C., Cunliffe, C., and Tudhope, D. (2002). Qualitative evaluation of a thesaurus-based retrieval system. In: *Proceedings of the 6th European conference on research and advanced technology for digital libraries* (pp. 346–361). Berlin: Springer.

Cousins, S. A. (1992). Enhancing access to OPACs: Controlled vs natural language. *Journal of Documentation*, 48(3), 291–309.

Dubois, C. P. R. (1987). Free text vs controlled vocabulary: A reassessment. *Online Review*, 11(4), 243–253.

Efthimiadis, E. N. (2000). Interactive query expansion: A user-based evaluation in a relevance feedback environment. *Journal of the American Society for Information Science*, 51(11), 989–1003.

Fidel, R. (1991). Searchers' selection of search keys: II. Controlled vocabulary or free-text searching. *Journal of the American Society for Information Science*, 42(7), 501–514.

Golub, K., Jones, C., Lykke Nielsen, M. et al. (2009). EnTag: Enhancing social tagging for discovery. In: F. Heath, M. L. Rice-Lively, and R. Furuta (Eds.), *Proceedings of the 2009 joint conference on digital libraries* (pp. 163–172). New York: ACM Press.

Harter, S., and Hert, C. A. (1998). Evaluation of information retrieval systems: Approaches, issues, and methods. In: M. E. Williams (Ed.), *Annual review of information science and technology* (Vol. 32, pp. 3–94). Washington, D.C.: American Society for Information Science.

Hsieh-Yee, I. (1993). Effects of search experience and subject knowledge on the search tactics of novice and experienced searchers. *Journal of the American Society for Information Science*, 44(3), 161–174.

Jones, S., Gatford, M., Hancock-Beaulieu, M., Robertson, S. E., Walker, W., and Secker, J. (1995). Interactive thesaurus navigation: Intelligence rules OK? *Journal of the American Society for Information Science*, 46(1), 52–59.

Malaise, V., Aroyo, L., Brugman, H. et al. (2006). Evaluating a thesaurus browser for an audio-visual archive. In: S. Staab and V. Svatek (Eds.), *Managing knowledge in a world of networks* (pp. 272–286). Berlin: Springer.

Markey, K., Atherton, P., and Newton, C. (1980). An analysis of controlled and free-text search statements in online searches. *Online Review*, 4(3), 225–236.

McKay, D., Preeti, S., Hunt, R., and Cunningham, S. J. (2004). Enhanced browsing in digital libraries: Three new approaches to browsing in Greenstone. *International Journal on Digital Libraries*, 4(4), 283–297.

McMath, C. F., Tamaru, R. S., and Rada, R. (1989). A graphical thesaurus-based information retrieval system. *International Journal of Man-Machine Studies*, 31(2), 121–147.

Muddamalle, M. R. (1998). Natural language versus controlled vocabulary in information retrieval: A case study in soil mechanics. *Journal of the American Society for Information Science*, 49(10), 881–887.

Perez, E. (1982). Text enhancement: Controlled vocabulary vs. free text. *Special Libraries*, 73(July), 183–192.

Robertson, S. E., and Beaulieu, M. (1997). Research and evaluation in information retrieval. *Journal of Documentation*, 53(1), 51–57.

Rowley, J. (1994). The controlled versus natural indexing languages debate revisited: A perspective on information retrieval practice and research. *Journal of Information Science*, 20(2), 108–119.

Saracevic, T. (1995). Evaluation of evaluation in information retrieval. In: E. A. Fox, P. Ingwersen, and R. Fidel (Eds.), *Proceedings of the 18th annual international ACM SIGIR conference on research and development in information retrieval* (pp. 138–146). New York: ACM.

Savoy, J. (2005). Bibliographic database access using free-text and controlled vocabulary: An evaluation. *Information Processing & Management*, 41(4), 873–890.

Shiri, A., and Revie, C. (2005). Usability and user perceptions of a thesaurus-enhanced search interface. *Journal of Documentation*, 61(5), 640–656.

Shiri, A., Ruecker, S., Bouchard, M. et al. (2011). User evaluation of Searchling: A visual interface for bilingual digital libraries. *Electronic Library*, 29(1), 71–89.

Shneiderman, B., and Plaisant, C. (2004). *Designing the user interface: Strategies for effective human-computer interaction*, 4th ed. Boston, MA: Addison Wesley.

Sugar, W. (1995). User-centered perspective of information retrieval research and analysis methods. In: M. E. Williams (Ed.), *Annual review of information science and technology* (Vol. 30, pp. 77–109). Medford, NJ: ASIS.

Sutcliffe, A. G., Ennis, M., and Watkinson, S. J. (2000). Empirical studies of end-user information searching. *Journal of the American Society for Information Science*, 51(13), 1211–1231.

Svenonius, E. (1986). Unanswered questions in the design of controlled vocabularies. *Journal of the American Society for Information Science*, 37(5), 331–340.

Tang, M. (2007). Browsing and searching in a faceted information space: A naturalistic study of PubMed users' interaction with a display tool. *Journal of the American Society for Information Science and Technology*, 58(13), 1998–2006.

Tudhope, D., Binding, C., Blocks, D., and Cunliffe, D. (2006). Query expansion via conceptual distance in thesaurus indexed collections. *Journal of Documentation*, 62(4), 509–533.

Vakkari, P. (2000). Cognition and changes of search terms and tactics during task performance: A longitudinal case study. In: *Proceedings of RIAO 2000, content-based multimedia information access RIAO conference* (pp. 894–907). Paris: C.I.D.

CHAPTER 9

Guidelines for the Design of Thesaurus-Enhanced Search User Interfaces

Drawing on the literatures of human-computer interaction, information architecture, information search behavior, and thesaurus construction standards, this chapter provides a focused set of guidelines and best practices for the design and search user interfaces enhanced with thesauri, and of the search and retrieval process.

The focus is on the ways in which thesauri can be incorporated into search user interfaces in order to support both the search process—in particular, search term selection and query formulation and reformulation—and various browsing options and strategies, using the hierarchical, alphabetical, and visual functionalities of thesauri.

9.1 Interface Design Process

Numerous user interface design guidelines and principles have been put forward by researchers. To provide a comprehensive perspective on the task of user interface design, researchers discuss the process and life cycle of interface design as an introduction to guidelines and principles.

Nielsen (1993) proposes the concept of *iterative user interface design* to emphasize the importance of iteration as the key activity in designing user interfaces. Involving users and conducting user-centered evaluations of designed interfaces are the focus of the iterative user interface design process. He notes that iterative design of user interfaces entails steady refinement of the design on the basis of user testing and evaluation methods.

He suggests that a typical process for user interface design is as follows:

- Complete a design.

- Record the problems that test users encountered.

- Fix the identified problems in a new iteration of the interface.

- Conduct user testing to ensure the "fixes" did solve the problems.

- Identify new usability problems introduced by the changed design.

To design and develop effective user interfaces, redesigning the interface is necessary. Nielsen (1993) notes that "it is virtually impossible to design a user interface that has no usability problems from the start. Even the best usability experts cannot design perfect user interfaces in a single attempt, so a usability engineering lifecycle should be built around the concept of iteration."

Rose (2006) suggests that, in order to reconcile information-seeking behavior with search user interfaces, "three key principles should be taken into account:

- Different interfaces (or at least different forms of interaction) should be available to match different search goals.

- The interface should facilitate the selection of appropriate contexts for the search.

- The interface should support the iterative nature of the search task, and in particular, it should invite refinement and exploration." (p. 799)

These principles highlight the importance of considering several aspects of good design: level of domain and subject knowledge, variety of search goals and tasks that users may bring to the search process, provision of contextual information, and the advantages of features that support query reformulation and deeper exploration of the collection and its conceptual structure.

The following sections discuss general design guidelines, specific search user interface design guidelines, and guidelines developed specifically for the design of thesaurus-enhanced search user interfaces.

9.2 Search User Interface Design Principles

Human-computer interaction researchers and developers have published a substantial body of literature on design principles and guidelines for user interfaces. Shneiderman et al. (1997) provide these general guidelines for effective user interfaces for information retrieval:

- Strive for consistency: terminology, font, layout, and so forth.

- Provide shortcuts for skilled workers.

- Offer informative feedback: informing the user of all aspects of the search.

- Offer simple error handling: clear and specific error messages.

- Permit easy reversal of actions: ease of getting back to the previous stage.

- Support user control: Users should have control over the search process rather than being provided with an enforced set of actions.

- Reduce short-time memory load: Search history and fewer screens are more effective.

- Design for closure: Users need to know when they have completed the search, and a broader tree with fewer levels is more effective than deep menu tree.

Shneiderman (1998) emphasizes the importance of thesaurus support for effective searching. In a discussion of user interface features for searching textual databases, he proposes a four-phase framework: formulation, initiation of action, review of results, and refinement. He suggests that in the search formulation phase, interfaces should provide broader, narrower, and synonymous terms from a thesaurus to help users clarify their search.

One of the key challenges in search user interface design is the amount of information provided on the interface. Decisions about how much information should be presented to the user affect the ways in which users interact with and make use of interface features and functionalities. In a discussion of design principles for user interfaces, Hearst (1999) suggests that there is always a trade-off between the amount of information shown to the user and the sophistication of interface functionalities. This trade-off, she notes, depends on the users' prior knowledge of the system, the interface, and the topic for which they are carrying out the search. She also notes that introducing novel interface features may be pleasing to some users but cumbersome to others. For this reason, user interface design should allow for flexibility in interaction style, and one should not expect new features to be equally helpful for all users.

In addition to the previously mentioned principles, Hearst (2009) provides a number of design guidelines specific to search user interfaces, taking into account current design trends:

- Show search results immediately, allowing users to be sure they are on the right track and providing them with suggestions of related terms for query reformulation.

- Show informative document metadata and highlight query terms, which may include titles, URLs, or textual summaries; also, visual highlighting of query terms, using a boldface or colored background, can be a useful feature of the interface.

- Allow sorting of results by various criteria, which may include relevance, recency, author, price, and so forth.

- Show query term suggestions, which may be in the form of spelling corrections, semantically related query terms for users to choose from, or dynamic suggestions as the user types a term into a search system.

- Use relevance indicators sparingly, recognizing that graphical indicators can be more useful than textual or numerical indicators, as the notion of relevance is vague.

- Support rapid response, recognizing it is critical for the interface to provide fast response related to dynamic search result suggestions and query reformulation activities.

- Suggest the search action in the entry form; that is, rather than showing a blank entry form, the designer places text within the entry form to indicate the action that will result from using that form.

- Support simple history mechanisms, a feature that allows users to view their search navigation, or term selection activities.

- Integrate navigation and search, with navigation interfaces allowing the user to interleave keyword queries within existing information structures, thereby smoothly integrating navigation with search; browsable information structures such as links on the website, table of contents, and flat, hierarchical, or faceted category systems allow searchers to navigate, gain an overview of the collection, or narrow down their search.

- Avoid empty results sets, one mechanism being to use query previews to show how many documents will result if a particular navigation step is taken.

- Address the vocabulary problem, which refers to the great variety of search terms that users may use to search for a given piece of information; choice of interface terminology and terms for a category system is important and should take into account the variety of users' search terms.

In a discussion of appropriate design for dynamic taxonomies and faceted search user interfaces, Stefaner et al. (2009) identify a number of useful features. The key features proposed are clear instructions on Boolean search functions across facets; provision of clear visual structure and hierarchy; user control for hiding or showing partial and full sets of facets; availability of a free-form keyword search, with clear instructions on whether the user is searching within facets or the collection; and clear marking of the current focus and the resulting effects, to allow users to keep track of the changes that take place in the appearance of facets and in the results after their query formulation or reformulation.

Kules and Shneiderman (2008) studied how users make use of high-level categories or categorized overviews of web search results and proposed the following design guidelines for web search user interfaces that relate to various search and retrieval tasks:

- Provide overviews of large sets of results: This feature will allow users to gain a more comprehensive perspective of the collection and provide them with opportunities for reformulation of their query.

- Organize overviews around meaningful categories: Categories should be meaningful and can be based on such metadata elements as document format, language, topic, and geography.

- Clarify and visualize category structure: If categories are drawn from a classification, taxonomy, or ontology, the structure should be made visible. This visualization will provide users with the context of individual categories, as well as with their relationship to other categories.

- Tightly couple category labels to result list: The use of this technique allows users to quickly switch between the categories and the retrieved results and assists the users in clarifying the meaning and relevance of a given category.

- Ensure that the full category information is available: If the search interface makes use of deep hierarchies, designers should ensure that full category information (that is, the complete label or descriptor) is available to searchers. The category labels in the overview indicate which categories the results are in, but this information may be limited to the top few levels because of limited display space.

- Support multiple types of categories and visual presentations: A variety of categories and presentation styles should be provided in order to allow searchers to customize the categories or presentation styles according to their own needs.

- Use separate facets for each type of category: If the interface makes use of multiple categories, such as topical and geographical, facets within each category should be visually separated to assist users in clarifying the meanings and relationships.

- Arrange text for scanning or skimming: To support fast scanning and skimming, category labels, titles, URLs, and snippets of text should be designed in a consistent manner, such as linear lists, columns, or matrices. They should be visible rather than require interaction such as moving the pointer over an item.

As can be seen from these guidelines, there is a particular focus on the style of results presentation and on the integration of categories for browsing and results examination.

Resnick and Vaughan (2006) describe the best practices for the design of search user interface, noting that domain-specific thesauri should be used for query expansion. In their view, the key best practices for search user interface design are as follows:

- Provide a large query entry box when longer queries will be effective.

- Brief search hints are more likely to be used than advanced search dialogues.

- In the results descriptions, show the keywords in context.

- Organize large sets of results into categories.

- If no results are found, provide suggestions for improving the query.

- On the results page, provide the original query in a format that can be edited.

- The user interface should facilitate iterative searching, by supporting the modification of queries and allowing users to search within and across existing results sets.

9.3 Information Architecture Design Guidelines and Principles

Information architecture and web usability studies have provided a variety of design principles and best practices that may relate to the use and integration of thesauri into websites. For instance, Krug (2006) emphasizes the importance of having a clear visual hierarchy to show directly and accurately the relationships among the items on the page. He refers to three characteristics of a clear visual hierarchy:

- The more important something is, the more prominent it is.

- Things that are related logically are also related visually.

- Things are "nested" visually to show what's part of what.

In a discussion of search patterns from the perspective of information architecture and web design, Morville and Callender (2010) propose several key design principles:

- Input hints or prompts near or within the box should show the "what" and the "how" of search, and the box should provide autocompletion features and a forgiving format.

- Progressive disclosure: design the interface in such a way that advanced features are revealed to searchers as they progress through their search.

- Users should be able to receive immediate response through autocomplete and autosuggest features.

- Users' intentions drive search behavior, so it is important to provide a variety of choices and alternative views of the collection.

- Users should know what will happen next—predictability ensures usability.

- Users should be provided with some options in addition to search function; a right balance is needed between showing and hiding options.

- The interface should minimize disruption, such as when users are switching between pages and windows.

In a discussion of effective information architecture design, Morville and Rosenfeld (2007) provide another list of guidelines:

- Have a ubiquitous search box that is clear and easy to use.

- Provide advanced search functions for expert searchers,

- Allow users to revise their search by repeating it in the results page, explaining where results come from (e.g., the search is carried out on a single collection or on multiple collections; describe what the user did; and show the sorting feature, number of results, and filters such as date range.

- Integrate searching with browsing to allow users to jump back and forth between these functions.

- Provide a means of revising the search, and offer advice on how to improve it.

9.4 Guidelines Specific to the Information Search Process

In her model of cascading interactions in the digital library, Bates (2002) suggests the user interface may provide vocabulary support systems that present additional or related terms for use in searching. Query expansion capabilities should incorporate a core feature of the intellectual structure of faceted vocabularies, namely, facet combination, a feature that is crucial to effective operation for many real queries. She suggests that interface design should not only follow good criteria but also be based on a key understanding of various options in the provision of search capabilities for the user, including front end. Designers should ensure the underlying indexing and metadata structure is represented and used effectively in the interface.

In a discussion of the ways in which control over the search process should be divided between the user and the interface, Bates (1990) notes that, because of the variety of user preferences for searching versus browsing and because of the vague or ill-defined nature of some queries, the provision of search strategies and tactics within the user interface will be effective in supporting users' search behavior and thinking about the search process.

In a series of experiments on interfaces that support query expansion with a thesaurus, Beaulieu (1997) found that both implicit (automatic) and explicit (interactive) use of the thesaurus are beneficial for query reformulation and that the terms explicitly selected by users are valuable. She suggests that the interface should allow users to view and select from system-generated terms. Also, the use of thesaurus terms for interactive and automatic query expansion has been specifically investigated for the type of thesaurus terms that could be useful for each approach. The findings suggest that broader terms and related terms in thesauri are good candidates for interactive query expansion. Also, narrower terms could be good candidates if precision is desired (Greenberg, 2001).

Greenberg (2001) emphasizes further that interactive query expansion research should address issues related to interface design and human-computer interaction, such as how thesaurus terms should be displayed to end users and how to initiate thesaurus-based query expansion support. Research has also found that in the context of interactive thesaurus-based query expansion, users with extensive domain knowledge choose narrower and synonymous terms, whereas users with limited knowledge of the domain select broader and related terms (Shiri and Revie, 2006). These findings indicate that thesaurus terms may provide different benefits for searchers with varying levels of domain knowledge.

Wildemuth (2006) suggests that there are important findings from studies of information search behavior that can be used as evidence to inform the design of search user interfaces. She places particular emphasis on search strategies and query formulation. Based on an analysis of numerous studies, she suggests that search user interfaces should provide mechanisms for supporting search strategy reformulation and query modification. Her main design ideas are as follows:

- Provide tips for reformulating the search with some customization based on the size of the previously retrieved set.

- Accommodate a control mechanism for deleting the first term shown while retaining the second term.

- Conduct stemming of search terms entered by the searcher and query expansion.

- Add narrower and related terms from a controlled vocabulary or terms from documents judged to be relevant in an initial or previous search cycle.

- Provide access to a controlled vocabulary (if available) from which searchers can select terms directly to add to their searches.

- Display potential terms from which the user can select in order to expand the query.

9.5 Design Guidelines Specific to Thesaurus-Enhanced Search Interfaces

A number of researchers have discussed user interface design features for thesaurus management software and have provided general interface design guidelines (Ganzmann, 1990; Milstead, 1991;

Riesland, 2004; Will, 2010). However, these guidelines have a particular focus on thesaurus construction, thesaurus editing and updating, and thesaurus management software. The guidelines, for instance, offer software developers a set of recommendations for creating features and functionalities that make use of various thesaural elements such as relationship types; scope notes; hierarchical organization of terms; adding, deleting, and updating terms; and the format and structure of the output of the created thesaurus.

This section reviews the guidelines and principles that are proposed specifically for the design and development of thesaurus-enhanced interfaces for search and retrieval. Milstead (1997) notes that the provision of effective thesaurus navigation will not only increase searcher use, but will also support seamless switching between thesaurus navigation and database searching to improve access. This is a key design decision and challenge, as there is always a trade-off between the amount of information provided on the interface and the way in which the user is invited to interact with the thesaurus and the document collections.

As well, the author notes that interfaces should be designed in such a way that users need not interact directly with the thesaurus to any greater extent than they wish or need to. This recommendation implies the flexibility of the user interface in terms of providing basic and advanced thesaurus-based functionalities for users with different interaction styles and mental models.

Weinberg (1998) stresses the importance of usability of thesaurus interfaces for searchers and argues for the use of user-centered design techniques in developing thesaurus interfaces:

> The thesaurus must be brought to the user instead of the user having to request it. A thesaurus should be designed for usability—otherwise users will not consult it. When the user inputs a term, the system should suggest other related search terms. Users need to see how their search terms are expanded and select the appropriate terms from a suggested list. The expansion should not be done automatically; otherwise, entering a term such as "counselors" could lead to obtaining information about "lawyers" by mistake, when information on camp counselors is sought. (p. 13)

These statements point to the interactive, rather than the automatic, use of thesauri in support of searching. Research by Shiri and Revie (2005) into the interaction between thesaurus usability and interface usability found that interface usability was a factor affecting thesaurus browsing and navigation, together with other information-searching behaviors. Users who evaluated the learning or use of the interface as very easy also rated thesaurus browsing and navigation as very easy. Usability was also found to have a relationship to the time users spent searching for their topic, with those who evaluated the use of the interface as very easy requiring significantly less time to carry out searches (Shiri and Revie, 2005).

Williamson (2007) notes that there is an urgent need for the design of more user-friendly interfaces for thesauri and that there should be greater emphasis on human-computer interaction to assist searchers in facilitating successful searches.

The Institute for Learning and Research Technology (2000) in the U.K. conducted a research project called DESIRE, which focused on the development of several subject gateways for organizing subject-based access to internet resources. A set of guidelines was suggested for the user interfaces for these subject gateways, a number of which were associated with thesaurus interfaces and focused on how thesauri should be used for browsing and searching the content of subject gateways. These guidelines are as follows:

- Ability to search for the selected term together with all "child" terms, a feature often known as an Explode option

- Ability to browse through the hierarchical structure of the thesaurus as well as to search it by keyword

- Alphabetical index of terms with links to the thesaurus, with thesaural browsing accomplished through hypertext links between related terms, and parent, child, related, and non-preferred terms listed with the currently selected term

- Use of the thesaurus for access to catalog records so as to produce a list of all records that contain the currently selected term

- Necessity of ensuring the thesaurus has a very different look and feel from the catalog itself, so that users are not confused about which one they are searching

Shiri et al. (2002) investigated several research prototype and commercial search user interfaces enhanced with thesauri and proposed the following features for the design of such interfaces:

- Offer an explicit thesaurus search option on the main search page in an easy-to-use way for end users; use tabs such as Suggested Terms, Thesaurus, and Subject Headings to show the availability of a thesaurus facility in the interface.

- Provide easy and understandable terminology to describe the relationships between descriptors and terms.

- Supply hierarchical, alphabetical, and permuted lists to support different browsing and searching strategies.

- Allow for flexible ways of choosing terms for posting to the search system, such as drag and drop, checkboxes, hypertext features, and double clicking.

- Facilitate, via hypertext navigation, the process and understanding of moving from a descriptor to its hierarchical structure.

- Encourage the selection of alternative Boolean operators for combining different thesaurus terms.

- Provide feedback on terms not available in the thesaurus and suggest terms related in some way to the initial entered term.

- Include a Term Pool option for saving for later use the descriptors chosen by users during thesaurus browsing.

- Integrate thesaurus and retrieved document displays for more effective search and retrieval.

- Make the thesaurus option available in all stages of the search process, namely, query formulation, modification, and expansion.

A usability study of an online photographic collection with thesaurus-enhanced features suggests the following strategies and features in order to make effective use of thesauri in search user interfaces (Dalmau et al., 2005):

- Integrate the controlled vocabulary's cross-reference structure into the search engine, thereby allowing users to access images described with synonyms or variant names.

- The interface should support a structured form of browsing and searching, with links to term suggestions, in addition to keyword searching.

- Users' search terms should be matched against the descriptive fields of the records and the thesaurus.

- The search engine should carry out two automatic functions, mapping of lead-in terms to authorized terms and retrieval of all narrower terms.

Research into the design of digital library user interfaces has suggested another set of best practices (Davis, 2006):

- Inform the design through user focus group and observation.

- Allow flexibility in search options and provide free-text search as well as controlled vocabulary search.

- Integrate search and browsing activities.

- Present metadata-based results sets.

- Resolve the various controlled vocabularies used by different communities through the development of an overarching ontology.

Si and Chen (2009) suggest a number of strategies for optimizing thesaurus interfaces on the web. They recommend provision of support for different types of users, including both new and frequent users; provision of various search functions to allow users to carry out partial-match and exact-match searches; access to category browsing as well as alphabetical browsing; and accommodation of navigation strategies to support users' navigation around the thesaurus and the document collection.

9.6 Categorization of Design Guidelines for Thesaurus-Enhanced Search User Interfaces

The guidelines and best practices for designing thesaurus-enhanced search user interfaces can be made coherent through categorization.

The categorization is derived from a multiplicity of sources: human-computer interaction research, search user interface design studies and analyses, information architecture research, information search behavior studies, and guidelines and recommendations from national and international standards for the construction of thesauri and controlled vocabularies.

These sources have produced several comprehensive sets of guidelines for developing search user interfaces enhanced with thesauri. However, because of the absence of communication among the relevant research and practice communities, a unified structure for presenting a coherent set of guidelines has not hitherto been developed. This section addresses that deficiency.

The categorization is arranged on the basis of the general stages of the search process of the models reviewed in Chapter 2. All these process models involve three common stages: query formulation, results examination, and query reformulation.

Because of the complex nature of specific features associated with those interfaces that are enhanced with thesauri, this classification provides a more specific description of the activities in the search process, including activities such as browsing, query term suggestion, and the principles associated with the general search process. All of the guidelines and recommendations forming this classification are tailored to suit the design and development of thesaurus-enhanced search interfaces.

Accordingly, Table 9.1 organizes design guidelines into the following categories:

- Query formulation
- Term suggestion
- Query reformulation
- Browsing
- Search or query history
- Results presentation
- Visual representations
- Integration of querying and browsing
- General search process

Table 9.1 Categorization of guidelines and best practices in the design of thesaurus-enhanced search user interfaces

Action	Guidelines
Query formulation	• Provide direct access to the thesaurus for query formulation • Suggest search action in both the thesaurus and database search bars • Provide clear instructions on Boolean search functions across facets and thesaurus terms • Provide keyword search option with clear instruction on whether the user is searching within the thesaurus or the collection • Provide flexible term selection features, such as drag and drop, checkboxes, hypertext features, and double clicking • Provide large query entry box for both the thesaurus and the collection search features • Provide a feature to select all the narrower terms of a term known as Explode option • Provide keyword search for the thesaurus, which would be particularly useful for compound terms and their display to the user • Provide a usable approach to various thesaurus-based searching (for example, the use of such terms as *starting with*, *containing*, and *exact match*) to allow various types of searches in thesauri • Provide access to synonymous terms, variant names, and narrower terms through the integration of cross-references in the search engine
Term suggestion	• Show query term suggestions based on exact or partial matches of user terms to thesauri • Provide quick and dynamic term suggestions based on the structure of the thesaurus • Provide spelling suggestions or alternative term suggestions • Provide term suggestions for searches with no exact match results based on users' initial query terms • Provide term suggestion based on the descriptive fields in which thesaurus matches were successful
Query reformulation	• Provide the original query in an editable format on the results page • Provide query modification. facilities to improve the initial query and to facilitate search within and across result sets • Provide term suggestions from thesauri to support interactive query expansion and modification; depending on the target audience and their desire for recall and precision, broader, narrower, and related terms can be suggested to support various search tasks • Provide tips for reformulating queries based on some customization of the previously retrieved results; in thesauri, the retrieved terms can be provided along with additional related terms for narrowing down or broadening the search • Conduct stemming of the user's term and query expansion based on various thesaural relationships • Show user potentially useful terms from thesauri for query expansion
Browsing	• Organize overviews around meaningful categories so the thesaurus facets or top terms can provide a high level and informative view of the collection • Arrange the text (including the thesaurus and the results) for scanning and skimming to make it easy for users to scan and skim without having to hover a mouse • Provide hierarchical and alphabetical browsing based on the structure of the thesaurus and its broader/narrower term relationships • Show the first three levels of the hierarchy for browsing • Provide shortcut or path to thesaurus browsing from suggested or selected terms • Provide navigational features to allow switching between terms and create hyperlinks between synonymous and related terms • Provide browsing and navigation strategies around the thesaurus and the collection • Provide faceted and classified views of the thesaurus where applicable
Search or query history	• Keep and provide access to search history, which may include a user's thesaurus browsing history, history of selected terms, and the results viewed as well as the sessions' general history; search history can be provided within the same session or longitudinally • Provide a real time search term pool for users to be able to select or deselect terms

Table 9.1   (*cont.*)

Results presentation	• Show results immediately, which should apply to both results from the thesaurus and from the collection as well • Show informative document surrogates and highlight query terms • Provide result sorting criteria and an indication of the number of records available for which term in the collection • Use graphical representation of relevance, and for the relevance of thesaurus terms, exact and partial matches may have different relevance indicators • Avoid empty result sets, which in the thesaurus search function, can be achieved through the use of stemming and partial matching of user terms and through submitting the user's term as a free-text search; an indication of the number of results per thesaurus term is useful for this purpose • Provide overviews of large sets of results, to which faceted thesauri lend themselves very well • In the results, show keywords in their context, which will help users see the context of the word and will be particularly useful for multi-term descriptors in thesauri • Organize large sets of results into categories; organizing results based on a set of thesaurus facets and terms can be one way of achieving this purpose • Provide access points to thesauri in the retrieved results through hyperlinked descriptors • Provide metadata-based result sets
Visual representations	• Provide clear visual structure and hierarchy and user control for hiding or showing partial and full sets of facets or thesaurus terms • Clarify and visualize category structure, as the high level facets of a thesaurus or its structure should be visible to users in order for them to form a context for individual terms • Ensure that the full category information is available; depending on the size of the thesaurus, a few levels of the hierarchy can be shown on the interface • Support multiple types of categories and visual presentations, as in thesauri, there are several types of displays, namely alphabetical, hierarchical, and permuted, that can be provided on the interface • Provide easy control for switching between different thesaural displays
Integration of querying and browsing	• Integrate searching and browsing, and provide the facility to allow user to switch between thesaurus browsing and thesaurus searching and searching within various subsets of the collection • Tightly couple category labels to result list, and allow users to browse and select terms and view the results simultaneously • Integrate thesaurus browsing and results examination to allow seamless access to the thesaurus and the retrieved results
General search process	• Offer informative feedback, which may be associated with the availability of the term in the thesaurus or instructions on what would be the next step for the user to take; if no results are found, provide suggestions for improving the query • Clearly mark the current focus and the resulting effects of the user's action, for instance, what part of the thesaurus hierarchy is consulted by the user • Provide brief search hints as they are more likely to be used than advanced search dialogs; for thesaurus interfaces, this could imply that rather than offering thesaurus search as advanced feature, brief hints can be designed to encourage and engage users • Provide explicit thesaurus search option on the interface • Use an easy to understand terminology to show the availability of the thesaurus and suggested terms and their relationships • Make the thesaurus available at all stages of the search process • Provide thesaurus search and browsing options for novice and advanced searchers, which may require thesaurus developers to create two versions of the thesaurus for these two groups

It should be noted that these categories were created as organizing principles to facilitate the presentation of guidelines and do not necessarily represent a sequential view of the various stages of search. The typical approach to search is iterative, multidimensional, and nonlinear and depends on a broad range of searcher dynamics, including task, context, subject knowledge, and search expertise.

In addition to the best practices and guidelines synthesized in Table 9.1, designers of thesaurus-enhanced search user interfaces need to take into account usability and accessibility standards and best practices. Much has been written on usability and usability testing. One of the most widely consulted sources for information on usability is Nielsen's useit.com website. Another useful website for accessibility is Web Accessibility Initiative (WAI; World Wide Web Consortium), and a European website that provides both usability and user-centered design resources to practitioners, managers, and European projects is called UsabilityNet (European Union Framework V Information Society Technologies Programme, 2003).

9.7 Conclusion

This chapter discusses general user interface design processes and guidelines, and summarizes the principles, guidelines, and best practices for the design of user interfaces for search and retrieval. The chapter also reviews studies on information search behavior that have focused on the use of controlled vocabularies, and it presents a detailed account of guidelines and recommendations for designing thesaurus-enhanced search interfaces. Drawing on the various literatures of human-computer interaction, information search behavior, and thesaurus construction standards, a number of design guidelines and recommendations have been identified and organized. This categorization follows the well-known stages of the search process in order to allow designers and developers of thesaurus-enhanced search user interfaces to contextualize more holistically the role of thesauri in the total search process and to provide design ideas for effective and useful integration of thesauri into search user interfaces.

References

Bates, M. J. (1990). Where should the person stop and the information search interface start? *Information Processing and Management*, 26(5), 575–591.

Bates, M. J. (2002). The cascade of interactions in the digital library interface. *Information Processing & Management*, 38(3), 381–400.

Beaulieu, M. (1997). Experiments of interfaces to support query expansion. *Journal of Documentation*, 53(1), 8–19.

Dalmau, M., Floyd, R., Jiao, D., and Riley, J. (2005). Integrating thesaurus relationships into search and browse in an online photograph collection. *Library Hi Tech*, 23(3), 425–452.

Davis, L. (2006). Designing a search user interface for a digital library. *Journal of the American Society for Information Science*, 57(6), 788–791.

European Union Framework V Information Society Technologies Programme. (2003). UsabilityNet. www.usabilitynet.org (accessed June 9, 2012).

Ganzmann, J. (1990). Criteria for the evaluation of thesaurus software. *International Classification*, 17(3/4), 148–157.

Greenberg, J. (2001). Optimal query expansion (QE) processing methods with semantically encoded structures thesauri terminology. *Journal of the American Society for Information Science and Technology*, 52(6), 487–498.

Hearst, M. A. (1999). User interfaces and visualization. In: R. Baeza-Yates and B. Ribeiro-Neto (Eds.), *Modern information retrieval* (pp. 257–323). New York: ACM Press.

Hearst, M. A. (2009). *Search user interfaces*. Cambridge, UK: Cambridge University Press.

Institute for Learning and Research Technology, University of Bristol (2000). DESIRE information gateways handbook. Retrieved from web.archive.org/web/20061010105450/http://www.desire.org/handbook/3-2.html (accessed June 18, 2012).

Krug, S. (2006). *Don't make me think: A common sense approach to web usability*. Indianapolis, IN: Que.

Kules, B., and Shneiderman, B. (2008). Users can change their web search tactics: Design guidelines for categorized views. *Information Processing and Management*, 44(2), 463–484.

Milstead, J. L. (1991). Specifications for thesaurus software. *Information Processing and Management*, 27(2/3), 165–175.

Milstead, J. L. (1997). Use of thesauri in the full-text environment. In: P. A. Cochrane and E. H. Johnson (Eds.), *Visualizing subject access for 21st century information resources: Proceedings of the 34th annual clinic on library applications of data processing* (pp. 28–38). Champaign, IL: Graduate School of Library and Information Science, University of Illinois.

Morville, P., and Callender, J. (2010). *Search patterns*. Sebastopol, CA: O'Reilly.

Morville, P., and Rosenfeld, L. (2007). *Information Architecture for the World Wide Web: Designing Large-Scale Web Sites*, 3rd ed. Sebastopol, CA: O'Reilly.

Nielsen, J. (1993). Iterative user interface design. *IEEE Computer*, 26(11), 32–41. Retrieved from www.useit.com/papers/iterative_design (accessed June 18, 2012).

Nielsen, J. useit.com. Retrieved from www.useit.com (accessed July 13, 2011).

Resnick, M. L., and Vaughan, M. W. (2006). Search user interfaces: Best practices and future visions. *Journal of the American Society for Information Science and Technology*, 57(6), 777–780.

Riesland, M. A. (2004). Tools of the trade: Vocabulary management software. *Cataloging & Classification Quarterly*, 37(3/4), 155–176.

Rose, D. E. (2006). Reconciling information-seeking behaviour with search user interfaces for the web. *Journal of the American Society for Information Science and Technology*, 57(6), 797–799.

Shiri, A., and Revie, C. (2005). Usability and user perceptions of a thesaurus-enhanced search interface. *Journal of Documentation*, 61(5), 640–656.

Shiri, A., and Revie, C. (2006). Query expansion behaviour within a thesaurus-enhanced search environment: A user-centered evaluation. *Journal of the American Society for Information Science and Technology*, 57(4), 462–478.

Shiri, A. A., Revie, C., and Chowdhury, G. (2002). Thesaurus-enhanced search interfaces. *Journal of Information Science*, 28(2), 111–122.

Shneiderman, B. (1998). *Designing the user interface: Strategies for effective human-computer interaction*, 3rd ed. Reading, MA: Addison-Wesley.

Shneiderman, B., Byrd, D., and Croft, W. B. (1997). Clarifying search: A user-interface framework for text searches. *DL Magazine*. Retrieved from www.dlib.org/dlib/january97/retrieval/01shneiderman.html (accessed June 9, 2012).

Si, L., and Chen, H. (2009). An investigation of functions and some optimizing strategies of thesauri with web interface. In: *Proceedings of the 2nd IEEE international conference on computer science and information technology* (pp. 580–584). Beijing, China, August 8–11, 2009.

Stefaner, M., Ferré, S., Perugini, S., Koren, J., and Zhang, Y. (2009). User interface design. In: G. Sacco and Y. Tzitzkas (Eds.), *Dynamic taxonomies and faceted search: Theory, practice, and experience* (Vol. 25, pp. 75–112). Berlin, Germany: Springer.

Weinberg, B. H. (1998). Thesaurus design for information systems. *Newsletter of the American Society of Indexers*, 6(6), 12–15.

Wildemuth, B. M. (2006). Evidence-based practice in search interface design. *Journal of the American Society for Information Science and Technology* 57(6), 825–828.

Will, L. (2010). Thesaurus management software. In: *Encyclopedia of library and information sciences*, 3rd ed. (pp. 5238–5246). New York: Taylor & Francis.

Williamson, N. J. (2007). Knowledge structures and the internet: Progress and prospects. *Cataloging & Classification Quarterly*, 44(3/4), 329–342.

World Wide Web Consortium (WC3). Web accessibility initiative. www.w3.org/WAI (accessed June 9, 2012).

CHAPTER 10

Current Trends and Developments

As we have seen through the preceding chapters, thesauri have come a long way since the middle of the 20th century; in particular, they have been a growing dimension of research and development in numerous areas. In the more than 50 years since Vickery (1960) wrote about the new term *thesaurus* in the fledgling intellectual domain of documentation, many information retrieval thesauri have been built and used by researchers and practitioners. In fact, the past five decades have witnessed the incremental and evolutionary development and use of thesauri in many different domains and disciplines.

In writing this book I have made use of a broad array of sources on thesauri, ranging from books, journal articles, and standards to conference proceedings, internet websites, and research reports. A quick glance at the sources cited throughout the book documents the multidimensional and versatile nature of thesauri in various systems, contexts, and technologies. The publications cited have appeared in a considerable variety of journals, notably, *Journal of the American Society for Information Science and Technology*, *Journal of Information Science*, *Journal of Documentation*, *Information Processing and Management*, *Online Information Review*, *Knowledge Organization*, and *Cataloguing and Classification*. Through conference proceedings, several organizations have also documented research in this area, particularly the American Society for Information Science and Technology (ASIST) Annual Meetings, the Association for Computing Machinery (ACM) Special Interest Group on Information Retrieval, and the International Society for Knowledge Organization. A significant number of digital library conferences held in the U.S. and Europe are also cited.

This simple mapping of the publications in which thesaurus research has appeared over the past half-century points to the emergent interest of various research and practice communities in this area and to the relevance of research in this area to information access improvement. The mapping also reveals a collection of disparate and sometimes unrelated, sometimes overlapping intellectual traditions of thesaural research.

Thesauri have been a primary dimension of the research and development interests of experts in information retrieval, online searching, user interface design, knowledge organization in general, indexing and abstracting, cataloging and classification, and information search behavior studies. I trust you have found that this book has met the goal of bringing together the research, scholarship, and development in all these divergent areas in order to provide a solid basis for the effective use of thesauri in interfaces designed to serve many different information search and retrieval environments.

Developments in the age of the World Wide Web have paved the way for the increasingly more extensive use of knowledge organization systems such as thesauri. Illustrative of these developments are new web-related formats and standards; new internet programming languages and platforms; and more flexible and functional user interface design methodologies, along with significant increases in the speed, efficiency, and ubiquity of computer systems. We examined developments involving thesauri in Chapter 1.

These developments relate to the following areas of intellectual inquiry impacting thesauri:

- Digital libraries

- Interoperability

- Semantic web

- Simple Knowledge Organization System (SKOS)

- Linked data

- Taxonomies

- Social tagging and folksonomies

- Ontologies

- Query formulation and expansion

- Faceted and exploratory search

- Search user interfaces

- Information architecture

- Metadata

Figure 10.1 depicts these areas visually and perhaps more coher-ently. Note that these subject areas or categories are not mutually exclusive; rather, they are highlighted to demonstrate the consider-able variety of web initiatives and advances that have brought the-sauri to the forefront of information representation and retrieval.

10.1 Search User Interfaces

While user interface design for the web owes intellectual homage to human-computer interaction, web usability, and information retrieval research, it is important to highlight the widespread use of facet analysis techniques in the development of highly interactive and information-rich user interfaces.

The renewed recognition of facet analysis by the information architecture community stresses the importance of one of the key, and long established, principles of information organization and the-saurus construction. Many user experience designers, information architects, and web usability experts benefit from the principles of facet analysis, and as a result we have witnessed the emergence of hundreds of corporate, and noncorporate, websites that draw on this useful technique to design navigation, browsing, and searching func-tionalities. Almost all information architecture books have a chapter

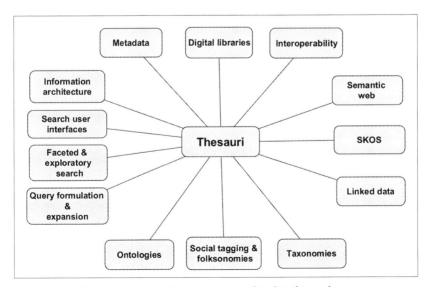

Figure 10.1   Research and development areas related to thesauri

or section on controlled vocabularies, and thesauri in particular, to inform information architects and user experience designers of the ways in which these tools can be incorporated into websites to organize and design information and ultimately to optimize search and browse capabilities. This, of course, is directly related to the business purposes and profit making of each company and to corporate success as defined by its customer base and by how efficiently and effectively its website satisfies users' needs and intentions.

The interfaces developed on the basis of facet analysis are called *faceted search user interfaces*. We reviewed examples of faceted search user interfaces in Chapter 1.

Some researchers have used the term *guided search user interfaces* to stress the importance of facets as guides for searchers. Other researchers have called them *exploratory user interfaces*, in recognition of the potential of faceted user interfaces to support browsing and information-seeking strategies that are not query-based and to highlight the support that these user interfaces provide for exploratory behavior of searchers who may browse facets and subfacets and change their browsing or searching strategies accordingly. From these developments, we can foresee continued use of facet analysis as the need for organized and consistent access to information becomes increasingly necessary on the web.

Search user interfaces have become more sophisticated in offering query formulation and reformulation support and in providing users with dynamic and interactive search term suggestions. These interfaces also make available spelling and auto-completion features that allow a user's initial search term characters to be completed as they are typed in and shown to the user. Thesauri have been used in search user interfaces both as a source of search term suggestion and as an auto-completion feature.

In addition, new user interface designs, such as the use of word clouds and tag clouds, are now finding their way into websites and search services. Recently, some digital libraries and online public access catalogs (OPACs) have started using tag clouds to show users the most popular or most frequently used subject terms from controlled vocabularies. Thesaurus terms, term relationships, and suggested terms based on thesauri can be visualized via tag clouds. Shiri et al. (2010) reported the design of a user interface that visualizes thesaurus relationships with word clouds whereby narrower, broader, and synonymous terms are distinguished by means of color, proximity, and opacity.

Further research should experiment with new visual techniques for presenting thesauri to users. Such techniques promise new opportunities for designers of interfaces to web-based thesauri and the thesauri attached to both commercial and noncommercial databases.

10.2 Digital Libraries

After almost two decades of research, development, and practice, the area of digital libraries is now mature, with a broad range of communities contributing to it, including library and information science, computer science, and database and networking groups.

The developments associated with metadata, a key component of digital libraries in the mid-1990s, demonstrated the need for, and the importance of, subject description and subject access to information. This need resulted in the exploitation of thesauri as sources of subject metadata, as well as in their use to create information-rich user interfaces. A large number of digital library initiatives, such as subject gateways, portals, subject repositories, and institutional as well as subject-based digital libraries and open archives, make use of thesauri in a wide variety of ways in order to facilitate access to digital information. We examined examples of such digital libraries, subject gateways, and portals in Chapter 4.

Almost all metadata protocols, formats, and standards include subject-based descriptive elements to allow for subject description of various digital information objects, ranging from text-based materials to archives, manuscripts, photographs, and multimedia content. Metadata standards such as Dublin Core, Metadata Encoding and Transmission Standards (METS), Learning Object Metadata (LOM), the Photo Metadata Project, Encoded Archival Description (EAD), and the Government Information Locator Service (GILS) are just a few examples of metadata formats that contain subject description elements.

Digital library projects currently make use of a broad range of thesauri and other types of controlled vocabularies to assign subject terms within such standards. It is predicted that thesauri will be used in new digital library collections and services that adopt a structured, controlled, and metadata-based approach to information organization and representation.

The large number and variety of metadata formats and controlled vocabularies used in digital libraries call for subject and semantic interoperability, a concept that is widely researched and reported in the literature of digital libraries. Ensuring subject interoperability allows searchers to cross-browse and cross-search multiple digital library collections without having to deal with individual subject schemes and thesauri. This development, in turn, has drawn attention to the importance of linking, reconciling, and merging several different controlled vocabularies to facilitate consistent description and discovery of digital information.

It should be noted that the discussion of issues related to the integration and mapping of thesauri, classification schemes, and other types of controlled vocabulary has a long history. Consideration and use of subject interoperability models in digital libraries has its roots in pre-web projects that investigated the reconciliation, merger, or creation of super-thesauri. A wide range of projects have investigated subject interoperability. In Chapter 7 we reviewed the literature and examined a number of major projects that have investigated subject and semantic interoperability.

The advent of the web and its associated technologies and languages, such XML provided new opportunities to create mapping and cross-walks of several different controlled vocabularies, including classification schemes, subject heading lists, and thesauri. These developments have resulted in the design of terminology services that can host multiple controlled vocabularies and their mappings and cross-walks in order to facilitate machine-to-machine and client-server interactions for cross-browsing and cross-searching of various digital library collections.

Metadata interoperability standards such as the Open Archives Initiatives Protocol for Harvesting Metadata include subject-based metadata elements to support subject-based federated searching of various repositories and digital collections. We discussed examples of terminology services that encompass multiple controlled vocabularies in Chapter 7.

These developments and trends point to the value and relevance of thesauri in digital libraries, open archives, and subject repositories. As the number of digitization projects in various academic, governmental, and public and private institutions increases, the need for subject metadata and thesauri is predicted to become more critical.

It would be helpful to put digital libraries and digitization in the broader context of cyberinfrastructure. The Pervasive Technology Institute at Indiana University (2007) defines cyberinfrastructure as follows:

> Cyberinfrastructure consists of computing systems, data storage systems, advanced instruments and data repositories, visualization environments, and people, all linked together by software and high performance networks to improve research productivity and enable breakthroughs not otherwise possible.

Several terms are used in association with cyberinfrastructure to demonstrate its application in relation to many different disciplines, including e-science, e-social sciences, and e-humanities. The National Science Foundation's Cyberinfrastructure Vision for the 21st Century (National Science Foundation, 2007) emphasizes the importance of digital libraries in support of many scientific breakthroughs and points to the significance of data, metadata, controlled vocabularies, and ontologies to ensure consistent and coherent access to information.

In a discussion of scholarship in the digital age, Borgman (2007) notes that maintaining the coherence of content in today's environment depends on information organization mechanisms such as name spaces, thesauri, ontologies, and models for metadata and data structures. The stability and control of the information infrastructure hinges on the existence and currency of these tools. She emphasizes that thesauri and taxonomies can be used for text and data mining in the sciences to facilitate new discoveries. She also argues that thesauri and ontologies must reflect changes in terminology in the fields they serve and that organizations and institutions should take responsibility for maintaining, controlling, and disseminating these essential components of the information infrastructure.

10.3 Query Formulation and Expansion

Thesauri have been used to support the information search process by various categories of users, ranging from indexers, online search professionals, and librarians to end users of all types. Many studies have investigated the ways in which users can understand and make use of thesauri to improve their search experience.

Thesauri have been used to support various stages of the search process, including initial query formulation, query reformulation, query expansion, and refinement of the results set. Both interactive (explicit) and automatic (implicit) query reformulation and expansion techniques have been used to explore users' impressions and understandings of and reactions to thesaurus terms.

In interactive or explicit thesaurus-based query reformulation, users are presented a list of suggested terms from the thesaurus to add to or modify their initial search terms. This provides an opportunity for the user to browse and select terms and to improve knowledge of the topic being searched. In automatic or implicit thesaurus-based query expansion, the user is not involved in deciding which terms should be added to the initial query terms.

The findings from a number of studies suggest that thesauri have the potential to support both approaches to query reformulation, and that various thesaural relationships may serve different types of tasks and users with different degrees of prior subject knowledge. We discussed details of studies on search term selection for query formulation and expansion in Chapter 3.

With the rapid growth of research and development activities involving multiple thesauri and controlled vocabularies, there will certainly be more opportunities to examine interactive and automatic thesaurus-based query reformulation. These opportunities will include the provision of larger entry vocabularies for users and the development of new ways of ranking and retrieving thesaurus terms based on semantic overlapping in multiple controlled vocabularies.

Thesauri have also been studied from usability and usefulness viewpoints and from the perspective of the interaction of users with both the interface and the thesaurus. These studies have found that thesauri and thesaurus interfaces are used if the presentation and integration of thesauri into the search user interface is seamless, easy to understand, and easy to use.

There are many challenges, however, associated with incorporating a thesaurus into the search process because of the iterative and multistage nature of the search process. For example, when should thesaurus-based search and browsing be provided—at the initial search stage, after the presentation of the first results set, or when the user is struggling to think up terms for formulating a query? At what stage should browsing be suggested or presented?

Would the integration of thesaurus-assisted searching and browsing always result in successful searches? Should users be provided with a simple set of suggested terms from the thesaurus and then left to choose and refine their queries without directly consulting the thesaurus? While this approach may be useful for novice searchers and those new to a particular subject area or discipline, what about more-expert searchers who expect more from a search system and would be willing to spend more time and interact with more-sophisticated features of a system, including its thesaurus?

To add another dimension of complexity, what about users who prefer browsing over searching? Search task is a key factor influencing the initiation as well as the progression of the search process, and it is recognized that certain tasks lend themselves better to browsing than to searching. With this in mind, should we pursue one simple type of search strategy?

Full or partial presentation and display of a thesaurus and its relationship types, such as broader, narrower, related, and synonymous terms, may be provided for various users. A visual presentation of thesaurus terms and their relationships can encourage and engage some users to explore the thesaurus to support their search process and task completion. As we discussed in Chapter 2, many search behavior and interactive information retrieval models suggest that to ensure successful searches, a variety of search strategies should be supported by the information retrieval system and interface so that users with different types of tasks can interact with the system and satisfy their information needs and search intentions.

In line with these studies, the visual display of hierarchical, alphabetical, or permuted lists of thesaural terms may serve various information search strategies and styles. In Chapter 8 we analyzed a number of usability and user-centered studies and suggested that both the user interface and the thesaurus itself affect the ways in which users interact with the information retrieval system.

In Chapter 6 we presented examples of prototype and operational search user interfaces that have incorporated thesauri. These interfaces have taken various approaches to either partial or full access to thesauri during the search process. Some interfaces have provided visualized representations of various thesaural data elements, while others have focused on presenting a list set of suggested terms. Some have integrated searching and browsing and have provided seamless access to both the thesaurus and the retrieved results.

We offered a collection of guidelines and best practices for the design and development of thesaurus-enhanced search user interfaces in Chapter 9. These design guidelines are based on the various information search and retrieval activities that users experience when they interact with information retrieval systems. To provide an inclusive perspective on the design guidelines, research and development activities are examined and evaluated in areas of intellectual inquiry such as human-computer interaction, information search behavior, thesaurus construction standards, information architecture, and web usability.

One of the key challenges that remains to be investigated further is how to separate the effects of a thesaurus from those of the search interface on the search process and search success. To allow a fair evaluation of a system and its thesaurus, new evaluation measures have to be developed that will objectively delineate these effects and thus allow us to effectively and accurately evaluate thesauri in support of searching and browsing. Some of the studies we discussed in Chapter 8, such as Jones et al. (1995), Shiri and Revie (2005), and Tudhope et al. (2006), introduced approaches to the evaluation of both the thesaurus and the user interface. The challenge for thesaural researchers in the new information environments is to focus on the creation of new measures and evaluation criteria.

10.4 Thesaurus Construction

Although thesaurus construction is not the focus of this book, there are a number of associated developments and trends that do, in fact, provide new ways of using and expanding thesauri. The revision of thesaurus construction standards was undoubtedly one of the main developments. Both the American National Standards Institute–National Information Standards Organization (ANSI/NISO) Z39.19 and the British 8723 thesaurus construction standards were revised to reflect web developments and to accommodate the flexible use of thesauri, not only in terms of their construction but also in terms of their use by various communities and categories of users.

These two standards make guideline recommendations for thesaurus construction and user interface design that help developers and designers create a wider variety of thesaurus-enhanced search systems. Of particular importance are the attention of these two standards to various categories of users, in particular nonspecialist searchers, and to interoperability across collections, domains, disciplines, and languages. We addressed the specific guidelines associated with user interfaces for thesauri in Chapter 5.

In addition to standards, various techniques and technologies have been introduced that could expand and enhance thesauri for more effective support of users' search behavior. For example, some attention has been paid to the development of conceptual clustering methods that take advantage of statistical, linguistic, and natural language processing techniques in order to expand and enhance thesauri (Ibekwe-SanJuan, 2006). One of the main advantages of this approach is its use in updating a thesaurus or creating a thesaurus de novo.

Similarly, others have noted that bibliometrics may aid in the creation and maintenance of thesauri using a semi-automatic approach. For instance, Schneider and Borlund (2004) propose a comprehensive methodology for thesaurus construction based on a set of strong techniques such as citation analysis, co-citation analysis, network analysis, multidimensional scaling, and cluster analysis. They argue that a combination of manual and automatic techniques will provide a well-rounded, solid basis for thesaurus development and construction. Other researchers suggested that terms found in the titles of documents might be used to glean terms that would be useful to include in the thesaurus (Wang, 2006).

Another line of research and development associated with the construction of thesauri using new techniques is attributed to the use of transaction logs. Zhang et al. (2008) analyzed transaction logs of a health information portal to investigate and compare users' search terms and those in medical thesauri. They found low similarity between a term set defined by user query terms and a vocabulary set defined by either the Medical Subject Headings (MeSH) thesaurus or the Systematized Nomenclature of Medicine—Clinical Terms (SNOMED-CT) thesaurus. They conclude that users' query terms extracted from transaction logs can be analyzed to identify terms for the construction and revision of thesauri and classification systems. Other transaction log studies, notably in the areas of nanoscience and technology (Shiri and Chambers, 2008) and media and audiovisual archives (Huurnink et al., 2010), have revealed greater variability in user vocabulary compared with standard thesauri.

With the increasing popularity of social tagging and folksonomies, a number of studies have investigated how social tags and controlled vocabularies can coexist. They conclude that controlled vocabularies and folksonomies have their respective advantages and disadvantages and that in order to enhance user experiences of various information retrieval systems, controlled vocabularies and folksonomies should be used in tandem. The rationale is that controlled vocabularies have semantic and linguistic capabilities that can bring order, consistency, and control to social tags. Social tags and folksonomies, on the other hand, can enhance and expand the terminology of controlled vocabularies and thereby create a large entry vocabulary to support various search strategies.

Taxonomies are now created and maintained by many different organizations and institutions, and the many taxonomies available electronically provide useful sources of terms for developing domain-specific taxonomies. It should be recognized that the construction of solid taxonomies for information architecture, navigation, and search can benefit from thesaurus construction principles. Thesauri and taxonomies have a significant number of commonalities, even though there may well be differences in the control of terms and relationships, the indexing of the content, in the visualization of browsing structures, and in the various types of displays. The level of flexibility to be adopted by a taxonomy developer will, to a large extent, depend on the target audience, the information collection, and the various types of information-seeking strategies the organization wants to support with the search user interface. Therefore, it will be useful for researchers and developers to be aware of the similarities and differences among various target audiences, information collections, and desired information-seeking strategies.

It is envisaged that many of the techniques and methods we've described in this book will be the subjects of numerous future studies to investigate the ways in which such functionalities can support the construction, revision, and expansion of thesauri and other types of controlled vocabularies.

10.5 Semantic Web

In 2001, Berners-Lee (2001) introduced the term *semantic web* to focus on the semantic aspects of the representation, discovery, and retrieval of distributed and decentralized information on the web. Common, flexible, and semantically rich data formats such as the Resource Description Framework (RDF) and XML allow for the machine-readable representation of a broad range of content types. These common formats alleviate the problems that arise from the use of several incompatible data presentation formats and structures.

Berners-Lee notes that the basic component of the semantic web is ontologies. He points out that an ontology has a taxonomy of objects and the relations among them and that ontologies can be used to support advanced and accurate searching of web content.

Over the decade following his introduction of the semantic web vision, several projects have investigated the encoding of ontologies and thesauri in the RDF format. Among the first was the initiation by Matthews and Miles (2001) of the RDF-based representation of thesaurus data and relationships. Their mode of thesaurus encoding accommodates various inter-thesauri mapping as well as a mapping and systematic approach to multilingual data.

Some researchers since then have investigated the enrichment of an ontology with semantic relationships held in thesauri (Huang et al., 2007), while others have made use of thesauri to create domain-specific ontologies (Wielinga et al., 2001; Nogueras-Iso et al., 2010). These developments hold great promise for the value and relevance of thesauri in the semantic web environment. Thesauri serve not only as a basis for developing domain-specific ontologies, but their integration into more general-purpose ontologies also enhances the structural and semantic nuances of ontologies.

One of the recent semantic web developments related specifically to thesauri and other types of controlled vocabularies is the introduction of SKOS, a standard launched by the World Wide Web Consortium for flexible and machine-readable encoding of thesauri and other kinds of controlled vocabularies. Within this standard thesaurus, relationships can be encoded in such a way as to be used by various web services and web search systems.

Pastor-Sanchez et al. (2009) suggest the following advantages of encoding thesauri in the SKOS format:

- Possibility of expanding hierarchical and associative relationships

- Expansion and adoption of thesauri for incorporation and reuse in information retrieval systems

- Integration of thesauri into ontologies and other knowledge organization systems

- Integration of thesauri within semantic web at descriptive levels

Currently, a considerable number of thesauri have been encoded in SKOS, including AGROVOC, an agricultural thesaurus developed and used by the Food and Agriculture Organization of the United Nations; EuroVoc, a multilingual thesaurus for the European Union; the National Agricultural Library (NAL) thesaurus; the GEneral

Multilingual Environmental Thesaurus (GEMET), and the Thesaurus for Economics (STW).

Because SKOS is a standard, it is predicted that a large number of thesauri will be brought into this new format to flexibly and consistently function within the semantic web environment.

Another important and relevant development associated with the semantic web, which has implications for thesauri, is the development of linked data sources. By means of uniform resource identifiers and HTTP protocol, the semantic web makes use of linked data to connect data that was not previously associated; this concept and its definition were discussed in Chapter 4. A good example of the use of thesauri in the context of linked data is attributed to PoolParty (Schandl and Blumauer, 2010), a SKOS-based thesaurus management tool that supports the creation, enrichment, and maintenance of thesauri by means of linked data sources. With PoolParty, a search can be conducted for a concept within a broad range of linked data sources, such as DBpedia, Geonames, Sindice, FreeBase, WordNet, and Yago.

Furthermore, the concept can be linked to similar or related concepts in those sources, thereby expanding and enriching an existing thesaurus and allowing organizations and institutions to create applications that broaden users' access to many different knowledge organization systems and services and that support searching, browsing, and navigation of all kinds of linked data sources.

SKOS and linked data provide new opportunities to do a number of things in the semantic web environment:

- Link several different thesauri

- Expand search functionalities through federated searching of multiple controlled vocabularies and linked data sources

- Allow for the integration of thesauri into many web-based search engines and services

- Provide semantically rich visualization of thesauri and links between and among thesauri

- Facilitate multilingual information access and retrieval

- Provide easy access to thesauri for indexing and information representation purposes

To sum up, the semantic web environment in general, and SKOS and the linked data initiatives in particular, open up new avenues for thesauri to be used in a broader range of web-based applications and services in support of semantic and more meaningful web search.

10.6 Conclusion

Five decades of research and development demonstrate the tremendous potential for continuing discoveries, advances, and innovations in powering search through thesaurus-enhanced search user interfaces. With the increasing number of domain-specific digital collections on the web, the need for consistent description and discovery of information becomes more important, and more urgent, than ever before.

This book has taken a new approach to thesauri by critiquing the relevant literatures of a variety of communities who share an interest in thesauri and their functions but who are not, it should be noted, closely collaborating at this time—research communities such as library and information science, information retrieval, knowledge organization, human-computer interaction, information architecture, information search behavior, usability studies, search user interface, metadata-enabled information access, interactive information retrieval, and searcher education.

Semantic web applications such as SKOS will provide new approaches to the use of thesauri for searching and browsing across a broad range of information retrieval systems, from bibliographic and full-text databases to digital libraries, web portals, digital archives, museums, subject gateways, and linked data repositories. Emerging initiatives such as digital humanities, e-science, and linked open data present new opportunities for reusing and repurposing thesauri.

It is confidently predicted that thesauri and other types of knowledge organization systems will be used in an increasingly wider variety of web services and applications. The potential is virtually unlimited for web-related developments and technologies to present new ways of both reconciling and exploiting multiple thesauri, and the knowledge structures inherent in thesauri, in support of information access and retrieval.

It is my sincere hope that you have discovered in this book a useful treatment of the evolution in theory, research, projects, systems, standards, functionalities, and best practices designed to advance the mission of designing and developing thesaurus-enhanced search user interfaces in the context of rapidly emerging information environments. Clearly, this book's publication is only a first step in this exciting journey.

References

Berners-Lee, T., Hendler, J., and Lassila, O. (2001). The semantic web. *Scientific American*, 284(5), 34–43.

Borgman, C. (2007). *Scholarship in the digital age: Information, infrastructure, and the internet.* Cambridge, MA: MIT Press.

Huang, J. X., Shin, J. A., and Choi, K. S. (2007). Enriching core ontology with domain thesaurus through concept and relation classification. In: *Proceedings of OntoLex 2007, workshop at ISWC07, 6th international semantic web conference.* November 11, 2007, Busan, South Korea.

Huurnink, B., Hollink, L., Heuvel, W. V., and de Rijke, M. (2010). Search behavior of media professionals at an audiovisual archive: A transaction log analysis. *Journal of the American Society for Information Science and Technology*, 61(6), 1180–1197.

Ibekwe-SanJuan, F. (2006). Constructing and maintaining knowledge organization tools: A symbolic approach. *Journal of Documentation*, 62(2), 229–250.

Jones, S., Gatford, M., Hancock-Beaulieu, M., Robertson, S. E., Walker, W., and Secker, J. (1995). Interactive thesaurus navigation: Intelligence rules OK? *Journal of the American Society for Information Science*, 46(1), 52–59.

Matthews, B., and Miles, A. (2001). Review of RDF thesaurus work: A review and discussion of RDF schemes for thesauri. Retrieved from www.w3.org/2001/sw/Europe/reports/thes/8.2/ (accessed June 10, 2012).

National Science Foundation. (2007). Cyberinfrastructure vision for the 21st century. Retrieved from www.nsf.gov/od/oci/CI_Vision_March07.pdf (accessed June 19, 2012).

Nogueras-Iso, J., Lacasta, J., Falquet, G., Guyot, J., and Teller, J. (2010). Ontology learning from thesauri: An experience in the urban domain. In: F. Gargouri and W. Jaziri (Eds.), *Ontology theory, management and design: Advanced tools and models* (pp. 247–260). Hershey, PA: IGI Global.

Pastor-Sanchez, J. A., Martinez, F. J., and Rodriguez, J.V. (2009). Advantages of thesaurus representation using the Simple Knowledge Organization System (SKOS) compared with proposed alternatives. *Information Research*, 14(4), paper 422. Retrieved from InformationR.net/ir/14-4/paper422.html (accessed June 19, 2012).

Pervasive Technology Institute at Indiana University. (2007, March). IU cyberinfrastructure news. Retrieved from pti.iu.edu/ci/iu-cyberinfrastructure-news-march-2007 (accessed July 16, 2011).

Schandl, T., and Blumauer, A. (2010). PoolParty: SKOS thesaurus management utilizing linked data. In: L. Arroyo (Ed.), *The semantic web: Research and applications* (Lecture notes in computer science, pp. 421–425). Berlin: Springer.

Schneider, J. W., and Borlund, P. (2004). Introduction to bibliometrics for construction and maintenance of thesauri: Methodical considerations. *Journal of Documentation*, 60(5), 524–549.

Shiri, A., and Chambers, T. (2008). Information retrieval from digital libraries: Assessing the potential utility of thesauri in supporting users' search behaviour in an interdisciplinary domain. In: C. Arsenault and J. Tennis (Eds.), *Proceedings of the 10th international conference of the International Society for Knowledge Organization* (pp. 184–189). Würzburg, Germany: Ergon Verlag.

Shiri, A., and Revie, C. (2005). Usability and user perceptions of a thesaurus-enhanced search interface. *Journal of Documentation*, 61(5), 640–656.

Shiri, A., Ruecker, S., Fiorentino, C., Stafford, A., and Bouchard, M. (2010). Exploratory interaction with information through visualization and semantics: Designing a visual user interface using the UNESCO multilingual thesaurus. In: E. Ménard, V. Nesset, and S. Mas (Eds.), *Proceedings of the 38th Canadian Association for Information Science annual conference*. Concordia University, Montreal, Quebec, Canada. June 2–4, 2010.

Tudhope, D., Binding, C., Blocks, D., and Cunliffe, D. (2006). Query expansion via conceptual distance in thesaurus indexed collections. *Journal of Documentation*, 62(4), 509–533.

Vickery, B. C. (1960). Thesaurus—A new word in documentation. *Journal of Documentation*, 16(4), 181–189.

Wang, J. (2006). Automatic thesaurus development: Term extraction from title metadata. *Journal of the American Society for Information Science and Technology*, 57(7), 907–920.

Wielinga, B., Wielemaker, T. J., and Sandberg, J. A. C. (2001). From thesaurus to ontology. In: Y. Gil, M. Musen, and J. Shavlik (Eds.), *K-CAP '01: Proceedings of the 1st international conference on knowledge capture* (pp. 194–201). Victoria, BC, Canada, October 21–23, 2001. New York: ACM Press.

Zhang, J., Wolfram, D., Wang, P., Hong, Y., and Gillis, R. (2008). Visualization of health subject analysis based on query term co-occurrences. *Journal of the American Society for Information Science and Technology*, 59(12), 1933–1947.

About the Author

Ali Shiri is an associate professor in the School of Library and Information Studies at the University of Alberta, Edmonton, Canada. He joined the University of Alberta as an assistant professor in 2004. Before joining the University of Alberta, Ali worked as senior researcher in the Centre for Digital Library Research at the University of Strathclyde in Glasgow, Scotland, and was project officer for the NHS Glasgow Health Information Gateway. He teaches courses on digital libraries and knowledge organization. He obtained his associate's degree in library science from Shahid Chamran University, Ahvaz, Iran, and his bachelor's and master's degrees in library and information science from the University of Tehran. He holds a doctorate in information science from the Department of Computer and Information Sciences, University of Strathclyde, in Glasgow. His research areas include user search and interaction behavior, digital library user interfaces, and knowledge organization systems and social tagging in digital libraries. He has published widely on thesaurus-enhanced search user interfaces.

Index

Figures and tables are indicated by f and t following page numbers.

More Titles of Interest from Information Today, Inc.

ASIST Thesaurus of Information Science, Technology, and Librarianship, Third Edition

Edited by Alice Redmond-Neal and Marjorie M. K. Hlava

The *ASIST Thesaurus* is the authoritative reference to the terminology of information science, technology, and librarianship. An optional CD-ROM includes the complete contents of the print thesaurus along with Data Harmony's Thesaurus Master software. In addition, the CD-ROM allows users to add, change, and delete terms, and to learn the basics of thesaurus construction.

Book with CD-ROM: 272 pp/softbound/ISBN 978-1-57387-244-7
ASIST members $63.95 • Nonmembers $79.95
Book only: 272 pp/softbound/ISBN 978-1-57387-243-0
ASIST members $39.95 • Nonmembers $49.95

Information Representation and Retrieval in the Digital Age, Second Edition

By Heting Chu

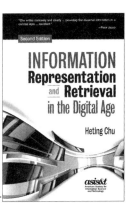

This second edition features many updates and revisions, including coverage of taxonomies, folksonomies, ontologies, social tagging, and next generation OPACs. She reviews key concepts and major developmental stages of the field, and then examines information representation methods, IRR languages, retrieval techniques and models, and internet retrieval systems. In addition, she explains the retrieval of multilingual, multimedia, and hyper-structured information and explores the user dimension and evaluation issues.

320 pp/hardbound/ISBN 978-1-57387-393-2
ASIST Members $39.60 • Nonmembers $49.50

Information Need

A Theory Connecting Information Search to Knowledge Formation

By Charles Cole

Charles Cole digs deep into the need that motivates people to search for information and articulates a theory of information need as the basis for designing information retrieval (IR) systems that engage the user's knowledge/belief system. Cole describes how such systems use signals from the user's own information environment to reduce overload, improve search results, and enhance the usefulness of information delivered on mobile devices. *Information Need* is an important text for researchers and students in information science, computer science, and HCI, and for anyone interested in current IR theory, practice, and systems design.

240 pp/hardbound/ISBN 978-1-57387-429-8
ASIST Members $47.60 • Nonmembers $59.50

Introduction to Information Science and Technology

Edited by Charles H. Davis and Debora Shaw

This guide to information science and technology presents a clear, concise, and approachable account of the fundamental issues, with appropriate historical background and theoretical background. Topics covered include information needs, seeking, and use; representation and organization of information; computers and networks; structured information systems; and more.

288 pp/softbound/ISBN 978-1-57387-423-6
ASIST Members $47.60 • Nonmembers $59.50

To order or for a complete catalog, contact:

Information Today, Inc.

143 Old Marlton Pike, Medford, NJ 08055 • 609/654-6266
email: custserv@infotoday.com • website: www.infotoday.com